Interactions 1

READING

Elaine Kirn
Pamela Hartmann

Lawrence J. Zwier
Contributor, Focus on Testing

Pamela Hartmann
Reading Strand Leader

Interactions 1 Reading, Silver Edition

ISBN 13: 978-0-07-313811-4 (Student Book)
ISBN 10: 0-07-313811-8
1 2 3 4 5 6 7 8 9 10 VNH 11 10 09 08 07 06

ISBN 13: 978-0-07-332964-2 (Student Book with Audio Highlights)
ISBN 10: 0-07-332964-9
1 2 3 4 5 6 7 8 9 10 VNH 11 10 09 08 07 06

Editorial director: Erik Gundersen
Series editor: Valerie Kelemen
Developmental editors: Mary Sutton-Paul, Terre Passero
Production manager: Juanita Thompson
Production coordinator: Vanessa Nuttry
Cover designer: Robin Locke Monda
Interior designer: Nesbitt Graphics, Inc.
Artist: Bradley Clark
Photo researcher: Photoquick Research

The credits section for this book begins on page iv and is considered an extension of the copyright page.

Cover photo: Steve Allen/Creatas Images

www.esl-elt.mcgraw-hill.com

The McGraw·Hill Companies

A Special Thank You

The Interactions/Mosaic Silver Edition team wishes to thank our extended team: teachers, students, administrators, and teacher trainers, all of whom contributed invaluably to the making of this edition.

Macarena Aguilar, **North Harris College**, Houston, Texas ■ Mohamad Al-Alam, **Imam Mohammad University**, Riyadh, Saudi Arabia ■ Faisal M. Al Mohanna Abaalkhail, **King Saud University**, Riyadh, Saudi Arabia; Amal Al-Toaimy, **Women's College, Prince Sultan University**, Riyadh, Saudi Arabia ■ Douglas Arroliga, **Ave Maria University**, Managua, Nicaragua ■ Fairlie Atkinson, **Sungkyunkwan University**, Seoul, Korea ■ Jose R. Bahamonde, **Miami-Dade Community College**, Miami, Florida ■ John Ball, **Universidad de las Americas**, Mexico City, Mexico ■ Steven Bell, **Universidad la Salle**, Mexico City, Mexico ■ Damian Benstead, **Sungkyunkwan University**, Seoul, Korea ■ Paul Cameron, **National Chengchi University**, Taipei, Taiwan R.O.C. ■ Sun Chang, **Soongsil University**, Seoul, Korea ■ Grace Chao, **Soochow University**, Taipei, Taiwan R.O.C. ■ Chien Ping Chen, **Hua Fan University**, Taipei, Taiwan R.O.C. ■ Selma Chen, **Chihlee Institute of Technology**, Taipei, Taiwan R.O.C. ■ Sylvia Chiu, **Soochow University**, Taipei, Taiwan R.O.C. ■ Mary Colonna, **Columbia University**, New York, New York ■ Lee Culver, **Miami-Dade Community College,** Miami, Florida ■ Joy Durighello, **City College of San Francisco**, San Francisco, California ■ Isabel Del Valle, **ULATINA**, San Jose, Costa Rica ■ Linda Emerson, **Sogang University**, Seoul, Korea ■ Esther Entin, **Miami-Dade Community College**, Miami, Florida ■ Glenn Farrier, **Gakushuin Women's College**, Tokyo, Japan ■ Su Wei Feng, Taipei, Taiwan R.O.C. ■ Judith Garcia, **Miami-Dade Community College**, Miami, Florida ■ Maxine Gillway, **United Arab Emirates University**, Al Ain, United Arab Emirates ■ Colin Gullberg, **Soochow University**, Taipei, Taiwan R.O.C. ■ Natasha Haugnes, **Academy of Art University**, San Francisco, California ■ Barbara Hockman, **City College of San Francisco**, San Francisco, California ■ Jinyoung Hong, **Sogang University**, Seoul, Korea ■ Sherry Hsieh, **Christ's College**, Taipei, Taiwan R.O.C. ■ Yu-shen Hsu, **Soochow University**, Taipei, Taiwan R.O.C. ■ Cheung Kai-Chong, **Shih-Shin University**, Taipei, Taiwan R.O.C. ■ Leslie Kanberg, **City College of San Francisco**, San Francisco, California ■ Gregory Keech, **City College of San Francisco**, San Francisco, California ■ Susan Kelly, **Sogang University**, Seoul, Korea ■ Myoungsuk Kim, **Soongsil University**, Seoul, Korea ■ Youngsuk Kim, **Soongsil University**, Seoul, Korea ■ Roy Langdon, **Sungkyunkwan University**, Seoul, Korea ■ Rocio Lara, **University of Costa Rica**, San Jose, Costa Rica ■ Insung Lee, **Soongsil University**, Seoul, Korea ■ Andy Leung, **National Tsing Hua University**, Taipei, Taiwan R.O.C. ■ Elisa Li Chan, **University of Costa Rica**, San Jose, Costa Rica ■ Elizabeth Lorenzo, **Universidad Internacional de las Americas**, San Jose, Costa Rica ■

Cheryl Magnant, **Sungkyunkwan University**, Seoul, Korea ■ Narciso Maldonado Iuit, **Escuela Tecnica Electricista**, Mexico City, Mexico ■ Shaun Manning, **Hankuk University of Foreign Studies**, Seoul, Korea ■ Yoshiko Matsubayashi, **Tokyo International University**, Saitama, Japan ■ Scott Miles, **Sogang University**, Seoul, Korea ■ William Mooney, **Chinese Culture University**, Taipei, Taiwan R.O.C. ■ Jeff Moore, **Sungkyunkwan University**, Seoul, Korea ■ Mavelin de Moreno, **Lehnsen Roosevelt School**, Guatemala City, Guatemala ■ Ahmed Motala, **University of Sharjah**, Sharjah, United Arab Emirates ■ Carlos Navarro, **University of Costa Rica**, San Jose, Costa Rica ■ Dan Neal, **Chih Chien University**, Taipei, Taiwan R.O.C. ■ Margarita Novo, **University of Costa Rica**, San Jose, Costa Rica ■ Karen O'Neill, **San Jose State University**, San Jose, California ■ Linda O'Roke, **City College of San Francisco**, San Francisco, California ■ Martha Padilla, **Colegio de Bachilleres de Sinaloa**, Culiacan, Mexico ■ Allen Quesada, **University of Costa Rica**, San Jose, Costa Rica ■ Jim Rogge, **Broward Community College**, Ft. Lauderdale, Florida ■ Marge Ryder, **City College of San Francisco**, San Francisco, California ■ Gerardo Salas, **University of Costa Rica**, San Jose, Costa Rica ■ Shigeo Sato, **Tamagawa University**, Tokyo, Japan ■ Lynn Schneider, **City College of San Francisco**, San Francisco, California ■ Devan Scoble, **Sungkyunkwan University**, Seoul, Korea ■ Maryjane Scott, **Soongsil University**, Seoul, Korea ■ Ghaida Shaban, **Makassed Philanthropic School**, Beirut, Lebanon ■ Maha Shalok, **Makassed Philanthropic School**, Beirut, Lebanon ■ John Shannon, **University of Sharjah**, Sharjah, United Arab Emirates ■ Elsa Sheng, **National Technology College of Taipei**, Taipei, Taiwan R.O.C. ■ Ye-Wei Sheng, **National Taipei College of Business**, Taipei, Taiwan R.O.C. ■ Emilia Sobaja, **University of Costa Rica**, San Jose, Costa Rica ■ You-Souk Yoon, **Sungkyunkwan University**, Seoul, Korea ■ Shanda Stromfield, **San Jose State University**, San Jose, California ■ Richard Swingle, **Kansai Gaidai College**, Osaka, Japan ■ Carol Sung, **Christ's College**, Taipei, Taiwan R.O.C. ■ Jeng-Yih Tim Hsu, **National Kaohsiung First University of Science and Technology**, Kaohsiung, Taiwan R.O.C. ■ Shinichiro Torikai, **Rikkyo University**, Tokyo, Japan ■ Sungsoon Wang, **Sogang University**, Seoul, Korea ■ Kathleen Wolf, **City College of San Francisco**, San Francisco, California ■ Sean Wray, **Waseda University International**, Tokyo, Japan ■ Belinda Yanda, **Academy of Art University**, San Francisco, California ■ Su Huei Yang, **National Taipei College of Business**, Taipei, Taiwan R.O.C. ■ Tzu Yun Yu, **Chungyu Institute of Technology**, Taipei, Taiwan R.O.C.

Author Acknowledgements

To my father, Isadore Fendelman, 1917-2004

— Elaine Kirn

Photo Credits

Table of Contents

Introducing Interactions/Mosaic Silver Edition

NEW to the Silver Edition:

- **World's most popular and comprehensive academic skills series**—thoroughly updated for today's global learners
- **Full-color design** showcases compelling instructional photos to strengthen the educational experience
- **Enhanced focus on vocabulary building, test taking, and critical thinking skills** promotes academic achievement
- **New strategies and activities for the TOEFL® iBT** build invaluable test taking skills
- **New "Best Practices" approach** in Teacher's Edition promotes excellence in language teaching

NEW to Interactions 1 Reading:

- **All new content:** Chapter 10 Sports
- **Enhanced design**—featuring larger type and 50% more instructional photos—ensures effective classroom usage
- **Transparent chapter structure**—with consistent part headings, activity labeling, and clear guidance—strengthens the academic experience:

  > Part 1: Reading Skills and Strategies
  > Part 2: Reading Skills and Strategies
  > Part 3: Vocabulary and Language Learning Skills
  > Part 4: Focus on Testing

- **Dynamic vocabulary acquisition program**—systematic vocabulary introduction and practice ensures students will interact meaningfully with each target word at least four times
- **New focus on vocabulary from the High-Frequency Word List** offers additional practice with words students are most likely to encounter in social interactions and academic text
- **Line numbering and paragraph lettering** in reading passages allows students and teachers to easily find the information referred to in activities.
- **Expanded audio program** includes all reading selections, vocabulary words, and selected listening activities to accelerate reading fluency
- **New *Vocabulary index*** equips student and instructors with chapter-by-chapter lists of target words

---

* TOEFL is a registered trademark of Educational Testing Service (ETS). This publication is not endorsed or approved by ETS.

Interactions/Mosaic
Best Practices

Our Interactions/Mosaic Silver Edition team has produced an edition that focuses on Best Practices, principles that contribute to excellent language teaching and learning. Our team of writers, editors, and teacher consultants has identified the following six interconnected Best Practices:

Making Use of Academic Content

Materials and tasks based on academic content and experiences give learning real purpose. Students explore real world issues, discuss academic topics, and study content-based and thematic materials.

Organizing Information

Students learn to organize thoughts and notes through a variety of graphic organizers that accommodate diverse learning and thinking styles.

Scaffolding Instruction

A scaffold is a physical structure that facilitates construction of a building. Similarly, scaffolding instruction is a tool used to facilitate language learning in the form of predictable and flexible tasks. Some examples include oral or written modeling by the teacher or students, placing information in a larger framework, and reinterpretation.

Activating Prior Knowledge

Students can better understand new spoken or written material when they connect to the content. Activating prior knowledge allows students to tap into what they already know, building on this knowledge, and stirring a curiosity for more knowledge.

Interacting with Others

Activities that promote human interaction in pair work, small group work, and whole class activities present opportunities for real world contact and real world use of language.

Critical Thinking

Strategies for critical thinking are taught explicitly. Students learn tools that promote critical thinking skills crucial to success in the academic world.

Highlights of Interactions 1
Reading Silver Edition

Full-color design showcases compelling instructional photos to strengthen the educational experience.

Interacting with Others
Questions and topical quotes simulate interest, activate prior knowledge, and launch the topic of the unit.

Chapter

10

Sports

Connecting to the Topic

1. Look at the photo below. Where do you think this game is taking place?
2. What is your favorite Olympic event to watch? Why?
3. What do you think are some of the issues and problems with competitive sports?

In This Chapter

The readings in this chapter offer information and opinions about competitive sports. The first reading compares and contrasts the ancient Greek Olympic Games with the modern worldwide Olympics. In opinion-letter form, the second reading offers opposing views on controversial issues in sports competition, such as the use of banned drugs, and the effects of commercialism on professional sports.

❝ The goal of the Olympic movement is to contribute to building a peaceful and better world by educating youth through sport practiced without discrimination of any kind. ❞

—The Olympic Charter, paraphrased by the
Amateur Athletic Foundation of Los Angeles, California

Activitating Prior Knowledge
Prereading activities place the reading in context and allow the student to read actively.

Making Use of Academic Content
Magazine articles, textbook passages, essays, and website articles explore stimulating topics of interest to today's students.

Part 1 Reading Skills and Strategies

How the Visual Media Affect People

Before You Read

 1 Previewing the Topic Look at the photos and read the questions below. Discuss them in small groups.

1. What are the people doing?
2. How are the photos similar? How are they different?
3. Are any of the scenes similar to a scene in your home? Why or why not?

▲ A family watching TV

▲ A family reading

 2 Predicting Discuss possible answers to these questions. If you don't know the answers, make predictions. You can look for the answers when you read "How the Visual Media Affect People."

1. What are some examples of visual media?
2. How might the amount of time spent in front of a TV or computer have a negative effect on family life? In what ways can watching television be helpful in people's lives?
3. What might low-quality programming do to the human brain? What might it do to people's lives?
4. What are some possible effects of violent movies or TV programs on people's personalities and behavior?
5. What are some signs of possible addiction to visual media like TV and computers?

3 Previewing Vocabulary Read the vocabulary items below from the first reading. Then listen to the words and phrases. Put a check mark (✓) next to the words you know. You can learn the other words now or come back to them after you read.

Nouns	Verbs	Adjectives
❏ addiction	❏ concentrate	❏ addicted
❏ behavior	❏ envy	❏ aural
❏ disadvantages	❏ focus	❏ average
❏ hospitals	❏ improve	❏ boring
❏ images	❏ practice	❏ dissatisfied
❏ personalities	❏ reduce	❏ elderly
❏ programming	❏ replace	❏ envious
❏ reality	❏ scares	❏ exciting
❏ stars	❏ shout	❏ immoral
❏ tension		❏ nursing
❏ viewers		❏ unlimited
❏ violence		
❏ visual media		

Read

4 Reading an Article Read the following article. Then read the explanations and do the activities that follow.

How the Visual Media Affect People

Introduction: Benefits of the Visual Media

A   How do television and the other visual media affect the lives of individuals and families around the globe? The media can be very helpful to people (and their children) who carefully choose what they watch. With high-quality programming in various fields of study—science, medicine, nature, history, the arts, and so on—TV, videotapes, and DVDs increase the knowledge of the average *and* the well-educated person; they can also improve thinking ability. Moreover, television and other visual media benefit elderly people who can't go out often, as well as patients in hospitals and residents of nursing facilities. Additionally, it offers language learners the advantage of "real-life" audiovisual instruction and aural comprehension practice at any time of day or night. And of course, visual media can provide almost everyone with good entertainment—a pleasant way to relax and spend free time at home.

Scaffolding Instruction
Instruction and practice with reading skills helps students increase their reading fluency.

aging body. It's a folk remedy, not a proven medical therapy. Nevertheless, science is beginning to figure out why sour cherry juice might work to improve the health of patients with arthritis. The secret is in the substance that gives the cherries their dark red color. It belongs to a classification of natural nutrients that color blueberries, strawberries, plums, and other fruits—and vegetables too. Moreover, these coloring substances may help to prevent serious health disorders like heart disease and cancer. In other words, vitamins and fiber are not the only reasons to eat fruits and vegetables. "To take advantage of natural whole foods," advise nutritionists and health researchers, "think variety and color."

Which sentence best states the point of the facts and beliefs in Paragraph C?
- (A) Color makes people happy, so it improves their health and state of mind; therefore, families should wear colorful clothes at meals.
- (B) Like vitamins and fiber, the substances in foods that give them color may offer an important health advantage.
- (C) Dark red foods are the best for nutrition, but bright yellow and green vegetables are more effective for elderly people that have arthritis pain.

Which title best tells the topic of Paragraph D?
- (A) Claims of the Advantages of Genetic Research and Engineering
- (B) Defects in Gene Structure and Insect Damage to Foods
- (C) Characteristics of Folk Remedies vs. Beliefs of Geneticists

D   What are *genes* and why are medical researchers always trying to find out more about them? Genes are part of the center (that is, the *nucleus*) of every living cell; in the form of DNA (deoxyribonucleic acid), this biological *genetic* material determines the characteristics (features) of every living thing—every plant, animal, and human being—on Earth. Medical *geneticists* are scientists that study DNA and genes for many purposes: (1) to learn how living things such as parasites, viruses, and bacteria cause illness; (2) to find the gene or combination of genes that cause certain diseases to pass from parents to their children; (3) to prevent or correct (repair) birth defects; (4) to change gene structure to improve health and increase the length of human life (longevity); and (5) to change the biological characteristics of animals and humans in ways that are beneficial to society. Another use of genetic technology that some scientists support is

▲ A DNA strand

144   Chapter 7 ■ ■ ■

changing the genes of the food farmers grow. Genetic engineers claim that these differences in DNA structure will increase food production, prevent damage from insects, and improve world health; in contrast, others oppose the use of genetic engineering not only in plants but also in animals and humans.

Which sentence best states the point of the facts and beliefs in Paragraph D?
- (A) Deoxyribonucleic acid is not as beneficial as DNA—the biological material related to genetics—in research on the causes of birth defects.
- (B) Genetic engineers and other specialists claim that research into the gene structure of living things can improve human health in many ways.
- (C) Because there is a natural limit to the length of human life, only changes in gene structure can increase longevity in senior citizens that drink cherry juice.

After You Read

Strategy

Summarizing Using a Mind Map
You learned how to summarize in previous chapters. Another way to summarize is to use a mind map.
- First, figure out the topic, the main ideas, and the supporting details. You can make a mind map showing the relationship of the points to one another.
- Then create a short summary from the items in the map.

Below is an example of a mind map of Paragraph A from the reading "Claims to Amazing Health." A summary based on the mind map follows.

■ ■ ■ Health   145

Cultivating Critical Thinking
Critical thinking strategies and activities equip students with the skills they need for academic achievement.

Organizing Information
Graphic organizers provide tools for organizing information and ideas.

Part 3 Vocabulary and Language-Learning Skills

Strategy

Getting Meaning from Context: Definitions and Italics
You can often find the meanings of words and phrases in the context. The context is the other words in the sentence or paragraph.

- **Look for a definition.** Definitions give the meaning of a word or phrase. A definition can be a short or long phrase. In a reading, a definition often comes in a sentence after the verbs *be* or *mean*.
- **Look for words in *italics*.** Defined words are sometimes in *italics*. The definitions or meaning explanations can be in quotation marks.

Example

> The definition of a *university* is "an institution of higher education with one or more undergraduate colleges and graduate schools." The word *college* means "a school of higher education."

1 Getting Meaning from Context In the reading "International Students" on pages 5–6, find the words for the definitions below. Write the words on the lines. The letters in parentheses ( ) are the letters of the paragraphs.

1. *an international student* = a postsecondary student from another country (A)
2. _____ = of a different country or culture (A)
3. _____ = in a foreign place (B)
4. _____ = the parties or people who run countries (C)
5. _____ = the cost or charge for instruction (D)

Now find definitions or meaning explanations for these words from the same reading. Write them on the lines.

6. international student = _a college student from another country_ (A)
7. postsecondary = _____ (A)
8. developing nations = _____ (B)
9. private schools = _____ (D)
10. citizens and immigrants = _____ (D)

Part 4 Focus on Testing

TOEFL® iBT

ANSWERING NEGATIVE FACT QUESTIONS ON TESTS
Similarity of meaning (see Part 3 of this chapter) is tested on many reading tests. Questions may ask you to choose the closest synonym or the most exact paraphrase for some part of the reading passage. Another type of question approaches the same skill in a different way. A negative fact question asks you to judge which of several choices is NOT similar to the rest. The TOEFL® iBT frequently asks negative fact questions. The structure of these questions uses such common expressions as *is not mentioned*, *except*, and *is not true*. Can you think of other phrases that are common in negative fact questions?

Answering Negative Fact Questions Read the following short passage and answer the questions that follow it. Then compare your answers with those of one or two other students.

Sharing the Water

A   Every community of humans faces a life-or-death question: How do we distribute water? Some water has to be held as a community resource if a town, city, or even nation is to survive. Many early human settlements were based on irrigation systems. These exist because earlier people agreed where the water should flow and to whom. Wells in desert lands are protected by cultural traditions that make them a shared resource among traveling peoples. Many large lakes, such as Lake Michigan in the United States, are mostly reserved for public use, not for the people who own houses on their shores.

B   Water-use laws can prevent a few powerful people from gaining control over all available water. But water laws do not make water freely available in equal amounts to everyone. Farmers need huge amounts of it. So do many industries. Families, however, do not need nearly that much. There is also the issue of pollution. Water laws must prevent careless (or intentional) pollution by some users before the water reaches all users.

C   Problems occur when government is not strong enough to make and enforce laws. Often, the water in dispute is an international (or interstate) resource. For example, the Mekong River in Southeast Asia starts in China and then winds through Laos, Cambodia, and Vietnam. The Vietnamese government, no matter how conscientious it is, has little control over how much of the Mekong water reaches Vietnam and what kind of condition it is in. The upstream nations, especially China, determine that. As upstream dams take more of the

Scope and Sequence

Chapter	Reading Selections	Reading Skills and Strategies
1 Academic Life Around the World pg. 2	*International Students* *University Life Around the World*	Recognizing reading structure in a textbook Recognizing main ideas Recognizing supporting details Recognizing topics Getting meaning from context
2 Experiencing Nature pg. 20	*The Powerful Influence of Weather* *Global Climate Changes*	Identifying cause and effect Recognizing titles and paragraph topics Identifying main ideas Recognizing supporting details
3 Living to Eat, or Eating to Live pg. 40	*Global Diet Choices* *Facts About Food*	Recognizing reading structure: main-idea questions for paragraph topics Recognizing one-or two-sentence statements of the main idea Matching paragraph titles with topics
4 In the Community pg. 60	*How Can I Get to the Post Office?* *The Laws of Communities*	Identifying paragraph and whole reading topics Identifying main ideas by asking questions Using punctuation to recognize supporting details Skimming for topics and main ideas

Critical Thinking Skills	Vocabulary Building	Language Skills	Focus on Testing
Synthesizing and discussing ideas from a reading Summarizing a reading Predicting the content of a reading Drawing conclusions Analyzing Internet information on higher education	Getting meaning from context: definitions and italics Identifying words with similar meanings Guessing words from context Focusing on high frequency words	Stating preferences and identifying reasons for preferences	**TOEFL® iBT** Summarizing
Distinguishing between beliefs and scientific facts Summarizing information in paragraph Synthesizing and discussing ideas from the reading	Getting meaning from context from parentheses and words with similar meanings Recognizing words with the same or similar meanings Matching vocabulary items with examples	Understanding weather reports; comparing weather conditions Stating and explaining opinions	**TOEFL® iBT** Finding main ideas and vocabulary clusters
Evaluating and comparing advice and opinions about food Summarizing paragraphs	Getting meaning from context: italics and punctuation Recognizing vocabulary categories	Making diet choices based on personal preferences and culture Finding and following recipes	**TOEFL® iBT** Understanding schematic tables
Understanding and giving directions Paraphrasing information	Getting the meaning from context: finding illustrations of words Recognizing words with similar meanings and meaning categories Recognizing nouns and verbs Finding definitions of vocabulary items	Comparing, contrasting, and evaluating different laws	**TOEFL® iBT** Answering negative fact questions

Critical Thinking Skills	Vocabulary Building	Language Skills	Focus on Testing
Evaluating and predicting family structures and social trends	Recognizing topics in readings about history Getting meaning from context: punctuation and phrase clues Recognizing nouns and adjectives	Researching and discussing family structures in different cultures	**TOEFL® iBT** Understanding definitions and explanations
Interpreting and discussing anecdotes Summarizing a short story	Understanding new vocabulary in context Recognizing nouns, verbs, and adjectives Understanding adverbs of manner	Recognizing and discussing cultural attitudes and customs Researching and reporting on unfamiliar cultures	**TOEFL® iBT** Practicing vocabulary questions
Choosing information to complete a mind map Summarizing using a mind map	Figuring out new or difficult vocabulary Identifying synonyms Identifying part of speech from suffixes	Giving advice about health Evaluating and agreeing or disagreeing with health tips	**TOEFL® iBT** Practicing for timed readings
Completing an outline with reading material Classifying different types of stories Evaluating the advantages and disadvantages of the media Summarizing a story	Understanding suffixes (nouns, adverbs, adjectives) Understanding word families	Retelling a story plot Discussing and justifying media choices Persuading others to watch a particular show	**TOEFL® iBT** Focusing on comparison and contrast

Critical Thinking Skills	Vocabulary Building	Language Skills	Focus on Testing
Identifying pros and cons Interpreting proverbs	Understanding negative prefixes Figuring out vocabulary from prefixes and suffixes	Discussing and comparing proverbs Researching poems, quotes, and proverbs	**TOEFL® iBT** Understanding inferences and points of view in readings
Recognizing point of view Distinguishing opinion from fact Classifying supporting details Comparing and contrasting the ancient and modern Olympics	Understanding and working with prefixes, stems, and suffixes Identifying antonyms	Researching and supporting points of view on competitive sports Convincing others to understand a point of view	**TOEFL® iBT** Taking notes and recognizing contrasts in reading passages

Academic Life Around the World

In This Chapter

You will read about international students in higher education around the world. You will also look at experiences of college life. What is higher education like where you're from? Do many students from other countries come to study in your country? In the first reading, "International Students," you'll find out why many students choose to study in other countries and why universities want international students. In the second reading, "University Life Around the World," you'll learn about the similarities and differences in university life around the world and about the different facilities universities offer.

" Education is not preparation for life; education is life itself. "

—John Dewey, U.S. educator, psychologist, philosopher (1859–1952)

Connecting to the Topic

1. What do you think some of the benefits are to studying in another country?

2. In some places classrooms are very formal, in others they are informal. Which do you prefer? Why?

3. Look at the picture below. Where are these students? What do you think they are doing?

International Students

Before You Read

1 Previewing the Topic Look at the photos and discuss the questions in small groups.

1. Describe the place and the people in each photo. Where are they? Where are they from? What are they doing?

2. Imagine the conversation in one of the photos. In your opinion, what are the people saying to each other?

3. Make comparisons. How is this place like your school? How is it different?

▲ Please keep the cafeteria clean.

▲ Are there any questions?

▲ I wonder if this will be on the test.

2 **Predicting** Work in groups of three. Think about and discuss possible answers to these questions. Write down your answers. If you don't know the answers, you can guess. Then you can look for the answers when you read "International Students."

1. What are *international students*? What is *postsecondary*?
2. Where do most international students go to school?
3. Why do students attend colleges and universities far from home?
4. Why do institutions of higher education want foreign students?

3 **Previewing Vocabulary** Read the vocabulary items below from the first reading. Then listen to the words and phrases. Put a check mark (✓) next to the words you know. You can learn the other words now or come back to them after you read.

Nouns

- ❑ campus
- ❑ charge
- ❑ citizens
- ❑ college degrees
- ❑ developing nations
- ❑ engineering
- ❑ experience
- ❑ governments
- ❑ immigrants
- ❑ industrialization
- ❑ institutions of higher education
- ❑ internationalism
- ❑ level
- ❑ nations
- ❑ postsecondary
- ❑ recreation
- ❑ skills
- ❑ subjects
- ❑ technology
- ❑ tuition
- ❑ universities

Verbs

- ❑ attend
- ❑ charge
- ❑ leave
- ❑ save
- ❑ spend
- ❑ supported by

Adjectives

- ❑ abroad
- ❑ expensive
- ❑ foreign
- ❑ international
- ❑ legal
- ❑ private

Adverb

- ❑ abroad

Read

4 **Reading an Article** Read the following article. Then do the activities that follow.

International Students

Introduction and Definitions

A   All around the world, there are **international** students at *institutions of higher education*. The definition of an *international student* is "a post-secondary student from another country." The meaning of *postsecondary* is "after high school." Another phrase for international students is "foreign students." The word **foreign** means "of a different country or culture."   5
Even so, some people don't like the word *foreign*. Instead, they use the phrase "international students." For an institution of higher education, they say "university," "college," or "school."

Where International Students Attend School

B   International students leave their home countries. They go to school **abroad**. One meaning of the word *abroad* is "in a foreign place." Probably, the country with the most students from abroad is the United States. Canada, Great Britain, and some other European countries also have a lot of students from other countries. But more and more, international students **attend** colleges and **universities** in the **developing nations** of Latin America, Asia, and Africa. Developing nations are countries without a high level of industrialization or technology.

Why Students Attend School Abroad

C   Why do high school and college graduates go to colleges and universities far from their homes? Undergraduates are postsecondary students without college degrees. Often, undergraduates want the **experience** of life in new cultures. Maybe they want to learn another language well. Many students want degrees in business, **engineering**, or technology. These subjects are not always available in their home countries. Some **governments** and companies send their best graduate students and workers to other countries for new knowledge and **skills**. And some international students from expensive **private** schools at home save money through study abroad programs, especially in developing nations.

Why Universities Want Foreign Students

D   Why do institutions of higher education want international students? Students from other countries and cultures bring internationalism to the classroom and campus. They bring different languages, customs, ideas, and opinions from many places. Also, educational institutions need money. **Tuition** is the fee or charge for instruction. Private schools are colleges and universities not supported by government money. They charge high tuition. International students are not **citizens** or **immigrants**. (One definition of *citizens* and *immigrants* is "legal members of a nation or country.") International students pay full tuition and fees to state or government schools. And all students away from home have to spend money for housing, food, recreation, and other things. For these reasons, many schools and groups of schools want students from other countries.

Conclusion and Summary

E   For different reasons, many high school and college graduates want or need to study abroad. For other reasons, many nations want or need students from other countries and cultures on their college and university campuses.

RECOGNIZING READING STRUCTURE IN A TEXTBOOK

Most reading material has reading structure. The word *structure* means "organization or form." This book, *Interactions 1 Reading,* has a structure. It has a title, chapters, two readings within each chapter, paragraphs, and a heading for each paragraph.

5 **Recognizing Reading Structure in *Interactions 1 Reading*** Read the information below about the structure of this book and answer the questions.

1. A *title* is the name of something to read. What is the title of this book?

2. *Interactions I Reading* contains 10 chapters. *Chapters* are the largest divisions of the book. What is the title of Chapter 1?

3. Each chapter of this book contains two *readings*. What is the title of the first reading in Chapter 1?

4. The information of most reading selections is in paragraphs. A *paragraph* is a division or part about one idea or one kind of information. How many paragraphs are in the reading "International Students"?

5. Each paragraph has a heading. The *heading* of the first paragraph is "Introduction and Definitions." What is the heading of the last paragraph in the first reading?

Strategy

Recognizing the Main Ideas

- The main idea tells the main point, or idea, about the topic. Sometimes one or two sentences of a paragraph tell the main idea.
- The main idea is often found in the first sentence of a paragraph, but not always.
- The main idea can also be in the middle or at the end of the paragraph.
- The other sentences in the paragraph usually give supporting details for the main idea.

6 **Recognizing the Main Ideas** Read the following main ideas for the five paragraphs in the reading "International Students." Match each main idea with the related paragraph. Write the letter of the paragraph next to each main idea.

1. _C_ International students go to school *abroad* for different reasons.

2. _____ Some important words in international education are *international students* and *institutions of higher education*. *International students* are postsecondary students from other countries. *Institutions of higher education* are colleges and universities.

3. _____ Institutions of higher education usually want students from other countries because they bring internationalism and money to their schools.

4. _____ Most foreign students attend school in the United States and Canada, in Great Britain and parts of Europe, and in developing nations around the world.

5. _____ The conclusion of the reading is that students choose to study abroad, and many nations want international students.

Strategy

Recognizing Supporting Details
The information in each paragraph of a reading selection tells more than the main idea. It also gives details about the main idea. *Details* are "single or specific pieces of information." Some kinds of details are definitions, examples, facts, and reasons.

7 **Recognizing Supporting Details** Read the five main-idea questions below about the reading "International Students." Three details correctly answer each question. Cross out the untrue, unrelated detail. The first item is an example.

1. What are some of the meanings of some words and phrases in international higher education?
   a. The definition of an *international student* is "a postsecondary student from another country."
   b. The meaning of *postsecondary* is "after high school."
   c. ~~The word *school* usually means "a large group of fish."~~
   d. Another phrase for *international students* is "foreign students."

2. Where do most international students go to school?
   a. The United States has the most students from other countries.
   b. Developing nations have a very high level of industrialization or technology.
   c. Many foreign students attend school in Canada, Great Britain, and some European nations.
   d. More and more students from abroad attend school in the developing nations of Latin America, Asia, and Africa.

3. Why do students attend colleges and universities far from home?
   a. Maybe they want the experience of life and language in another country.
   b. They need technological information and skills not available at home.
   c. They can't afford tuition to state or government universities in their native countries.
   d. In developing nations, they can save money through lower tuition and living costs.

4. Why do institutions of higher education want foreign students?
   a. They don't want to send their students to universities in other countries.
   b. International students bring internationalism to the classroom and campus.
   c. Educational institutions need money from tuition.
   d. Foreign students put money for housing, food, and other things into the economy.

5. What are the main points of the reading selection "International Students"?
   a. International students have many reasons to attend school abroad, and institutions of higher education have many reasons to accept them.
   b. Some high school or college graduates want to or need to study in other countries.
   c. Many nations want or need foreign students at their colleges and universities.
   d. After graduation from high school, legal citizens and immigrants don't usually want more education.

Now, go back to Activity 2 on page 5 and look at the questions again. Now look at the answers you wrote down before you read the article. Change them if necessary.

- Give definitions in your answer to Question 1.
- Give facts in your answers to Question 2.
- Give reasons in your answers to Questions 3 and 4.

 8 Discussing the Reading Talk about your answers to the following questions.

1. On the subject of higher education, what are some other important vocabulary items? (Some possible examples are *degree, visa, program, enrollment, registration, assignment,* and *sponsor*.) What are some definitions of these words and phrases? Why are the items important to you?

2. Are you an *international student, a citizen,* or *an immigrant*? Are you studying at a *secondary* or a *postsecondary* school? Are you an *undergraduate* or a *graduate* student? Give details for your answers.

3. If you are an international student, do you like attending school abroad? If you are not an international student, do you want to study in another country? Give reasons for your answer.

4. Does your school want or need international students on campus? Give facts and reasons for your answer.

University Life Around the World

Before You Read

1 Previewing Vocabulary Read the vocabulary items below from the next reading. Then listen to the words and phrases. Put a check mark (✓) next to the words you know. You can come back to the other words after you read.

Nouns
- ❑ academic lectures
- ❑ assignments
- ❑ atmosphere
- ❑ certificates
- ❑ distance learning
- ❑ equipment
- ❑ exit exam
- ❑ facilities
- ❑ financial aid
- ❑ instructors
- ❑ learning resource centers
- ❑ loans

- ❑ materials
- ❑ methods
- ❑ points
- ❑ public transportation
- ❑ quizzes
- ❑ requirements
- ❑ resources
- ❑ scholarships
- ❑ scores
- ❑ services
- ❑ social lives
- ❑ software programs
- ❑ styles
- ❑ tennis courts
- ❑ views

Verbs
- ❑ complete
- ❑ differ

Adjectives
- ❑ audio
- ❑ available
- ❑ formal
- ❑ individual
- ❑ relaxed
- ❑ similar

Adverb
- ❑ casually

RECOGNIZING TOPICS, MAIN IDEAS, AND SUPPORTING DETAILS

- The word *topic* means "the subject of speech or writing." A paragraph usually tells about one topic. The heading of a paragraph gives information about its topic.

- The *main idea* tells the main point, or idea, about the topic. Sometimes one or two sentences of a paragraph tell the main idea.

- The *supporting details* give examples or more information about the main idea.

Example

Kinds of University Classes in the United States

There are several different kinds of classes on university campuses in the United States. Professors usually teach large undergraduate classes with formal lectures. Students listen and write things down. Then students may attend discussion groups with teaching assistants. In graduate seminars, small groups of students discuss information and ideas with their professor and classmates.

Finally, another type of class takes place off campus. **Distance-learning** and online students do most of their work individually in other places. But they sometimes go to a campus for group meetings.

Topic: In the example above, the title is the topic. The topic of the paragraph is "Kinds of University Classes in the United States."

Main idea: The first sentence is underlined. It is the main idea of the paragraph. It gives the main point of the whole topic.

Supporting details: Some other sentences tell the kinds of classes: undergraduate classes (formal lectures and discussion groups), graduate seminars, distance and online learning with group meetings. The remaining sentences give details about these three kinds of classes.

---

2 **Recognizing the Topics and Main Ideas of Paragraphs** Read the following article. Then answer these questions about the article.

   1. What is the topic of the article? _____

   2. What is the topic of each paragraph? (Hint: Look at the paragraph heading.)

      A: _____

      B: _____

      C: _____

      D: _____

   3. What is the main idea of each paragraph? Underline it and then read it aloud. Remember: the main idea is not always the first sentence. The main idea in Paragraph A has been underlined.

 Read

University Life Around the World

Similarities in Student Life

A   At colleges and universities around the world, students from other places live in student housing on campus, in apartments, or in the private homes of other people. They walk to school or get there by bicycle or by car. Sometimes they take **public transportation** like the bus or subway. They attend classes and take **quizzes** or tests or exams. They **complete** necessary course   5 **requirements**. After years of study, they get **certificates** or college degrees. These are proof of completion of courses of study. Outside school, they have other interests and family or social lives. <u>In some ways, life on the campuses of institutions of higher education is the same everywhere in the world.</u>

Systems of Higher Education

B   Maybe student *life* is **similar**, but the system of higher education differs in   10
countries around the world. For example, in the United States, postsecondary
students can live at home and go to community colleges for two years or
more. Or they can choose four-year state or private colleges or universities.
They can get **financial aid**, like **scholarships**, grants, or **loans**. This money
helps students to pay college tuition and other charges. (Loans have to be   15
paid back.) With undergraduate degrees, they can attend graduate school. The
system is different in some countries of Asia or the Middle East, like Iran.
There, students take an **exit exam** in their last year of high school. The
people with the highest **scores** attend the best universities in the country.
Other students can go to other kinds of colleges or get jobs.   20

Differences in Teaching and Learning Styles

C   But not only the system of higher education can vary. Teaching and
learning **methods** and **styles** differ in various cultures, at different colleges
and universities, and in **individual** courses. For example, the **atmosphere**
in many classrooms is very formal. Students use titles such as "Professor
Gonzalez" or "Mrs. Wong" for their **instructors**. Some teachers wear busi-   25
ness clothes and give **academic lectures**. Students respect the knowledge
and **views** of their "master teachers." Other classrooms have an informal
atmosphere. Instructors dress casually, and students use instructors' first
names. In this **relaxed atmosphere**, class members work together in
groups. They tell their individual experiences, give their opinions, and talk   30
about their ideas. Some teachers always follow a course plan or the
textbook. They give a lot of **assignments**. They give **points**, scores, or
grades for homework. In their courses, students take many quizzes, tests,
and exams. All over the world, there are teaching and learning differences.

Campus Facilities and Services

D   And what about the **facilities** and services available to students at   35
college and university campuses around
the world? At many institutions of
higher education, resources for learning
and recreation are available to students.
At libraries, they can read and study   40
books and other materials. At **learning
resource centers**, they can often work
on computers. Maybe they can use
educational software programs or the
Internet. Sometimes **audio** or video   45
equipment is available. And people can
buy books, supplies, and other things at

▲ Students in a computer lab

campus stores. Also, learners can get advice from counselors and individual help with their courses from tutors. Maybe they can relax and have fun on campus, too. Some schools have swimming pools, tennis courts, and other sports facilities. Most have snack bars, cafeterias, or other eating places. And at some schools, not all students go to the campus. They take Internet courses by computer, see and hear lectures on television, or use other kinds of **distance learning**.

50

After You Read

Strategy

Summarizing

How can you show your understanding of reading material? You can summarize it. Here is some information about summaries:

- A summary is a short statement of the main points and important details of reading material.
- A summary has some words from the reading and some not from the reading.
- A summary of a paragraph or short article has only a few sentences. It is much shorter than the original.
- A good summary tells the main idea and the important details in your own words.

Example

Summary of Paragraph A from the reading "University Life Around the World":

> In many ways, university life is the same in different places around the world. Students live in similar kinds of places and get to school in similar ways. They attend classes, study, and get certificates or degrees for their hard work. And they have interests and lives outside school, too.

3 **Summarizing a Paragraph** Work in groups of three. Have each person choose one of the remaining paragraphs from the reading "University Life Around the World." Read it carefully. Write a summary of your paragraph. Begin with a sentence about the topic or title. Then read your summary to your group.

4 **Discussing the Reading** Discuss the following questions with your group.

1. Talk about your student life: Where do you live? How do you get to school? What do you do there? What other interests and family or social life do you have?

2. Talk about the system of higher education in your country or culture: What kinds of colleges and universities are there? What are the requirements for admission? Do they charge tuition? Is there financial aid?

3. Talk about the teaching styles and methods of your instructors: Are they formal or relaxed? Do they use course plans and textbooks? Do they give assignments, tests, and grades? Talk about your learning style.

4. Talk about your school: What campus facilities and services does your school have? What learning and recreational resources do you use? Where are they?

 5 **Talking It Over** What do you like about student life? From each box below, check (✓) one or two preferences. In groups, tell your preferences and the reasons for them. Compare your choices with the choices of your classmates.

1. Housing	2. Transportation	3. Activities
❑ Home life with family ❑ Student housing ❑ Apartment life ❑ Private home ❑ Other: _____	❑ Walking ❑ Bicycling ❑ Driving ❑ Taking the bus, subway, or other public transportation ❑ Other: _____	❑ Courses and classes ❑ Individual study, homework, and projects ❑ Clubs with academic or political purposes ❑ Student recreation or sports ❑ Other interests outside school ❑ Other: _____
4. Kinds of Schools	**5. Charges and Payments**	**6. Teaching and Learning Styles**
❑ High school or secondary school ❑ A community or technical college ❑ A public or state university ❑ A private school ❑ Online courses or distance learning ❑ Other: _____	❑ Free government education ❑ Low education charges ❑ Scholarships, loans, and other financial aid ❑ Private, individual payment of costs ❑ High tuition ❑ Other: _____	❑ Formal lectures and atmosphere ❑ Respect for professors as "masters" ❑ Informal classes with discussions of individual experiences, ideas, and opinions ❑ A course plan and textbook ❑ Quizzes, tests, exams, and final grades ❑ Course credit for graduation ❑ Other: _____
7. Facilities	**8. Services for Students**	**9. Other Choices and Preferences**
❑ A library with books and other reading material ❑ A learning center with audio, visual, and computer equipment ❑ Swimming pools, tennis courts, and other sports facilities ❑ A snack bar, cafeteria, or other eating places ❑ Other: _____	❑ Academic counseling ❑ Tutoring help or study groups ❑ Individual counseling about personal problems ❑ A student store with educational supplies ❑ A general store for groceries, clothing, and other things ❑ Other: _____	❑ A casual, relaxed student life ❑ Many fun years as a student ❑ A hard program of study ❑ A quick, efficient education ❑ Active political participation ❑ A good family or social life ❑ Other: _____

Getting Meaning from Context: Definitions and Italics

You can often find the meanings of words and phrases in the context. The context is the other words in the sentence or paragraph.

- **Look for a definition.** Definitions give the meaning of a word or phrase. A definition can be a short or long phrase. In a reading, a definition often comes in a sentence after the verbs *be* or *mean*.

- **Look for words in *italics*.** Defined words are sometimes in *italics*. The definitions or meaning explanations can be in quotation marks.

Example

> The definition of a *university* is "an institution of higher education with one or more undergraduate colleges and graduate schools." The word *college* means "a school of higher education."

1 **Getting Meaning from Context** In the reading "International Students" on pages 5–6, find the words for the definitions below. Write the words on the lines. The letters in parentheses ( ) are the letters of the paragraphs.

1. _an international student_ = a postsecondary student from another country (A)

2. _____ = of a different country or culture (A)

3. _____ = in a foreign place (B)

4. _____ = the parties or people who run countries (C)

5. _____ = the cost or charge for instruction (D)

Now find definitions or meaning explanations for these words from the same reading. Write them on the lines.

6. international student = _a college student from another country_ (A)

7. postsecondary = _____ (A)

8. developing nations = _____ (B)

9. private schools = _____ (D)

10. citizens and immigrants = _____ (D)

2 Matching Vocabulary Words with Definitions Look at the columns below. Match each vocabulary word on the left with the correct definition on the right. The vocabulary words are from "University Life Around the World," on pages 11–13. The letters in parentheses ( ) are the letters of the paragraphs.

Vocabulary Words

1. __l__ complete (A)
2. _____ public transportation (A)
3. _____ requirements (A)
4. _____ certificates and degrees (A)
5. _____ similar (B)
6. _____ score (B)
7. _____ financial aid (B)
8. _____ tuition (B)
9. _____ an exit exam (B)
10. _____ academic lectures (C)
11. _____ facilities (D)
12. _____ learning resource centers (D)
13. _____ distance learning (D)
14. _____ audio (D)

Definitions

a. proof of completion of courses of studies
b. necessary courses
c. the points or grade a student gets on a test
d. the bus or subway
e. the cost for educational instruction
f. the buildings and equipment of a school, college, or university
g. just about the same
h. courses by video, video conferencing, or computers to students in different places
i. money for students from scholarships, grants, or loans
j. having to do with things you can hear
k. a test for leaving high school
l. to finish or end something
m. formal talks by professors or instructors on subjects of study
n. places with computers and audio and video equipment for learning

For more vocabulary practice, give the reasons for your answers. Then cover the vocabulary words on the left. Read the definitions on the right and guess the vocabulary word. You can also give explanations of the meanings of the items on the left in your own words.

RECOGNIZING WORDS WITH THE SAME OR SIMILAR MEANINGS

Some words in a definition can have the same or a similar meaning as the vocabulary word. The word *similar* means "alike but not exactly the same."

3 Recognizing Words with Similar Meanings In each group of vocabulary items from Chapter 1, find the three words with the same or similar meanings. Which word doesn't belong? Cross it out, as in the example.

1. country   nation   ~~software~~   culture
2. students   atmosphere   learners   class members
3. teachers   instructors   professors   undergraduates
4. higher   ways   methods   styles

5. individual   casual   informal   relaxed

6. a quiz   a cafeteria   a test   an exam

7. a score   a textbook   points   a grade

8. scholarships   titles   loans   financial aid

4 **Focusing on High-Frequency Words** Read the paragraph below and fill in each blank with a word from the box. When you finish, check your answers on page 6, Paragraph C.

abroad	engineering	experience	international
attend	especially	governments	skills

Why Students _____ School Abroad
₁

C   Why do high school and college graduates go to colleges and universities far from their homes? Undergraduates are postsecondary students without college degrees. Often, undergraduates want the _____ of life in new cultures. Maybe they want to learn
₂
another language well. Many students want degrees in business,   5 _____, or technology. These subjects are not always
₃
available in their home countries. Some _____ and
₄
companies send their best graduate students and workers to other countries for new knowledge and _____ . And some
₅
_____ students from expensive private schools at   10
₆
home save money through study _____ programs,
₇
_____ in developing nations.
₈

Using the Internet

Searching the Internet
Do an Internet search about foreign students in higher education. Type in something like this: *studying abroad in _____ (name of any country, state, and/or city).*

5 **Making Connections** Look up two or more of the colleges or universities in the country you chose. Choose one that looks interesting to you. Take notes below.

Name and location of the college or university: _____

Offerings for international students: _____

_____

Requirements to attend: _____

_____

What you like about it: _____

_____

Part 4   Focus on Testing

SUMMARIZING

The TOEFL® iBT includes summary tasks, but they are different from what most people do in academic classes. In the TOEFL® iBT, some reading passages are followed by a summary task. The first sentence of the summary is given, and you have to complete the summary by choosing correct sentences from a list. Some sentences do not belong in the summary because they express ideas that are not presented in the passage or are minor ideas in the passage.

Try to recognize the main ideas within the given list and decide whether an answer:

1. expresses an idea that is truly in the reading

2. expresses the idea accurately

3. states a main idea or only a supporting detail

Practicing Summaries An introductory sentence for a short summary of the reading passage "International Students" is provided on the next page. Complete the summary by selecting the THREE answer choices that express the most important ideas in the passage.

TOEFL is a registered trademark of Education Testing Service (ETS). This publication is not endorsed or approved by ETS.

Summary

Studying internationally (in a country other than one's own) can be very beneficial for both the student and other parties.

- (A) The economy of a developing nation is not highly technological.
- (B) Colleges and universities welcome the diversity, and the money, that foreign students bring.
- (C) Many international students go abroad in search of new experiences.
- (D) It is both difficult and dangerous to study in a foreign country.
- (E) Sponsored by companies or governments, some foreign students have been sent abroad to develop skills or gain knowledge that is hard to get in the home country.

Self-Assessment Log

Read the lists below. Check (✓) the strategies and vocabulary that you learned in this chapter. Look through the chapter or ask your instructor about the strategies and words that you do not understand.

Reading and Vocabulary-Building Strategies

- ❏ Previewing the topic
- ❏ Previewing vocabulary
- ❏ Recognizing reading structure in a textbook
- ❏ Recognizing topics, main ideas, and supporting details
- ❏ Summarizing
- ❏ Getting meaning from context: definitions and italics
- ❏ Recognizing words with the same or similar meanings

Target Vocabulary

Nouns

- ❏ academic lectures
- ❏ assignments
- ❏ atmosphere
- ❏ certificates
- ❏ citizens*
- ❏ developing nations
- ❏ distance learning
- ❏ engineering*
- ❏ exit exam
- ❏ experience*
- ❏ facilities
- ❏ financial aid
- ❏ governments*
- ❏ immigrants
- ❏ instructors
- ❏ learning resource centers
- ❏ loans*
- ❏ methods
- ❏ points*
- ❏ public transportation
- ❏ quizzes
- ❏ requirements
- ❏ scholarships
- ❏ scores
- ❏ skills*
- ❏ styles
- ❏ tuition
- ❏ universities*
- ❏ views*

Verbs

- ❏ attend*
- ❏ complete*

Adjectives

- ❏ abroad*
- ❏ audio
- ❏ foreign*
- ❏ individual
- ❏ international*
- ❏ private*
- ❏ public*
- ❏ relaxed
- ❏ similar

* These words are among the 2,000 most frequently used words in English.

2

Experiencing Nature

In This Chapter

You will read about the effects of weather on people. You will also learn about possible global changes in climate. In the first reading, you will learn about the influence weather can have on people's health. You will also find out why people's moods (emotions) may change according to the season and weather. In the second reading, you will read about different changes to the earth's climate, such as global warming, and the causes of these changes.

❝ A change in the weather is sufficient to recreate the world and ourselves. **❞**

—Marcel Proust
French novelist (1871–1922)

Connecting to the Topic

1. Look at the photo below. Where do you think these people are? What are the weather conditions?

2. Do you find that your mood changes depending on the weather? If so, how?

3. Have you noticed any changes to the climate during your lifetime? If so, what are they?

The Powerful Influence of Weather

Before You Read

1 **Previewing the Topic** Look at the photos and discuss the questions in your groups.

1. Describe the people and their actions. What are they doing? What are they wearing? How do you think they are feeling? Why?

2. Describe the kinds of weather in the photos. Which kinds do you like? Which do you dislike? Why?

3. Make comparisons. How is the weather in the photos like the weather in your area? How is it different?

▲ Hot weather

▲ Rainy weather

▲ Windy weather

▲ Snowy weather

2 Predicting Think about and discuss possible answers to these questions with your group. Write down your answers. If you don't know the answers, make predictions. You can look for the answers when you read "The Powerful Influence of Weather."

1. What are the meanings of the following words related to weather? What are *biometeorologists*? What is the *atmosphere*? What is the *weather*?

2. How can some kinds of wind affect people's health?

3. In what ways might other weather conditions influence human health?

4. What effects might the weather have on people's moods and emotions?

3 Previewing Vocabulary Read the vocabulary items below from the first reading. Then listen to the words and phrases. Put a check mark (✓) next to the words you know. You can come back to the words you don't know after you read.

Nouns

- ❑ asthma
- ❑ atmosphere
- ❑ biometeorologists
- ❑ blood pressure
- ❑ diseases
- ❑ disorder
- ❑ effects
- ❑ flu (influenza)
- ❑ headaches
- ❑ heart attacks
- ❑ humidity
- ❑ moods
- ❑ personalities
- ❑ pneumonia
- ❑ researchers
- ❑ scientists
- ❑ strokes
- ❑ temperature
- ❑ weather

Verbs

- ❑ affects
- ❑ causes
- ❑ increase
- ❑ influence

Adjectives

- ❑ depressed
- ❑ depressing
- ❑ drier (dry)
- ❑ forceful
- ❑ humid
- ❑ irritable
- ❑ moody
- ❑ nervous
- ❑ physical
- ❑ powerful
- ❑ sudden
- ❑ warmer

Read

4 Reading an Article Read the following article. Then do the activities that follow.

The Powerful Influence of Weather

Biometeorologists and Their Research

A   **Weather** has a **powerful** impact on the physical world. It also **affects** people's personalities. How do we know about the **effects** of weather on people? We know from **biometeorologists**. These **scientists** study weather. They study how atmospheric conditions affect human health and emotions. The word **atmosphere** means "the air around the earth." *Atmospheric conditions at a time or place"* is a definition of the word *weather*. Some examples of these conditions are sun, wind, rain, snow,   5

humidity (the amount of moisture in the air), and air pressure (the force of air). The weather conditions of the atmosphere greatly **influence** (or affect) people's health, thinking, and feelings. 10

How Wind Can Affect Health

B   All over the world, winds come down from high mountain areas. The winds fall faster and faster, and the air becomes warmer and drier. What do scientists say about the health effects of this kind of weather? According to biometeorologists in Russia, powerful winds from the mountains **increase** the number of **strokes** (blood vessel attacks in the brain). Also, sometimes 15 strong southern winds blow north over Italy. During these times, researchers say, Italians have more **heart attacks** (sudden stopping of the heart). People everywhere have bad **headaches** during times of **forceful** winds. And Japanese weather scientists say there is an **increase** in the number of **asthma** attacks. (Asthma is a lung **disorder**. It causes breathing problems.) 20

Possible Effects of Other Kinds of Weather

C   Do other kinds of weather influence physical health? Sudden **temperature** changes in winter are often associated with a cold or the **flu**. (The *flu*, or *influenza*, is a viral **disease**.) However, colds and flu probably increase because people are 25 in close contact (near one another) indoors in cold weather. Colds and flu may even lead to **pneumonia** (another lung disease). Other illnesses also increase during long periods (times) of cold weather. In most places, 30 diseases of the blood and heart attacks are more common in winter. But in some very hot and humid (wet) regions, there are more heart attacks in summer. Many people have high blood pressure (a health condition). In three 35 out of four people, blood pressure falls (goes down) in warm weather. But some people have lower blood pressure in the cool or cold times of the year.

▲ Colds and flu are common in winter.

Weather and Mood

D   These forces of nature greatly affect people's **moods** (emotional conditions and feelings) too. For many people, winter in the northern 40 regions is very depressing. They eat and sleep a lot, but they usually feel tired. They are **nervous** and can't work well. They are irritable (not very nice to other people). Biometeorologists even have a name for this condition. The name is Seasonal Affective Disorder (SAD). Scientists think the cause of this mood disorder is the long periods of darkness. Even 45 during the day, it is often cloudy or gray. What can people with SAD do about their moods? Naturally, they need more light! On bright days they feel better. But people don't work very well on sunny, hot, and humid days. The best weather for good work and thinking is cool and clear.

Conclusion and Summary

E   Are the people around you becoming sick more often? Are they getting   50
more colds or the flu or even pneumonia? Are they having more health problems like headaches or asthma attacks or heart disease? Or are *you* becoming **moody**? Are you getting more tired or **depressed** (low in mood) or sad? Remember—according to biometeorologists and other weather scientists—the cause may be the atmosphere!   55

After You Read

Strategy

Using a Diagram to Show Cause and Effect
To clearly organize your ideas on why things happen, you can use a diagram. Write notes on the *causes* of your topic on the left side and include details on its *effects* on the right side. See the example below:

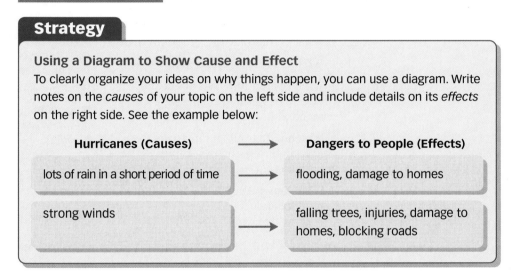

Hurricanes (Causes) ⟶ **Dangers to People (Effects)**

| lots of rain in a short period of time | ⟶ | flooding, damage to homes |
| strong winds | ⟶ | falling trees, injuries, damage to homes, blocking roads |

5 **Identifying Cause and Effect** This diagram shows the effects of different kinds of weather on people's health and emotions. Complete the chart by filling in the five blank lines in the boxes.

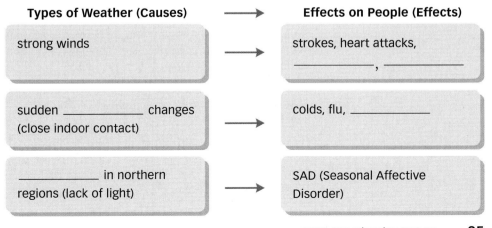

Types of Weather (Causes) ⟶ **Effects on People (Effects)**

strong winds	⟶	strokes, heart attacks, _____, _____
sudden _____ changes (close indoor contact)	⟶	colds, flu, _____
_____ in northern regions (lack of light)	⟶	SAD (Seasonal Affective Disorder)

RECOGNIZING READING STRUCTURE: TITLES AND PARAGRAPH TOPICS

Usually, a reading selection is about one general subject or topic. The information in each paragraph is about a different topic within the subject of the whole reading. Remember: Titles often tell topics in a general way.

6 **Recognizing Reading Structure: Titles and Paragraph Topics** Match the questions on the left with the answers on the right. Write the correct letter on the line.

1. __*f*__ What is the title of Chapter 2 of *Interactions I Reading?*

2. _____ What is the title of the first reading selection in Chapter 2?

3. _____ What is the title of Paragraph A?

4. _____ What is the topic of Paragraph B?

5. _____ What is Paragraph C about?

6. _____ Which paragraph tells about the effects of weather on people's moods?

7. _____ Which paragraph summarizes the information in the other four paragraphs?

8. _____ What general subject is the whole reading about?

a. "How Wind Can Affect Health"

b. "The Powerful Influence of Weather"

c. Paragraph E

d. Paragraph D

e. "Biometeorologists and Their Research"

f. "Experiencing Nature"

g. possible effects of some kinds of weather other than wind

h. ways weather can influence people's physical and emotional health

7 **Recognizing the Main Ideas** Read the possible statements about the main ideas of the paragraphs in the reading "The Powerful Influence of Weather." The letters in parentheses ( ) refer to paragraphs in the reading. Read each one and determine if it is the main idea of that paragraph. Write *T* (true) or *F* (false) on each line. Then change each false statement to a true statement.

Example

1. __*F*__ *Biometeorologists* study human responses to academic lectures. A definition of *weather* is "places on the earth like mountains, countries, and communities." (A)

   Biometeorologists are "researchers of human responses to weather." A definition of __weather__ is "atmosphere conditions like sun, wind, and temperature."

2. _____ During times of fast, strong winds from high mountain areas, there are more health problems like strokes, heart attacks, headaches, and asthma. (B)

3. _____ Sudden winter temperature changes, long cold periods, or heat and humidity can bring illnesses like colds, flu, or pneumonia. (C)

4. _____ The atmosphere and weather don't affect people's moods. People in the northern regions just like to eat and sleep a lot, work badly, are tired, and feel depressed all the time. (D)

5. _____ According to scientists, the cause of health problems and sad moods may be higher education around the world! (E)

8 **Recognizing Supporting Details** Read the five main-idea questions that follow about the information in the reading. Three details correctly answer each question. Cross out the untrue, unrelated detail. The first item is an example.

1. What are the meanings of some words and phrases related to the topic of weather?
   a. A definition of *biometeorologists* is "researchers with interest in human responses to the weather."
   b. The word *atmosphere* means "the air around the earth."
   c. *Atmospheric conditions* is another phrase for weather.
   d. ~~Sun, wind, temperature, air pressure, and the amount of moisture in the atmosphere have no effect on human health and emotions.~~

2. How can some kinds of winds affect people's health?
   a. Strong, fast winds from mountain regions warm and dry the air and can cause strokes.
   b. Most biometeorologists are in the developing nations of Latin America, Asia, and Africa.
   c. Bad headaches and asthma attacks are some other possible examples of the effects of the winds.
   d. Maybe there are more strokes and heart attacks during windy weather of this kind.

3. In what ways might other kinds of weather influence human health?
   a. Biometeorologists are always sad or depressed or moody. Weather isn't important to them.
   b. Sudden winter temperature changes might bring colds, flu, or pneumonia.
   c. During long cold periods, people have more blood diseases and heart attacks.
   d. Air temperature affects people's blood pressure in different ways.

4. What effects might the weather have on people's moods and emotions?
   a. In northern areas of the earth, the long periods of darkness influence many people's moods.
   b. No one likes cool, clear weather because it makes it hard to work or think well.
   c. Bright, hot days with high humidity can also affect human emotions.
   d. People with SAD (Seasonal Affective Disorder) may feel hungry, tired, nervous, and depressed.

5. What is the conclusion of the reading selection about the influence of weather on people's physical and mental health?

    a. Foreign students don't do well in countries without changes in atmospheric conditions.

    b. Weather conditions in the atmosphere can greatly influence people's health, thinking, and feelings.

    c. Some kinds of illnesses and health problems increase with some kinds of weather or weather changes.

    d. The weather affects people's moods and emotions, too.

Now, go back to Activity 2 in the *Before You Read* section on page 23. Look at the answers you wrote down before you read the article. Change them if necessary.

- Give definitions in your answer to Question 1.
- Give examples in your answers to Questions 2, 3, and 4.

 9 Discussing the Reading In small groups, talk about your answers to the following questions.

1. Is the study of the effects of weather on people useful research? Why or why not?

2. Do some kinds of weather (wind, sun, temperature, humidity, rain, snow, air pressure, and other conditions) seem to affect your health, feelings, or mood? In what ways?

3. In your opinion, do atmospheric conditions influence world events in important ways? Give reasons for your opinion.

Part 2   Reading Skills and Strategies

Global Climate Changes

Before You Read

 1 Previewing Vocabulary Read the vocabulary items on page 29 from the next reading. Then listen to the words and phrases. Put a check mark (✓) next to the words you know. You can come back to the other words after you read.

Nouns

- ❏ blizzards
- ❏ carbon dioxide (CO_2)
- ❏ climate
- ❏ damage
- ❏ desert
- ❏ droughts
- ❏ floods
- ❏ gases
- ❏ global warming
- ❏ the globe

- ❏ hurricanes
- ❏ meteorologists
- ❏ plants
- ❏ storms
- ❏ tornadoes
- ❏ tropical rain forests

Verbs

- ❏ cutting down
- ❏ follow
- ❏ vary

Adjectives

- ❏ average
- ❏ common
- ❏ extreme
- ❏ global
- ❏ major
- ❏ natural
- ❏ typical
- ❏ worse
- ❏ yearly

Adverbs

- ❏ generally
- ❏ slowly

Phrases

- ❏ at least
- ❏ from season to season
- ❏ in contrast (to)
- ❏ more and more

GETTING THE TOPIC FROM TITLES AND HEADINGS

The title of a reading selection often gives the general subject or topic of the whole reading. Each paragraph of the reading is about a more specific (narrower) topic within the general (wide) subject. For example, below are four paragraph headings for the next reading selection "Global Climate Changes." The headings tell the paragraph topics in phrases, not full sentences. The important words begin with capital letters.

---

2 **Recognizing Topics and Main Ideas** Quickly read each paragraph of the article below. Then choose the best heading from the list below and write it above the paragraph. Then underline the main idea in each paragraph.

- ▪ General Changes in the Nature of Weather
- ▪ The Powerful Effect of People on Nature
- ▪ Climate in Regions of the Globe
- ▪ Global Warming and the "El Niño" Effect

Read

3 **Reading an Article** Read the following article.

Global Climate Changes

Climate in Regions of the Globe

A   The word *weather* means "the atmospheric conditions at a specific place and time." The weather can vary from day to day. In contrast to weather, *climate* is "the general or average atmospheric conditions of a region." *In different areas of the globe, the climate generally stays the same from year to year.* For example, the climate in the **desert** is usually very dry. It may be cold in winter and hot in summer, but there is very little rain or humidity. In contrast, in tropical rain forests, there is very high

    5

humidity. In most other areas of the world, the weather is cool or cold and wet or dry in the winter season. It is warm or hot and dry or humid in the summer months.

10

B According to some **meteorologists** (weather researchers), the earth's climate is changing **slowly**. In most places on the earth, the weather varies from season to season or even from day to day. In contrast, the **typical** climate is similar every year. Even so, there may be global climate changes from one long time period to another. What are these changes? Some scientists believe the weather is becoming more **extreme**. There are longer periods of very cold and very hot **temperatures**. There are more and more powerful **hurricanes** and tornadoes (**storms** with strong, fast winds) and **blizzards** (heavy snowstorms). **Floods** (large amounts of water on dry land) and long droughts (times without enough **rain**) are causing greater and greater physical **damage** to the human communities on Earth. These extreme forces of nature will get even **worse** in the future, say some people. And every change in climate in one part of the globe will bring more extreme changes in other areas.

15

20

25

▲ A storm

C Global warming and *El Niño* are having major effects on the earth's atmosphere, weather, and climate. At least that's the opinion of many researchers and scientists. What is global warming? It is a slow increase in the average yearly temperature of the planet. The cause is an increase of gases in the atmosphere. What is El Niño? The Spanish phrase means "The Little Boy" or "The Christ Child." It names a weather condition most common in the month of December. This "seasonal weather disorder" is a change in the atmosphere of the tropical areas of the Pacific Ocean. It increases the amount of rain in the Americas and can bring strong winds and hurricanes. In contrast, El Niño may cause drought in the southern and western Pacific (Asia). Blizzards, snow, and long periods of low temperatures may follow in the northern regions of the globe.

30

35

40

D   Not all meteorologists believe there is much natural global warming. According to these scientists, the El Niño effect is not getting stronger. So why is the temperature of the earth going up? Why are tropical storms like 45 hurricanes causing more and greater flood and wind damage? Probably, human beings are the main cause of the extreme effects of weather and climate changes. Cars and factories are putting more and more gases like **carbon dioxide (CO$_2$)** into the earth's atmosphere. Coal and oil add carbon dioxide to the air, too. Trees and plants take in carbon dioxide, but 50 humans are cutting down the rain forests and putting up buildings where green plants used to grow. The world has a lot of people now, and it will have a lot more people in the future.

After You Read

Strategy

Summarizing a Paragraph

In Chapter 1, you learned that a summary is a short statement of the important information in a reading. How can you learn to summarize better? Here are some suggestions:

- In English, think about the meaning of the information.
- In your own words, begin with the most general point about the paragraph topic. Tell the main idea in your own words.
- Then give only the important supporting details (definitions, examples, facts, and reasons) for that point.
- To shorten your summary, put similar ideas in the same sentence.

Example

Here is a possible summary of Paragraph A from the reading "Global Climate Changes."

All over the world, the typical climate of an area is generally similar every year. It is dry in the deserts and wet in the tropics. In most places, it is colder in winter and warm or hot in summer.

4 Summarizing a Paragraph Work in groups of three. Have each person choose one of the remaining paragraphs from the reading "Global Climate Changes." Read it carefully. Summarize the main idea and the important supporting details. Then tell or read your summary to your group.

 5 Discussing the Reading Work in groups of three. Read and discuss the questions below.

1. Describe the typical climate in your area of the world. Does the weather change in the various seasons? If so, how?

2. Do you think the earth's climate is changing? If so, how and why is it changing? If not, why not?

3. What are your predictions for the future of the atmosphere and nature on earth? Give reasons for your predictions.

 6 Talking It Over People have many different beliefs about nature and the weather. Some ideas come from scientific fact. Others come from people's experiences or culture. In your opinion, which of the following statements are true? Check (✓) the true statements and explain your opinions to a small group. Give reasons for your opinions.

❑ In nature, there is no good or bad. There is no right or wrong. There is only the power of cause and effect.

❑ Why does it rain? It's useless to ask. It just does.

❑ Meteorologists and other researchers can study the weather, but they can't know or tell about future weather.

❑ A lot of people complain about the weather. Do they have the power to change it? Of course not.

❑ Nature doesn't listen to criticism or complaints. Do human beings have to listen to them? No, they can be like nature.

❑ If you ask for rain, don't be surprised if you get thunder and lightning.

❑ Why do people get depressed about the rain? Without rain, there would be no rainbows.

❑ Two people can never see exactly the same rainbow. But they can take a picture of it.

❑ Do you want sunshine today? Carry a big umbrella and wear a heavy raincoat. Then it won't rain.

❑ Is your arthritis pain increasing? This means wet weather is coming.

Strategy

Getting Meaning from Contexts, Parentheses, and from Words with Similar Meanings

You can often find the meanings of new vocabulary words from the context (the other words in the sentence or paragraph).

- The meaning can be in parentheses ( ). As explained in Chapter 1, a definition can come after the words *be* or *mean*. Here are examples for the words *biometeorologists* and *atmosphere*.

Example

We know about the effects of weather from *biometeorologists* (weather researchers). These scientists study human health and emotions in response to atmospheric conditions. The word *atmosphere* means "the air around the earth."

- There might be other words with the same or similar meanings as the item in the sentence or paragraph. In the following example, the adjectives *powerful, strong,* and *forceful* have similar meanings.

Example

Powerful winds from the mountains of Russia may increase the number of strokes. In times of *strong* winds in Italy, Italians have more heart attacks. People everywhere have bad headaches during times of *forceful* winds.

---

1 **Getting Meaning from Context** Complete the following sentences with words from the reading "The Powerful Influence of Weather" on pages 23–25. Some definitions appear following *be* or *mean*; some are in parentheses. There are also words with the same or similar meanings. The letters in parentheses ( ) refer to the paragraphs of the reading.

1. These weather researchers study health and emotions in response to atmospheric conditions. They are ___biometeorologists___ . (A)

2. This word means "the air around the earth." It is the _____. (A)

3. Some examples of kinds of atmospheric conditions are sun, wind,

   _____ , _____ , _____ , and

   _____ . (A)

4. Another word for "atmospheric conditions at a time or place" is

_____. (A)

5. A word for "blood vessel attacks in the brain" is _____. (B)

6. A heart attack is a _____. (B)

7. A short word for "influenza, a viral disease" is _____. (C)

8. Asthma and pneumonia are disorders or diseases of the _____

_____. (B, C)

9. The meaning of the word *moods* is _____. (D)

10. The name SAD means "_____." (D)

This condition is caused by _____. (D)

2 Recognizing Words with the Same or Similar Meanings

In each group of vocabulary items below from Chapters 1 and 2, find the three words with the same or similar meanings. Which word doesn't belong? Cross it out, as in the example.

1. region   area   ~~real life~~   place

2. the world   countries and cultures   the globe   earth

3. condition   affect   influence   have an effect on

4. global   powerful   physically strong   forceful

5. human emotions   feelings   moods   physical health

6. fall   go down   get lower   increase

7. diseases   sicknesses   health disorders and problems   science

8. sad   common   depressed   low in mood

9. season   time of year   air pressure   three-month period

10. human beings   meteorologists   weather researchers   scientists

For more practice, compare your answers with a partner. Give a reason for each answer.

3 **Matching Vocabulary Items with Examples** Sometimes examples can explain the meaning of a word or phrase. For example, *sun*, *rain*, and *wind* are examples of *kinds of weather*. Look at the columns below. Match each vocabulary word or phrase in the first column with the examples in the second column.

Vocabulary

1. __d__ atmospheric conditions

2. _____ kinds of extreme weather

3. _____ air temperatures

4. _____ Earth's natural materials and gases

5. _____ countries of the world

6. _____ the largest areas of the globe

7. _____ diseases or health disorders

8. _____ how people feel (adjectives)

9. _____ seasons of the year

10. _____ natural areas or regions of the earth

Examples

a. the ocean, seas, islands, deserts, forests

b. coal, oil, carbon dioxide, air, water

c. Asia, Europe, the Middle East, Africa, the Americas

d. sun, rain, snow, wind, humidity

e. happy, tired, sad, depressed, nervous, moody

f. blizzards, tornadoes, hurricanes, floods, droughts

g. Japan, China, Russia, Italy, Mexico, the United States

h. winter, spring, summer, fall

i. hot, warm, cool, cold

j. stroke, asthma, influenza, pneumonia, headaches, high blood pressure, arthritis

For more practice, give more examples for the items in the vocabulary column above.

4 **Focusing on High-Frequency Words** Read the paragraph below and fill in each blank with a word from the box. When you finish, check your answers on page 30.

damage	floods	slowly	temperatures	weather
extreme	rain	storms	typical	worse

General Changes in the Nature of Weather

B   According to some meteorologists (_____ researchers),

the earth's climate is changing _____. In most places on the

planet, the weather varies from season to season or even from day to day.

In contrast, the _____ climate is similar every year. Even so,

there may be global climate changes from one long time period to another.   5

What are these changes? Some scientists believe the weather is becoming

more _____. There are longer periods of very cold and very
4

hot _____. There are more and more powerful hurricanes
5

and tornadoes (_____ with strong, fast winds) and blizzards
6

(heavy snowstorms). _____ (large amounts of water on dry   10
7

land) and long droughts (times without enough _____) are
8

causing greater and greater physical _____ to the human
9

communities on Earth. These extreme forces of nature will get even

_____ in the future, say some people. And every change in
10

climate in one part of the globe will bring more extreme changes in other   15

areas.

5 **Making Connections** Do an Internet search about the weather in two parts
of the world. You can type in *weather in* _____ *(name of the place)*
or *climate in* _____ *(name of the place)*.

Take notes on today's temperature and other weather conditions. Which weather
seems the most pleasant to you? Complete the chart below. Share your findings and
thoughts with the class.

	Place #1	Place #2
Date		
Temperature today		
Weather conditions today		
Is this weather pleasant to you? Why or why not?		

TOEFL® iBT

FINDING MAIN IDEAS AND VOCABULARY CLUSTERS

The reading passages on the TOEFL® iBT have titles, but the different paragraphs don't have headings. The paragraphs do not all have easy-to-find topic sentences. So one way to help find the main idea is to look at vocabulary clusters—sets of words or phrases similar to each other in meaning.

As an example, look again at the first reading in this chapter, "The Powerful Influence of Weather", on page 23. The first of many vocabulary clusters in the reading is in the first paragraph. *Biometeorologists, these scientists,* and the pronoun *they* are several ways of referring to the same thing. This variety helps you understand unfamiliar words in context. Many expressions for the same idea appear throughout the paragraph, so it could be a main idea. An idea that is stated only once or twice is unlikely to generate a vocabulary cluster and is unlikely to be a main idea.

Relating Vocabulary Clusters to Main Ideas Answer the questions that come after this short reading. (Remember that TOEFL® iBT readings are much longer than this.)

A   Meteorologists use the term *training thunderstorms* to describe an especially troublesome weather phenomenon. These storms usually cause at least moderate flooding and may be a serious threat to life and property. In August 1996, for example, several waves developed along a front in west Texas and dumped a total of seven inches of rain on some areas in four hours. The storms came one after another, each successive cell pouring more rain on the ground that had been thoroughly soaked by those before it. Two interstate highways were closed because of flooding, and several ranches were isolated by high water for several days.

B   In this context, *training* means "following each other along the same route," much like the cars of a passing train. Thunderstorms tend to train in two situations. One involves a front (boundary between different air masses) that is barely moving. The front is an atmospheric battle line, where contrasts in temperature and humidity can fuel the formation of thunderheads. Since the atmospheric battle line does not move very much, the same areas get rained on over and over again as storms continually form and then continue along the front.

C   Training also occurs with a so-called cut-off low. Such a low-pressure system moves unpredictably, and sometimes slowly, because it is not pushed along by high-altitude winds. Tropical storm systems, such as hurricanes, are the best-known type. Thunderstorms circulate repeatedly around the cut-off low, which may not move for a long time. Thunderstorms around Hurricane Mitch in 1998, for example, trained for several days over parts of Honduras. Cell after cell, swelled by moisture from the Caribbean Sea, rolled ashore and brought more than 20 inches of rain. Deadly floods and mudslides affected the areas that saw the most constant chain of storms.

1. List three words in this reading's vocabulary cluster for *thunderstorm(s)*:

   _____

   _____

   _____

2. List three words or phrases in this reading's vocabulary cluster for *train (*or *training)*:

   _____

   _____

   _____

3. List one phrase in this reading's vocabulary cluster for *hurricane(s)*:

   _____

4. Which of the following best expresses the main idea of the reading as a whole?

   - (A) Meteorologists call repetitive thunderstorms "training thunderstorms."
   - (B) The concept of "training thunderstorms" helps scientists understand hurricanes.
   - (C) Thunderstorms often train near slow-moving weather features, causing damage.
   - (D) Meteorologists are developing new ways to keep thunderstorms from training.

Self-Assessment Log

Read the lists below. Check (✓) the strategies and vocabulary that you learned in this chapter. Look through the chapter or ask your instructor about the strategies and words that you do not understand.

Reading and Vocabulary-Building Strategies

- ❏ Identifying cause and effect
- ❏ Recognizing reading structure: titles and paragraph topics
- ❏ Recognizing topics and main ideas
- ❏ Summarizing a paragraph
- ❏ Getting meaning from context, parentheses, and words with similar meanings
- ❏ Focusing on high-frequency words

Target Vocabulary

Nouns

- ❏ asthma
- ❏ atmosphere
- ❏ biometeorologists
- ❏ blizzards
- ❏ carbon dioxide (CO$_2$)
- ❏ damage*
- ❏ desert*
- ❏ disease*
- ❏ disorder
- ❏ effects*
- ❏ floods*
- ❏ flu (influenza)
- ❏ headaches
- ❏ heart attacks*
- ❏ humidity
- ❏ hurricanes
- ❏ meteorologists
- ❏ moods
- ❏ pneumonia
- ❏ rain*
- ❏ scientists*
- ❏ storms*
- ❏ strokes
- ❏ temperatures*
- ❏ weather*

Verbs

- ❏ affects
- ❏ increase*
- ❏ influence*

Adjectives

- ❏ depressed
- ❏ extreme*
- ❏ forceful*
- ❏ moody
- ❏ nervous
- ❏ powerful*
- ❏ temperature*
- ❏ typical*
- ❏ worse*

Adverb

- ❏ slowly*

* These words are among the 2,000 most frequently used words in English.

3

Living to Eat, or Eating to Live?

In This Chapter

Why do people choose to eat the way they do? What makes up a nutritious diet? Is it OK to eat junk food? In this chapter you will read about individual and cultural reasons for food choices around the world. You will also learn about changes in the global diet. In the first reading, you will learn some different definitions of the word *diet* and how and why people choose to eat what they do. In Part 2, you will read some interesting facts about food, what elements are necessary for human life, and how diets around the world are becoming more and more similar.

> ❝ To read without reflecting is like eating without digesting. ❞

—Edmund Burke
British political writer (1729–1797)

Connecting to the Topic

1. Look at the photo below. Where is this woman? What is she doing?

2. Look at the title of this chapter, *Living to Eat, or Eating to Live?* What do you think it means?

3. Many holiday celebrations involve special foods. Think of a holiday in your culture. What special foods do people prepare and eat on that day? Why?

Global Diet Choices

Before You Read

1 **Previewing the Topic** Look at the photos and read the questions below. Answer the questions in small groups.

1. Describe each photo. Where are the people? What are they doing? What are they saying to each other?

2. Talk about the foods in each photo. Are they packaged or prepared? Fresh, canned, or frozen? Healthy or unhealthy?

3. Make comparisons. How is the food in the photos like typical foods in your culture? How is it different?

▲ A couple at a fast food restaurant

▲ A man at a supermarket

▲ A family eating at home

2 Predicting Think about these questions and write down short answers. If you don't know the answers, make predictions. Then discuss them in small groups. You can look for the answers when you read "Global Diet Choices."

1. What are some meanings of the word *diet*?

2. Are fast-food places international? What types of foods are common fast foods?

3. How do most people make decisions about food and diet?

4. What are some examples of diets based on location, history, tradition, or religion?

5. How are diet choices becoming more alike around the globe?

3 Previewing Vocabulary Read the vocabulary items below from the first reading. Then listen to the words and phrases. Put a check mark (✓) next to the words you know. You can learn the other words now or come back to them after you read.

Nouns
- ❑ additives
- ❑ atmosphere
- ❑ breakfast
- ❑ carbohydrates (carbs)
- ❑ complex carbohydrates
- ❑ convenience
- ❑ customs
- ❑ dairy
- ❑ diabetes
- ❑ diet
- ❑ dishes
- ❑ elements
- ❑ fast food
- ❑ fats
- ❑ habits
- ❑ insects
- ❑ low-carb diet
- ❑ minerals
- ❑ preferences
- ❑ protein
- ❑ soy products
- ❑ vitamins

Verbs
- ❑ diet
- ❑ lose (weight)
- ❑ prefer
- ❑ prohibit

Adjectives
- ❑ famous
- ❑ fried
- ❑ frozen
- ❑ healthy
- ❑ natural
- ❑ nutritious
- ❑ packaged
- ❑ permitted
- ❑ religious
- ❑ slim
- ❑ universal
- ❑ well-rounded

Adverb
- ❑ probably

Read

4 Reading an Article Read the article on the next page. Then do the activities that follow.

Global Diet Choices

Meanings of the Word *Diet*

A   Most words in the English language have more than one simple, or basic, meaning. One example is the word *diet*. The most general definition of the noun is "a person's or a group's usual food choices and **habits**." In a more specific definition, *diet* means "an eating plan with only certain kinds or amounts of food." For instance, a **diet** is often a plan to lose weight. And   5 as a verb, **diet** means "to lose weight." People can "go on a diet," meaning they are starting a program to lose weight.

International Fast Food

B   All over the world, the global diet includes **fast food**—prepared items from inexpensive restaurants, snack bars, or food stands. Some examples of typical American fast food are *hamburgers, hot dogs, sandwiches,* and *fried*   10 *chicken.* Some common international fast foods might be German *sausage* and *schnitzel,* Italian *pizza* and *pasta,* Mexican *tacos* and *burritos,* Middle Eastern *shish kebab* and *falafel,* Japanese *sushi* and   15 *tempura,* and Chinese *egg rolls* and *noodles.* Why is this kind of food becoming even more **universal**, or worldwide? First, fast-food restaurants usually prepare and serve the items quickly. Second, many fast-food   20 restaurants are part of fast-food chains (eating places with the same name and company owner). For instance, the biggest and most famous American fast-food chain serves hamburgers in every continent on the   25

▲ Fast food from around the world

planet except Antarctica. Its menu items may not be exactly alike in all cultures, but its 25,000 restaurants all have the same look and style. The atmosphere seems comfortable and familiar. Third, the items at fast-food places usually cost less than meals in formal restaurants or special **dishes** made at home. And finally, people usually enjoy the taste of the food, even if it   30 is not very nutritious (healthy).

How People Make Individual Food Choices

C   How do most people make their diet decisions? Individual choices are often based on former habits, cost and convenience, beliefs about health and nutrition, and ideas about physical beauty. Some people learn to like certain foods in childhood, and they don't change later in life. Many people have   35 busy lives, so they buy or prepare food and eat it as quickly as possible. Some meal-planners think only fresh and "natural" food is nutritious, so they buy vegetables, fruits, and foods without additives (chemical substances) and prepare it in healthy ways. People with health problems—like high-blood pressure or **diabetes** (a blood-sugar disorder)—may be on special non-salt or non-sugar diets. The nutritional requirements of very young or very old people may be different from the needs of others. Some cultures prefer a slim body to a well-rounded one, so people are always trying to lose weight. They may follow popular diets, such as a **low-carb diet**—an eating system high in protein but low in refined carbohydrates.

Other Reasons for Diet Habits Around the World

D   Unlike individual food plans, the diets of whole cultures and regions come from location, history, and tradition. For example, the typical Mexican diet is a combination of foods from pre-Columbian, Spanish, and French cultures. It is rich in **complex carbohydrates** (corn, beans, rice, breads) and protein (beans, eggs, fish, meat). Fish and fish products from the seas around Japan are one of the most important parts of the traditional Japanese diet. Rich in vitamins and **minerals**, seafood is served grilled, baked, raw, dried, pickled, hot, and cold. **Soy products** (miso, tofu, and bean paste), fermented vegetables, and rice are also important in the typical Japanese diet. Religious practices may also greatly affect diet. For instance, some Jewish people *keep kosher* (follow the requirements of Jewish food preparation and eating). These laws prohibit eating pork or bacon or other meat from pigs, shellfish, snake, or **insects**. In addition, people should not eat meat and **dairy** (milk products) at the same meal. In a similar way, Muslims follow the laws of *eating halal*, an Islamic system of eating only permitted foods. Some foods, such as pork or insects, are not permitted. Though people can eat some meat such as beef from cows, the animals must be killed in a special way, according to ritual. Also, for religious reasons, some Christians eat fish instead of meat on Fridays. They also limit their food choices during Lent (the 40 days before Easter) in the spring.

Conclusion and Summary: The Global Diet

E   Universally, more and more meals include basic necessary food **elements**—*protein*, *carbohydrates*, and *fats*. Almost everywhere, some kind of meat, fish, dairy product, or another food with protein is part of a good **breakfast**, lunch, or dinner. There are also grains, breads, vegetables, fruit, and the like. Many dishes contain the necessary vitamins and minerals. A few families grow their own food, but most people buy food from eating places and markets in their communities. Food may be fresh, prepared, canned, **frozen**, or packaged. "Fast food" is very popular, and maybe it is becoming healthier. In some ways, diet choices are becoming more and more similar around the world. Even so, the variety of food choices is large now and is **probably** going to increase. Are cooking **customs**, eating habits, and food **preferences** all over the world becoming more or less healthy? Are they better or **worse** for human beings? These questions are interesting topics of research and **discussion**.

RECOGNIZING READING STRUCTURE: MAIN-IDEA QUESTIONS FOR PARAGRAPH TOPICS

A well-structured paragraph has a clear topic. The material in each paragraph answers a different main-idea question about that topic.

5 **Recognizing Reading Structure** Read each question below. Which paragraph in the reading "Global Diet Choices" answers each main-idea question? Write the paragraph letter, A, B, C, D, or E.

1. _____ How are diet choices becoming more alike around the world?

2. _____ How do most individuals make decisions about food and diet?

3. _____ What are some diets based on location, history, tradition, or religion?

4. _____ In what ways are fast-food places international?

5. _____ What are some definitions of the word *diet*?

RECOGNIZING ONE- OR TWO-SENTENCE STATEMENTS OF THE MAIN IDEA

You can usually find the answer to a main-idea question in the first one or two sentences of the reading. Those sentences tell the point, or message, of the paragraph.

6 **Recognizing One- or Two-Sentence Statements of the Main Idea**
Read the main-idea statements below about each of the paragraphs in the reading "Global Diet Choices." Write *T* (true) or *F* (false) on each line. Then change the false sentences to true sentences to express the main idea. Next, use them as answers to the five questions in Activity 2.

1. _____ The word *diet* has two basic definitions—"usual food choices" and "an eating plan." (Paragraph A)

2. _____ Fast food has very little variety around the world. It is always hamburgers, hot dogs, and fried chicken. But the atmosphere of fast-food chains varies a lot in different countries. (Paragraph B)

3. _____ Individual choices about food and eating are more often based on history, tradition, and culture than on habits, convenience, cost, and beliefs about health and beauty. (Paragraph C)

4. _____ The typical Mexican and Japanese diets are based on religious law. Some religious people choose foods according to their country's history and location. (Paragraph D)

5. _____ Not many meals around the world include the basic necessary food elements. Almost all families grow their own food, so the global diet is becoming less and less varied. (Paragraph E)

7 Recognizing Supporting Details As you learned in Chapters 1 and 2, each paragraph of a reading includes not only a main idea but also details about it. These details support the point of the paragraph with specific facts, examples, or reasons. Like a well-written main-idea statement, supporting details can answer a main-idea question.

Read the five main-idea questions below from Activity 5. Which three details answer each question? Circle those and cross out the unrelated sentence.

1. What are some definitions of the word *diet*?
   a. It means "ideas or information to think about."
   b. It's a person's or a group's usual food choices or habits.
   c. A diet can be an eating plan with only certain kinds or amounts of food.
   d. It can be a way to lose weight.

2. In what ways are fast-food places now international?
   a. You can find some of the same fast-food chains in different parts of the world.
   b. Quick and convenient items from America, Germany, Italy, Mexico, the Middle East, Japan, China, and other cultures are available.
   c. Formal restaurant meals can be expensive or cheap, natural or prepared, non-fat or non-salt, low-carb and high-fat, and so on.
   d. Fast-food chains often have a similar look and atmosphere in every country.

3. How do most individuals make decisions about food and diet?
   a. Some adults still choose food from their childhoods because that food seems comfortable and familiar.
   b. People with busy lives may choose fast convenience foods, and people with health problems may choose "natural" foods or special diets.
   c. Age and ideas about physical beauty can influence diet decisions.
   d. A well-rounded figure is healthier than a slim body image, so Americans prohibit popular diet plans.

4. What are some diets based on location, history, tradition, or religion?
   a. The typical Mexican diet contains a combination of foods from its pre-Columbian, Spanish, and French history and traditions.
   b. Some people don't eat sugar because they are diabetic.
   c. Because of the location of the country, fish and other seafood plays a major role in the Japanese diet—along with soy products, fermented vegetables, and rice.
   d. Religious Jews may "keep kosher," Muslims may follow the laws of "halal," and devout Christians may make diet decisions for religious reasons.

5. How are diet choices becoming more similar around the world?
   a. Typical meals in many cultures are healthy because they contain the necessary food elements—protein, carbohydrates, fats, vitamins, and minerals.
   b. Fast-food restaurants are more common.
   c. Most people can buy basic, natural, fresh, prepared, canned, frozen, or packaged foods from local markets and restaurants.
   d. Health disorders like heart disease, strokes, and cancer are no longer related to food and eating.

Now, go back to Activity 2 in the *Before You Read* section on page 43. Look at the answers you wrote down before you read the article and answer the questions again.

- Give definitions in your answer to Question 1.
- Give examples in your answers to Questions 2, 4, and 5.
- Give reasons in your answers to Question 3.

 8 Discussing the Reading In small groups, talk about your answers to the following questions.

1. What are your opinions of fast food and of fast-food restaurants? Give reasons for your answers.

2. What are your eating habits like? When and where do you eat? What kinds of food do you usually buy from machines, food stands, snack bars, restaurants, stores, and markets? How do you prepare your food?

3. What are some reasons for your individual diet choices? Are they based on habit, your culture, religion, convenience, beliefs about health and nutrition, ideas about body image, health problems, age, popular diet plans, or something else?

4. In general, do you think eating customs and habits in various places of the world are becoming more similar or more varied? Is the global diet changing? In good ways or bad? Give reasons for your opinions.

Part 2   Reading Skills and Strategies

Facts About Food

Before You Read

 1 Previewing Vocabulary Read the vocabulary items below from the next reading. Then listen to the words and phrases. Put a check mark (✓) next to the words you know. You can come back to the other words after you read.

Nouns
- ❏ bugs
- ❏ caffeine
- ❏ cancer
- ❏ cholesterol
- ❏ desserts
- ❏ discussion
- ❏ effects
- ❏ fiber
- ❏ grains
- ❏ heart disease
- ❏ ingredients
- ❏ medicine
- ❏ memory

- ❏ nutrients
- ❏ nutritionists
- ❏ opinions
- ❏ specialists
- ❏ strokes
- ❏ substances
- ❏ value
- ❏ whole grains

Verbs
- ❏ affect
- ❏ allow
- ❏ support

Adjectives
- ❏ available
- ❏ home-cooked
- ❏ industrialized
- ❏ opposite
- ❏ perfect
- ❏ related
- ❏ required
- ❏ spicy

Adverb
- ❏ financially

Phrases
- ❏ brain power
- ❏ in contrast

MATCHING PARAGRAPH TITLES WITH TOPICS

Often, the title of reading material tells its topic. But a title should look or sound interesting, and it should be short. For these reasons, readers might not know the meaning of a title—at first.

2 **Matching Paragraph Titles with Topics** On the left are four examples of interesting titles on the subject of food and eating. On the right are less interesting but clearer phrases about the topic. Match the titles to the topics with lines, as in the example.

Titles

1. Food for Thought
2. The Fat of the Land
3. Food Fights
4. Getting the Bugs Out

Topics

a. The Effects of Amounts of Dietary Fat in Different Cultures
b. Cooking and Eating Insect Foods for Good Nutrition
c. Opposite or Contrasting Opinions on the Best Eating Habits
d. Brain Foods and Other Nutrients for the Mind and Memory

 3 **Choosing Titles and Recognizing Topic Sentences** Read each paragraph of the article below. On the line above each paragraph, write a possible title from Activity 2. Also, underline the topic sentence in each paragraph. Remember—a topic sentence is a short statement of the main idea or point of a paragraph.

Facts About Food

Food Fights

A   Everywhere on earth there are "food specialists" with opposite (or different) opinions on the best kinds of nutrition for various purposes. A lot of people believe that the healthiest diets are high in fiber, vitamins, and minerals but low in fat, cholesterol, sugar, and salt. Some **nutritionists** say the perfect eating plan

▲ Food specialists disagree on the best kinds of nutrition.

contains mostly carbohydrates without much protein. In contrast, other scientists say people need high-protein meals with meat, chicken, fish, or milk products and only small amounts of **grains**, potatoes, breads, rice, and noodles. One famous diet plan allows only certain foods at certain times—protein with protein, carbohydrates with carbohydrates, fruits alone, and so on. Some eaters stay away from all meat and maybe even fish and milk products. They get their protein from plants, mostly beans. Others want only high-fiber food. These people may not eat white bread or white rice or even cooked vegetables. So what is the best way to eat and be healthy? The discussion of food facts will go on far into the future.

B   The necessary substances and elements for human life and health are water, protein, carbohydrates, fats, vitamins, and minerals. Most kinds of food contain some or all of the required nutrients, but these substances have different effects on people. Various ingredients and dishes affect the mind in different ways, and some kinds of nourishment have better effects on the brain than others. For instance, can broccoli increase brain power? Maybe so. Low levels of some of the B vitamins can cause a decrease in memory and thinking ability, nutritionists say, but dark green vegetables, like broccoli, contain a lot of these nutrients. Another example of a "memory helper" is lecithin—a substance from soybeans, also found in high-fiber foods like nuts and whole grains. High-protein foods influence the mind in more helpful ways than dishes high in sugar and carbohydrates. And the caffeine in coffee or tea may help thinking. Of course, its effects don't last long.

C   In many places outside big cities, food with more than four legs is part of good, healthy home cooking. Fried or grilled ants are a tasty but expensive snack in Colombia, South America. In various parts of Mexico, over 300 types of insects serve as food. In southern Africa, many people like to eat at least one kind of caterpillar or worm. They enjoy it fried, dried, or cooked in tomato sauce. In Thailand, cooks create a spicy hot-pepper sauce with water bugs. In Vietnam, grasshoppers filled with peanuts are a special dish. And in some regions of China, **bugs** are not only a part of meals but an important ingredient in medicine too. Most kinds of insects have high nutritional value. They contain a lot of protein, vitamins, and minerals. Many people like their taste. They are everywhere on the planet. They add to the variety of people's diets. For several reasons, insects are an important kind of food in the global diet, and they may become a more common ingredient in the future.

D   The growing similarities in diet and eating habits around the world are influencing people of various cultures in different ways. For example, Western foods are damaging health in the industrialized island country of Japan. Instead of small meals of seafood, rice, and vegetables, the typical Japanese diet now includes large amounts of meat, dairy products (like whole-milk ice cream), and **desserts** like tiramisu, a rich Italian dish full of chocolate, cheese, and sugar. According to Japanese health researchers, such changes in eating habits are related to a great increase in health problems such as heart disease, strokes, cancer, and diabetes. On the other hand, the changing global diet is having the opposite effect on the people in the Czech Republic. The government of this European nation no longer supports meat and dairy products financially, so the cost of these foods is going up. In contrast, fresh fruits and vegetables are becoming more widely available from private markets and stands. Cooks are even serving salads to schoolchildren, and families are eating healthier home-cooked meals. For these reasons, fewer Czech men are having heart attacks, the women are losing a lot of weight, and most people are living healthier lives.

After You Read

Strategy

More About Summarizing

In previous chapters, you learned some ways to summarize information. Here are some other ways to summarize a paragraph:

- First, say or write the title of the reading material. Then ask a question about the main idea that is answered in the paragraph you are summarizing.
- Begin your summary with a one-sentence general answer to your main-idea question.
- Which information and ideas (facts, examples, and reasons) from the reading support your first statement? Add those in a clear order to your summary.

Here is a possible summary of the first paragraph of the selection "Facts About Food."

What do food specialists around the world believe about nutrition? They may agree on the basics, but they can have very different opinions about the best kinds and amounts of foods for human health. For example, some people say to eat mostly carbohydrates; others believe in high-protein eating plans; still others think fiber is the most important element.

4 Summarizing Work in groups of three. Have each person choose a different paragraph (B, C, or D) from the reading "Facts About Food." Read it carefully. Begin with the title. Summarize the main idea and important supporting details. Then tell or read your summary to your group.

5 Discussing the Reading Work in groups of four. Each person gives the instruction and asks the questions in one of these items. That person takes notes on the other three people's answers. Later, he or she summarizes the discussion about that item for the class. Everyone can ask more questions and make comments.

1. Tell your ideas about good food and nutrition. Is there a "perfect" diet for health and long life? Why do you think this way?

2. Give examples of your experiences with food. In your opinion, do certain foods increase or decrease brainpower (memory and thinking ability)? If so, which ones? How do you feel when you eat them?

3. In big cities and industrialized areas of the world, people don't generally cook or choose insect dishes. What do you think about unusual foods of this kind? Why do you feel that way?

4. Tell about diet changes in your country or culture. What changes are going on? How are they affecting people? Why do you think so?

6 Talking It Over Read the statements below about food. Then write one of your own. From your knowledge and experience, which of these statements are true facts? Which are unproven opinions? Write *F* for fact or *O* for opinion on each line. Then explain your reasons to the group.

1. _____ Fresh, uncooked natural foods are always best for the health. Cooking takes away vitamins and other nutrients.

2. _____ Hot, spicy foods damage the stomach. Chili peppers or similar ingredients don't belong in family dishes, even if they are part of the culture.

3. _____ Nuts are bad for people because they contain fat. Avocados are unhealthy for the same reason.

4. _____ Many kinds of foods are related. For instance, prunes are dried plums, and raisins are dried grapes. Tofu looks like cheese, but it really comes from soybeans.

5. _____ More coffee comes from Brazil than from any other place, and most of the world's tea comes from India.

6. _____ For various reasons (color, taste, safety, etc.), companies add natural substances from seaweed, insects, trees, flowers, and so on to packaged foods.

7. _____ With added vitamins, minerals, and nutrients, snack foods like candy, cookies, chips, and soft drinks can and will become the new "health foods."

8. _____ Even a simple, basic food like rice has many varieties—such as white, brown, black, basmati, long-grain, short-grain, and so on. There are various ways to cook and include rice in menus and meals.

9. _____ The best diets are based on religious law—usually Jewish, Muslim, or Christian.

10. _____ For good health and long life, there are a number of "perfect" foods. Some examples are vegetables like broccoli and cabbage, citrus fruits and red grapes, onions, garlic, and soybeans.

Part 3 Vocabulary and Language-Learning Skills

Strategy

Getting Meaning from Context: Italics and Punctuation Clues

As you have learned in other chapters, often the context of reading material contains clues to the meanings of vocabulary items.

- New or unusual words or phrases may be in _italics_. Italics are a special kind of slanted type, _like this._

- Short definitions, similar words, explanations of the items, or examples of their meanings might come between certain kinds of punctuation marks, like quotation marks (" ") or parentheses ( ). They can also appear after a comma , or a dash (—).

1 Getting Meaning from Context: Italics and Punctuation Clues

In the reading selection "Global Diet Choices" on pages 44–45, some vocabulary items are italicized and some have short explanations of their meaning between or after punctuation marks. For each of these definitions or group of examples below, find the words or phrases in the reading. Write the word or phrase on the line. (The letters in parentheses are the letters of the paragraphs.)

1. a person's or group's usual food choices or habits: (A) _diet_

2. an eating plan with only certain kinds or amounts of food: (A) _____

3. prepared items from inexpensive restaurants, snack bars, or food stands:

   (B) _____

4. another word for _worldwide_: (B) _____

5. types of Mexican fast food: (B) _____

6. a blood-sugar disorder: (C) _____

7. an eating system high in protein but low in refined carbohydrates: (C)

   _____

8. corn, beans, rice, breads: (D) _____

9. miso, tofu, and bean paste: (D) _____

10. milk products: (D) _____

Strategy

Recognizing Vocabulary Categories

Most language learners want to learn a lot of vocabulary as quickly as possible. How can they do this?

- One way is to learn several words with the same or similar meanings at the same time. For example, another word for *worldwide* is *universal*.
- Another way is to learn words in categories. A *category* is a class or group of items in a system of classification. For instance, the items *meat, dairy products, vegetables,* and *fruit* are "kinds of food." *Protein, carbohydrates, fats, vitamins,* and *minerals* belong to the category "nutrients in food."

2 **Recognizing Vocabulary Categories** Below is a list of words and phrases from Chapters 1 to 3. They belong to various categories shown in the chart on page 55. Write the words from the list under the correct category in the chart. Four vocabulary items are done for you.

asthma
~~beef and pork~~
bugs
cancer
candy and cookies
chicken and poultry
citizens
classmates
a classroom
a college campus
~~college students~~
continents
Colombia,
  South America
The Czech Republic
dairy products
the desert
desserts
developing nations
diabetes
doctors
eating halal

emotions
European countries
flu or pneumonia
foreign students
fruit
graduates
grains and breads
hamburgers
headaches
heart disease
high blood pressure
home-cooked
hunger
ice cream
immigrants
insects
instructors
international
keeping kosher
language learners
meteorologists
moody

mountain areas
nutritionists
perfect health
pork or bacon
physical beauty
professors
researchers
restaurants
rice and pasta
sadness
salads
sandwiches
~~school~~
scientists
shellfish
~~sickness or illness~~
snack bars
soy products
southern Africa
specialists
a stroke
students

sushi and tempura
swimming pools
teachers
tennis courts
tiramisu
a tropical rain forest
a university
vegetables
Vietnam and Thailand
the whole world

CATEGORIES			
People	**Places**	**Possible Foods**	**Human Conditions**
college students	*school*	*beef and pork*	*sickness or illness*

3 **Practicing with Categories** Match the vocabulary items on the left with their category on the right. Then check your answers with a partner and add one or more example to each vocabulary item on the left.

Vocabulary Items

1. __d__ summer, fall (autumn),
   winter, spring

2. _____ breakfast, lunch, dinner, supper,
   snacks

3. _____ broccoli, corn, cabbage, beans,
   potatoes, onions, green peppers

4. _____ business, engineering,
   technology, computer science

5. _____ Canada, Brazil, Great Britain,
   Germany, Russia, Korea

6. _____ sun, rain, snow, ice, wind,
   humidity, drought, fog, clouds

7. _____ restaurants, fast-food chains,
   snack bars, food stands, markets

8. _____ protein, carbohydrates, fats,
   cholesterol, vitamins, minerals

9. _____ North America, South America,
   Europe, Asia, Africa

10. _____ water, coffee, tea, wine, beer,
    juice, soft drinks

Categories

a. continents

b. countries

c. subjects of college study

d. seasons of the year

e. weather
   conditions

f. eating places and
   food stores

g. kinds of meals

h. vegetables

i. beverages

j. nutrients and food elements

For more practice you can choose a new category and list typical vocabulary items for that category. Read the items (not the category) to your classmates. Ask them to guess the category. For example, you might say or write *sausage, schnitzel, pizza, tacos, burritos, shish kebob, falafel, sushi,* and *tempura.* The classmates might name a category such as *international fast foods.*

4 **Focusing on High-Frequency Words** Read the paragraph below and fill in each blank with a word from the box. When you finish, check your answers on page 45.

breakfast	dishes	grains	probably
customs	fats	minerals	worse
discussion	frozen	preferences	

The Global Diet

E   Universally, more and more meals include basic necessary food elements—*protein, carbohydrates,* and _____. Almost
                                                        1

everywhere, some kind of meat, fish, dairy product, or another food with

protein is part of a good _____, lunch, or dinner. There
                                            2

are also _____, breads, vegetables, fruit, and the like.   5
                       3

Many _____ contain the necessary vitamins and
                    4

_____. A few families grow their own food, but most
           5

people buy food from eating places and markets in their communities.

Food may be fresh, prepared, canned, _____, or
                             6

packaged. "Fast food" is very popular, and maybe it is becoming   10

healthier. In some ways, diet choices are becoming more and more

similar around the world. Even so, the variety of food choices is large

now and is _____ going to increase. Are cooking
                    7

_____, eating habits, and food _____
       8   9

all over the world becoming more or less healthy? Are they better or   15

_____ for human beings? These questions are interesting
    10

topics of research and _____.
            11

5 Making Connections Do an Internet search about food and nutrition. Type in the name of any food that you particularly like or that you want to eat more of. Look up two or more recipes that include that ingredient. Which recipe seems the most interesting to you? Tell the class your choice and your reasons for choosing it. Then try cooking it!

Recipe for: _____

Website: _____

Ingredients	Cooking Directions

(TOEFL® iBT) UNDERSTANDING SCHEMATIC TABLES

The TOEFL® iBT aims to test "global understanding" of a reading: Do you have a picture in your mind of the overall structure and meaning of a reading passage? One item that tests this kind of comprehension is the "schematic table" question. Each passage in the reading section has either a summary or a schematic table item as its last question.

A reader who sees interrelationships among ideas should be able to sort them into categories, like you did in Activity 2 on page 54. On the TOEFL® iBT, the things to be classified are more complex (reasons, events, characteristics, theories, etc.) but the idea is the same.

Practice

Based on the reading on pages 44–45, "Global Diet Choices," complete the chart below. Select the six appropriate phrases from the answer choices (*A* through *H*) below the chart. Write the letter under the type of dieting it relates to. (Two of the answer choices will NOT be used.) Then compare your answers with those of one or two other students.

Personal reasons for Choosing a Diet Item	Cultural reasons for Choosing a Diet Item
❏ _____	❏ _____
❏ _____	❏ _____
❏ _____	❏ _____

A. Fast food tastes good, even though it may not be healthy.

B. German fast food includes sausage and schnitzel.

C. Some Christians eat fish instead of meat on Fridays.

D. Diabetics have to avoid foods with sugar in them.

E. Seafood can be prepared in many different ways.

F. The Mexican diet reflects pre-Columbian and European influences.

G. People who want to lose weight often choose low-carb foods.

H. Muslims avoid foods that are prohibited within the system of *halal*.

Self-Assessment Log

Read the lists below. Check (✓) the strategies and vocabulary that you learned in this chapter. Look through the chapter or ask your instructor about the strategies and words that you do not understand.

Reading and Vocabulary-Building Strategies

- ❏ Recognizing reading structure: main-idea questions for paragraph topics
- ❏ Recognizing one-or two-sentence statements of the main idea
- ❏ Recognizing supporting details
- ❏ Matching paragraph titles with topics
- ❏ Choosing titles and recognizing topic sentences
- ❏ Summarizing
- ❏ Getting meaning from context: italics and punctuation clues
- ❏ Recognizing vocabulary categories

Target Vocabulary

Nouns

- ❏ breakfast*
- ❏ bugs
- ❏ complex carbohydrates
- ❏ customs*
- ❏ dairy
- ❏ desserts
- ❏ diabetes

- ❏ diet
- ❏ discussion*
- ❏ dishes*
- ❏ elements
- ❏ fast food
- ❏ fats*
- ❏ grains*
- ❏ habits*
- ❏ insects*

- ❏ low-carb diet
- ❏ minerals*
- ❏ nutritionists
- ❏ preferences*
- ❏ soy products

Verb

- ❏ diet

Adjectives

- ❏ frozen*
- ❏ universal*
- ❏ worse*

Adverb

- ❏ probably*

* These words are among the 2,000 most frequently used words in English.

4

In the Community

In This Chapter

In what ways do people in various places give directions? The first reading "How Can I Get to the Post Office?" will tell you how people in different places around the world give directions using gestures, landmarks, and distances. Next, you will find out about differences in local laws on issues such as driving, smoking, and personal relationships. Some laws may surprise you!

> ❝ The world is a book, and those who do not travel read only a page. ❞
>
> —Saint Augustine of Hippo
> philosopher and theologian (354–430)

Connecting to the Topic

1. Look at the musicians in the photograph. Where are they and why do you think they choose to play there?

2. Look at the title of this chapter. What and who do you think makes up a *community*?

3. What kinds of laws (rules) do communities usually have?

How Can I Get to the Post Office?

Before You Read

1 Previewing the Topic Discuss the picture in small groups. Be prepared to tell the class your ideas.

1. Who are the two travelers in the illustration? They have a problem. What is it?

2. What are the other people in the illustration doing? What do you think they are saying?

3. Does this situation ever happen to you? Do you use a map or ask for directions— or both? Do people sometimes ask you for directions? How do you answer?

▲ Two tourists asking for directions

2 Predicting Discuss possible answers to these questions. If you don't know the answers, make predictions. You can look for the answers when you read "How Can I Get to the Post Office?"

1. How do people in countries you know give directions?

2. What are street directions like on Internet websites? Give an example.

3. Sometimes you might ask for directions, such as, "How can I get to the post office?" What if a person doesn't know the answer? What can he or she do?

4. How can body language help you in getting around a new community?

3 **Previewing Vocabulary** Read the vocabulary items below from the first reading. Then listen to the words and phrases. Put a check mark (✓) next to the words you know. You come back to the other words after you read.

Nouns	Verbs	Adjectives	Adverbs
❑ advantages	❑ gesture	❑ confused	❑ rarely
❑ body language	❑ get lost	❑ flat	❑ seldom
❑ computer printout	❑ guess	❑ impolite	❑ straight
❑ countryside	❑ lead		
❑ directions	❑ measure		
❑ distances	❑ merge		
❑ expressions	❑ motion		
❑ gestures	❑ point		
❑ Interstate highway	❑ print out		
❑ landmarks	❑ turn		
❑ movements	❑ type in		
❑ residents			
❑ sense of direction			
❑ tourists			
❑ travelers			
❑ turn			

Read

4 **Reading an Article** Read the following article. Then read the explanations and do the activities that follow.

How Can I Get to the Post Office?

A   I have a special rule for travel: Never carry a map. I prefer to ask for directions. Sometimes I get lost, but I usually have a good time. And there are some other advantages: I can practice a new language, meet new people, learn new customs, and the like. I learn about different "styles" of directions every time I ask, "How can I get to the post office?" Here are   5 some illustrations of those differences.

B   Tourists are often confused in Japan. That's because most streets there don't have names. Outside big cities, people most often use **landmarks** in their **directions**. For example, the Japanese might tell **travelers** something like this: "Go straight down to the corner. **Turn** left at the big   10 hotel with the sushi bar and go past the fruit market. The post office is across from the bus stop—next to the fast food fried chicken place."

C   In the United States, people might give directions in different ways according to their region or community. In the countryside of the American Midwest, for example, there are not usually many landmarks. There are no mountains, so the land is very flat; in many places there are no towns or buildings for miles. Instead of landmarks, **residents** of the flatlands will tell you directions (like north, south, east, and west) and **distances**, like two miles. In the states of Kansas or Iowa, for instance, people will say things such as, "Take this road here. Go straight north for two miles. Make a right **turn**, and then go another mile in a northeast direction. Keep to the left around the curve. Then merge with Local Route 12." In most cities, however, people will name the streets, number of blocks, even the number of stoplights or stop signs. People in towns or cities might say, "Go straight for five blocks. Turn left at Main Street. Go to the third stoplight and turn right. That's Sixth Street. The post office is two blocks up on your left."

▲ Tourists anywhere in the world can feel lost and may need directions.

D   Many people around the world can get street directions on the Internet. People in Canada, the United States, and many European countries can go to a website to get directions. They enter (type in) a start point and an end point for their trip. Then they get instructions like these: "Take I-40 (the Interstate Highway) 26 miles." "Go straight (East)." "Enter Texas." "Keep left (Northwest) 8.7 miles." "Turn right." "Merge onto Turner Turnpike." "At Exit 5B, take Ramp (RIGHT) towards Oklahoma City, Oklahoma." They print out these directions and carry the papers with them, sometimes with a map.

E   Without a computer printout, on the other hand, some people in Los Angeles, California, may have no idea of distance on the map. Residents of this Pacific coast area are almost always in their cars, so they **measure** distance in time. "How far away is the post office?" you ask. "Oh," they might answer, "I guess it's about five minutes from here." You say, "Yes, but how many miles away is it—or how many kilometers or blocks?" They **rarely** know—or they can **seldom** say.

F   Sometimes, people in Greece do not even try to give directions; that's because tourists seldom understand the Greek language. Instead, a Greek person may **motion** or **gesture** or say, "Follow me." Then that person will lead you through the streets of a city to the post office.

G   What if a person doesn't know the answer to your question about the location of a place? A New Yorker might say, "Sorry, I have no idea" and walk away quickly. But in Yucatan, Mexico, not many residents answer, "I don't know." People in Yucatan may believe that a quick "I don't know" is impolite. They might stay and talk to you—and usually they'll try to give an answer, sometimes a wrong one. A tourist without a good sense of direction can get very, very lost in this southern region!

H One thing will help you everywhere—in Japan, the United States, 60
Greece, Mexico, or any other place. You might not understand a person's words, but you can probably understand the **body language**—like facial **expressions**, **gestures**, **movements**, and so on. He or she will usually turn and then point his or her finger in a particular direction. Go in that direction and you'll find the post office—maybe! 65

After You Read

IDENTIFYING PARAGRAPH AND WHOLE READING TOPICS

Reading material with a simple structure might begin with a general introductory paragraph and end with a short conclusion or summary. The several paragraphs between the first and the last might give the same kind of information—for instance, illustrations of the main point of the whole reading.

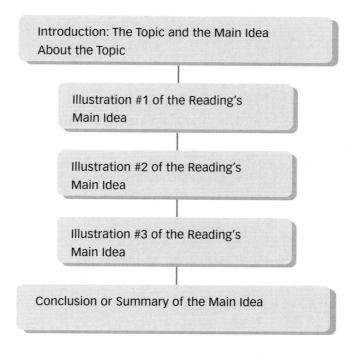

Introduction: The Topic and the Main Idea About the Topic

Illustration #1 of the Reading's Main Idea

Illustration #2 of the Reading's Main Idea

Illustration #3 of the Reading's Main Idea

Conclusion or Summary of the Main Idea

The topic, or subject, of a *whole* reading is more general than the specific topics of the individual paragraphs. The specific topic of each paragraph should clearly relate to the general topic of the reading.

---

5 **Identifying Topics of Paragraphs** In the reading "How Can I Get to the Post Office?" there is a capital letter next to each of the eight paragraphs. Write the specific topic of each paragraph next to its letter.

A. _____ *Introduction to the reading* _____

B. _____ *Directions in Japan* _____

C. _____

D. _____

E. _____

F. _____

G. _____

H. _____

Which phrase below best tells the subject of the whole reading "How Can I Get to the Post Office?" Circle it. Give reasons for your answer.

    a. the importance of body language for tourists and travelers

    b. how people give street directions in various places in the world

    c. different kinds of maps for travel and weather

Strategy

Identifying the Main Idea by Asking Questions
How can readers recognize the main idea of reading material? Here is one basic method:

- Ask and answer one question about the information in each paragraph.
- Then ask and answer a general question about the point of the whole reading.
- Your one- or two-sentence answer to each question gives the main idea.

6 **Identifying the Main Idea by Asking Questions** Complete the questions below about the article "How Can I Get to the Post Office?" Each question is about a different paragraph from the article. The last question is about the main idea of the whole article.

1. _____*What is*_____ the introduction to the article about? (A)

2. _____*How do people give*_____ directions in Japan? (B)

3. _____ directions in the region of the American Midwest? (C)

4. _____ typical directions like from websites on the Internet? (D)

5. _____ directions in the city of Los Angeles, California? (E)

6. _____ directions in the European country of Greece? (F)

7. _____ directions in some areas of Mexico like Yucatan? (G)

8. _____ the conclusion to the reading material? (H)

9. In what ways do _____ directions in various cultures around the world? (complete article)

7 **Changing False Statements to True Statements** Read the false sentences below about the main ideas in Paragraphs A–H of the reading and the main idea of the whole article. Change the nine false sentences to true statements. Then use them as correct answers to the nine questions in Activity 6.

1. If you don't carry a map on your travels, you won't have to ask for directions. (A)

2. In Japan, people most often use street names in their directions. (B)

3. In the mountainous land of the American Midwest, people will tell you directions with landmarks. (C)

4. Directions from websites on the Internet do not include distances. (D)

5. In Los Angeles, California, the most common way to give directions is in kilometers. (E)

6. Even if visitors to Greece don't understand the language, the people will usually give directions with a lot of words in long sentences. (F)

7. In some parts of Mexico, people may be impolite, so they always say, "I don't know" in answer to questions about directions. (G)

8. All over the world, words in sentences are easier to understand than body language. (H)

9. In various cultures around the world, people give directions to travelers and tourists in exactly the same way. (complete article)

Using Punctuation to Recognize Supporting Details

Punctuation marks might show the relationship between the main point of reading material and some of the supporting detail. For instance, a colon (:) can introduce a list of things—usually illustrations or examples of an idea. Commas (,) can separate the different items of the list or series.

Example

In Japan, people typically use *landmarks* in their directions: they talk about hotels, markets, bus stops, and so on. (What are some examples of landmarks for directions? *Hotels*, *markets*, and *bus stops*.)

A semicolon (;) can separate two closely related sentence parts. The second sentence part can explain or add useful information to the point of the first.

Example

In the American Midwest, there are no mountains and few hills; the land is very flat. (The word *flat* can mean "without mountains or hills.")

Quotation marks (" ") separate direct quotes (people's exact words) from the rest of the sentence.

Example

A Greek person will say, "Follow me." (What does a Greek often say instead of giving directions? "Follow me.")

---

8 **Using Punctuation to Recognize Supporting Details** Below are some questions about the supporting details of the article "How Can I Get to the Post Office?" Find the answers to these questions in the article. Look at the punctuation and related sentence parts. With words from the paragraphs and your own words, write the answers on the lines.

1. The writer has a special rule for travel. What is it? _____

_____

2. What are some advantages of travel without maps? _____

_____

_____

3. Why are foreign tourists often confused in Japan? _____

_____

_____

4. What are some illustrations of Japanese directions?

_____

_____

5. What directions might residents of the American Midwest give people? (Give some examples.)

_____

_____

6. What are some examples of street directions from websites like _mapquest.com_ and _mappoint.msn.com_? _____

_____

_____

7. Why don't people in Los Angeles give directions in miles, kilometers, or blocks?

_____

_____

8. Why do Greeks seldom give foreigners directions in words and sentences?

_____

_____

9. If a resident of New York City doesn't know the location of a place, how might he or she answer a question about directions?

_____

_____

10. Why won't a polite resident of Yucatan answer a lost tourist, "I don't know"?

_____

_____

11. How does a person give directions with body language? _____

_____

For more practice, turn back to Activity 2 in the _Before You Read_ section on page 62 and answer the four questions in your own words.

 9 **Discussing the Reading** In small groups, talk about your answers to the following questions. Each person can choose a number, ask the group the questions, and make sure that everyone answers.

1. Do you ever get lost—in our own town, city, region, or in new places? If so, do you ask for directions? Why or why not? If so, in what way?

2. How do most people give directions in your city or in the countryside? Do you give directions the same way? Why or why not?

3. In your opinion, why do people in different places give directions in different ways?

4. Do you have a good sense of direction? Can you find new places quickly and easily? Explain your answer with examples.

5. Do or can you use Internet websites or other computer equipment for driving or street directions? If so, how do you do this?

The Laws of Communities

Before You Read

 1 **Previewing Vocabulary** Read the vocabulary items below from the second reading. Then listen to the words and phrases. Put a check mark (✓) next to the words you know. You can learn the other words now or come back to them after you read.

Nouns

❑ action   ❑ lot   ❑ shopping   ❑ smoke

❑ activity   ❑ murder   ❑ smoking   **Adjectives**

❑ airline   ❑ offenses   ❑ steering wheels   ❑ illegal

❑ airports   ❑ order   ❑ teenagers   ❑ legal

❑ container   ❑ pedestrians   ❑ traffic   ❑ local

❑ dangers   ❑ procedures   ❑ vehicles   ❑ married

❑ drivers   ❑ regulations   ❑ wine   ❑ serious

❑ fine   ❑ relationships   **Verbs**   ❑ strange

❑ flights   ❑ restaurants   ❑ buy

❑ health   ❑ robbery   ❑ drive

❑ laws   ❑ safety   ❑ make sense

Read

Strategy

Skimming for Topics and Main Ideas

Topics: The title of a piece of writing may tell or suggest its topic. But sometimes there is no title. Readers then need to figure out the topic on their own. One way to quickly recognize a topic is to *skim*. *Skimming* is fast reading for a purpose.

Main Ideas: Another common reason to skim is to get the main idea. Not every piece of information contains one clear topic sentence, so readers may have to get the main idea or point of the material without it.

2 Skimming for Topics Read the four topic phrases or titles below. Then skim the four paragraphs in the reading "The Laws of Communities" that follows. Label each topic phrase with the paragraph letter A, B, C, or D.

——————— Strange or Unusual Laws About People's Relationships

——————— Traffic Laws for Drivers, Riders, and Pedestrians

——————— Drinking and Smoking Laws and Customs Around the World

——————— The Laws of Communities in Many Areas of Life

3 Skimming for Main Ideas Read Paragraphs A–D quickly a second time. Answer to the question about the main idea that follows each paragraph. Then explain the reason for each answer.

The Laws of Communities

A   **Laws** are rules for people in communities. For instance, in every country and culture of the world, there are laws against **serious** offenses: **murder**, **robbery**, violence against people, and the like. These laws make sense. They are necessary for safety and **health**, for community order, and for good human relationships in communities; they are probably similar all   5
over the world. On the other hand, many laws and rules differ from country to country, from area to area, or even from one community to another. Some common illustrations of this variety are laws about driving, drinking alcohol, eating, **smoking**, shopping, money, people's rights, and many others. For instance, a legal action in Lima, Peru, may be against the law in   10
Seoul, Korea—and an **illegal** activity in an Asian community may be perfectly legal in a European city. On the other hand, laws may be the same in various countries but vary in different cities or states of the same nation.

What is the main idea of Paragraph A?

(A) Laws should always make sense; if they don't, people won't follow them. They will drink alcohol, eat too much, and smoke.

(B) Laws in Lima, Peru, keep community order better than the laws in Seoul, Korea, and other communities or countries of Asia.

(C) Laws against the most serious crimes may be similar everywhere, but the rules of most areas of life differ from one place to another.

B   Every country has traffic rules and signs, but are they the same? In most countries, there are street and road signs with information about location, directions, dangers, cautions, and rules of the road. These signs tell drivers and **pedestrians** (walkers) what to do and what not to do, including speed and parking limits, places to stop, when to make turns, and other **procedures**. However, specific *local* traffic laws and practices usually differ around the world. For instance, in Japan, Indonesia, South Africa, the United Kingdom, and other countries, steering wheels are on the right side of **vehicles**, and cars and trucks drive on the left side of the road. In other countries, such as the United States, Saudi Arabia, Taiwan, Italy, and Mexico, steering wheels are on the left side of vehicles, and cars and trucks drive on the right side of the road. An illustration of a local traffic law is the regulations for pedestrian and school crossings in some Mexican cities: drivers rarely respect the rules, so for safety, people cross streets only at stop lights, on roads with little traffic, or on pedestrian-only bridges across wide avenues.

What is the main idea of Paragraph B?

(A) There are traffic rules all around the world, and for safety, it's important to learn local rules and practices for driving, riding, and walking.

(B) It's more difficult to drive and walk in Japan than in Taiwan, Mexico, or the United States; that's because vehicles with steering wheels on the right move on the left side of the road.

(C) What is the most important thing to know about driving in other countries? The largest vehicle is at fault in any accident.

C   What about regulations and customs in other areas of people's lives? Some communities have a **lot** of rules about legal and illegal individual activities—even drinking and smoking. For instance, in most places in the United States, no one under 21 can **buy** or drink alcohol legally—even beer or **wine**. In some communities, it's illegal to drink a can of beer on a public street; it's also against the law to have an open alcohol container in a car. Similarly, smoking is no longer legal in public places—such as workplaces, **restaurants**, airports, and on airline **flights** within the United States. In Japan and other countries, there is a legal age for smoking; in some Muslim countries, all smoking is against religious law. On the other hand, many

▲ A "No smoking" sign in the United States

people around the world drink and **smoke**—including more and more   45
teenagers and young people. Customs and habits do not always go along
with health or safety regulations or laws.

What is the main idea of Paragraph C?

(A) People should not drink, smoke, or eat too much. These are not good
health habits, but they are never against the law.

(B) Around the world, there are many laws about individual activities like
drinking and smoking; many people still do these things—sometimes
legally but not always.

(C) Workplaces, airports, airplanes, and restaurants are public places; for
this reason, people over the legal age can drink beer and wine and smoke
cigarettes there.

D   In the beginning, most local laws have a clear purpose or reason; even
so, after many years, these same regulations can seem very **strange** or
unusual. Here are some examples of old rules about personal relationships.   50
In the back country of New Zealand, a man with many sisters can have the
same number of wives. How is this custom legal? The man can give one
sister to each of his wives' families! In some Indian communities, it is illegal
for a young man and woman—married or not—to hold hands in a bus or
train station; if they do, they have to pay an expensive **fine**. The law in   55
some Chinese towns doesn't allow a man to give a woman a chicken leg
during a meal; he can give her other chicken parts, but not a leg. And in
Worland, Wyoming (a state in the United States), no married man may go
camping alone or with his friends; he has to take along his wife! These old
laws are probably still in effect, but not many people follow them.   60

What is the main idea of Paragraph D?

(A) After a long time, old local laws about relationships can seem very
strange; they may not make sense in today's world.

(B) All over the world, regulations for married men and women are different
from rules for unmarried people—especially in bus or train stations.

(C) Old local marriage and relationship rules are all the same: people follow
them everywhere because they make good sense.

Strategy

Learning to Paraphrase

In Chapter 3 you learned to summarize by asking questions that are answered in a paragraph. Another way to summarize is to *paraphrase* the main idea and the important supporting details. A paraphrase is a restatement of something using other words.

- First, be sure you understand the correct *meaning* of each important idea or piece of information in the reading.
- Think of words and phrases with similar meanings to express the same ideas. For example, below are phrases from the first paragraph of the reading "The Laws of Communities," with possible ways to paraphrase them.

  > *local law = legal rules of a community; rural, town, or city regulations*
  > *serious offenses = major illegal actions, very bad activities against the law*
  > *make sense = have a real purpose, necessary for good reasons*
  > *are different = differ, vary, appear in various forms*

- Then put your paraphrases together with other words in a short paragraph. Make sure your paragraph tells the main points of the original material in logical order. Here is an example of a possible paraphrased summary of Paragraph A.

In most communities in the world, the most serious offenses are illegal, so the necessary laws against these terrible acts are similar for good reasons. In contrast, the local rules about activities in everyday life in rural areas, towns, and cities may vary from place to place.

4 Paraphrasing Work in groups of three. Each student should choose a different paragraph (B, C, or D) from the reading "The Laws of Communities." Read it carefully. Reread the main idea. In a few sentences, summarize the paragraph, paraphrasing the main idea and important details. Then tell or read your summary to your group.

5 Discussing the Reading Work in small groups and talk about your answers to the following questions. Be prepared to tell the class some of the most interesting information.

1. Which community's or country's laws and rules do you know the best? Why are you familiar with these regulations?

2. Compare some traffic regulations and practices in two or more communities or cities. Tell about driving, bicycling, parking, walking, and so on. Why do you think different places have different traffic rules and customs?

3. What laws about smoking and drinking alcohol do you know about? Do most people follow these rules? Give examples for your answer.

4. What are some of the laws about relationships in your community? What is their purpose? Are they good laws to follow? Give examples and reasons for your answers.

6 Talking It Over All over the world, people like some laws and dislike others. Some rules seem reasonable while others don't seem to have a real purpose.

The following local laws may seem strange or unusual. From your knowledge and experience, which laws make sense? Which laws seem senseless or funny? Put an *X* next to the items that seem senseless or funny. Explain the reasons for your opinions and views.

1. _____ In Bangor, Maine (the United States), you can't put money into another car's parking meter—even to help another driver. If you do, you will pay a big fine.

2. _____ In Oslo, Norway, if you break a traffic law, you must pay a fine to the police officer right then. Then you get a receipt (a printed statement of money received).

3. _____ In Warsaw, Poland, it's against the law to do sit-ups or push-ups (kinds of physical exercise) in a bus inside the city.

4. _____ In Kaunas, Lithuania, a person may ride up in an elevator, but he or she must always walk down. Only three exceptions are allowed every day.

5. _____ In Pilsen, the Czech Republic, beer companies can use only ingredients from the state of Bohemia.

6. _____ In England, Sunday shoppers can buy canned dog food, but they can't buy food in cans for people—not even canned milk for babies.

7. _____ In Valencia, Spain, social dance parties are not allowed for young people.

8. _____ In Addis Ababa, Ethiopia, it's illegal for a person to spit on other people on the street. He or she mustn't spit on the bare feet of children, either.

9. _____ In many Mexican communities, it is against the law to walk around outside barefoot (without shoes).

10. _____ In Mexico City, students can keep many kinds of small animals but not scorpions (a member of the spider family) or tarantulas (a kind of spider).

| **Part 3** | Vocabulary and Language-Learning Skills |

Strategy

Getting Meaning from Context: Finding Illustrations of Words
Sometimes illustrations of the meaning of words that name categories are in another sentence or sentence part. The words *for example, for instance, as an illustration, like,* and *such as* can be clues to meaning through illustrations.

Example
People in Los Angeles talk about distance in time. They'll say such things as, "It's about five minutes from here."
(An illustration of the category *distance in time* is the phrase "about five minutes from here.")

1 **Finding Illustrations of Words** Read the vocabulary items below. Write illustrations (examples) of each one from the reading selection "How Can I Get to the Post Office?" on pages 63–65. (The letters in parentheses are the letters of the paragraphs.) Three items are done as examples.

1. landmarks: (B) _____ big hotel _____ , _____ ,

   _____ , _____ ,

   _____

2. street directions: (C, D) _____ take this road here _____ , _____ ,

   _____ , _____ ,

   _____ , _____

3. distances: (C, D) _____ go straight north for two miles _____ ,

   _____ , _____ ,

   _____ , _____

4. body language: (H) _____ , _____

   _____ .

For more practice, think of other illustrations of one of the categories above, for instance, *a church, a train station,* and *the local post office*. Tell your group the words in one category. Can your group name the category? (In this example, it is *landmarks*.) Or you can think of new categories and illustrations.

Strategy

Recognizing Words with Similar Meanings and Meaning Categories
To improve your vocabulary quickly, you can learn several new items at the same time. They should have something in common (be alike in some way). Here are two good ways to do this:

- Look at the words and phrases with the same or similar meanings together—like *pedestrian, walker, hiker,* and *passerby*.
- Learn items in categories. For example, the words *cars, trucks, motorcycles,* and *buses* are all in the category of *motorized vehicles*.

With both methods, the words and phrases in each grouping should be the same part of speech, such as *nouns, verbs, adjectives,* or *adverbs*.

2 **Identifying Similar Meanings and Meaning Categories** All the words and phrases in each of the groups below are the same part of speech. How do the vocabulary items belong together? Do they have the same (similar) meanings? If so, write *S* for *similar* on the line. Or are the vocabulary items members of the same meaning category? Then write *C* for *category* on the line and name the possible category.

1. __C__ walking / riding a bicycle / taking the bus / driving a car (*category: types of transportation*)

2. __S__ rules / laws / regulations / legal requirements

3. _____ Oslo, Norway / Tokyo, Japan / Mexico City, Mexico / Valencia, Spain

4. _____ not often / seldom / rarely / infrequently

5. _____ make sense / seem reasonable / have a purpose / be understandable

6. _____ directions / dangers / cautions / rules of the road

7. _____ northeast / southwest / northwest / southeast

8. _____ move / motion / gesture / body language

9. _____ a colon / a semicolon / a comma / a period

10. _____ against the law / wrong / illegal / not allowed

Strategy

Recognizing Nouns and Verbs

A very useful vocabulary-learning method is to recognize parts of speech. Some words can be more than one part of speech. As examples, in the first sentence below, the words *motions* and *gestures* are plural nouns; in the second sentence, the same words are verbs.

> Two examples of body language are *motions* and *gestures*. A person usually motions or gestures with the hands, arms, or other body parts.

On the other hand, some words in noun and verb pairs have different forms or endings. Here are some examples of related words from Chapter 4.

Noun	Verb	Noun	Verb
❑ movement	❑ move	❑ direction	❑ direct
❑ expression	❑ express	❑ illustration	❑ illustrate

3 **Recognizing Nouns and Verbs** Here are some sentences with two related words—one noun and one verb. In each blank, write the missing word—the noun related to the underlined verb or the verb related to the underlined noun.

1. I like to <u>travel</u> to distant places. My main rule for *travelers* is not to carry a map.

2. My <u>preference</u> is to ask for directions. What method of getting around do you _____?

3. Usually, residents like to <u>direct</u> tourists to various places; they give _____s in different ways.

4. An example of a street direction is "<u>Turn</u> left." This means "Make a left _____."

5. Many people want to <u>reside</u> on the Pacific coast of California; _____s of this area usually go places by car.

6. Some <u>measures</u> of distance are miles, kilometers, and city blocks; but people in Southern California usually _____ distance in time (minutes).

7. To direct tourists, Greek people often <u>motion</u>, or <u>gesture</u>; these _____s and _____s are illustrations of body language.

8. How do people <u>express</u> themselves without words? They <u>move</u> their hands. Facial _____s and body _____s are effective ways to communicate meaning.

9. Everywhere in the world, a few people <u>murder</u>, <u>rob</u>, and so on. Two examples of serious crimes are _____ and _____.

10. There are local laws against <u>smoking</u> and <u>drinking</u> in some communities; even so, some teenagers want to _____ and _____.

For more practice, tell or write more nouns from Chapters 1 to 4. Which nouns have related verb forms? What are they? Also, you can tell or write some verbs with their related noun forms. (You can check your guesses in a dictionary.)

4 **Finding Definitions of Vocabulary Items** Look at the columns below. Match each vocabulary word on the left with the correct definition on the right. The vocabulary words are from "The Laws of Communities," on pages 71–73. The letters in parentheses ( ) are the letters of the paragraphs.

Vocabulary Words

1. __d__ laws (A)

2. _____ make sense (A)

3. _____ illegal (A)

4. _____ pedestrians (B)

5. _____ procedure (B)

6. _____ vehicle (B)

7. _____ flight (C)

8. _____ teenager (C)

9. _____ strange (D)

10. _____ fine (D)

Definitions

a. people traveling on foot, walking

b. something like a car or truck used to transport people

c. a person over 12 and under 20 years old

d. rules or regulations

e. odd or unusual

f. against the law; not legal

g. a journey or trip on a plane

h. to be reasonable or necessary

i. money to be paid as a punishment

j. the way of doing something

5 **Focusing on High-Frequency Words** Read the paragraph below and fill in each blank with a word from the box. When you finish, check your answers on pages 72–73.

buy	habits	law	public	smoking
customs	health	lot	restaurants	wine

The Laws of Communities

c   What about regulations and _____ in other areas of people's lives? Some communities have a _____ of rules about legal and illegal individual activities—even drinking and _____. For instance, in most places in the United States, no one under 21 can _____ or drink alcohol legally—even   5 beer or _____. In some communities, it's illegal to drink a can of beer on a public street; it's also against the _____ to have an open alcohol container in a car. Similarly, smoking is no longer legal in _____ places—such as workplaces,

_____8, airports, and on airline flights within the United 10
States. In Japan and other countries, there is a legal age for smoking; in
some Muslim countries, all smoking is against religious law. On the other
hand, many people around the world drink and smoke—including more and
more teenagers and young people. Customs and _____
9
do not always go along with _____ or safety regulations 15
10
or laws.

6 Making Connections Do an Internet search about interesting local laws in the
world today. You can type in something like *unusual* (or *strange* or *weird*) *laws in*
_____ *(name of city, state, or country).* Look up two or more places. Take
notes on the laws.

Choose at least five laws that are the funniest or the strangest to you and write them in
the chart below. Tell the class these laws and the reasons for your choices.

Place	Unusual Law
1.	
2.	
3.	
4.	
5.	

TOEFL® iBT

ANSWERING NEGATIVE FACT QUESTIONS ON TESTS

Similarity of meaning (see Part 3 of this chapter) is tested on many reading tests. Questions may ask you to choose the closest synonym or the most exact paraphrase for some part of the reading passage. Another type of question approaches the same skill in a different way. A negative fact question asks you to judge which of several choices is NOT similar to the rest. The TOEFL® iBT frequently asks negative fact questions. The structure of these questions uses such common expressions as *is not mentioned, except*, and *is not true*. Can you think of other phrases that are common in negative fact questions?

Answering Negative Fact Questions Read the following short passage and answer the questions that follow it. Then compare your answers with those of one or two other students.

Sharing the Water

A   Every community of humans faces a life-or-death question: How do we distribute water? Some water has to be held as a community resource if a town, city, or even nation is to survive. Many early human settlements were based on irrigation systems. These exist because earlier people agreed where the water should flow and to whom. Wells in desert lands are protected by cultural traditions that make them a shared resource among traveling peoples. Many large lakes, such as Lake Michigan in the United States, are mostly reserved for public use, not for the people who own houses on their shores.

B   Water-use laws can prevent a few powerful people from gaining control over all available water. But water laws do not make water freely available in equal amounts to everyone. Farmers need huge amounts of it. So do many industries. Families, however, do not need nearly that much. There is also the issue of pollution. Water laws must prevent careless (or intentional) pollution by some users before the water reaches all users.

C   Problems occur when government is not strong enough to make and enforce laws. Often, the water in dispute is an international (or interstate) resource. For example, the Mekong River in Southeast Asia starts in China and then winds through Laos, Cambodia, and Vietnam. The Vietnamese government, no matter how conscientious it is, has little control over how much of the Mekong water reaches Vietnam and what kind of condition it is in. The upstream nations, especially China, determine that. As upstream dams take more of the river, Vietnam has a greater need to negotiate an effective water-rights agreement with other governments. International agreements have worked elsewhere. We will see if they will work along the Mekong.

1. Which of the following is NOT mentioned in Paragraph A as an example of water as a community resource?
   - (A) lakes
   - (B) rivers
   - (C) irrigation
   - (D) wells

2. All of the following are nations in Southeast Asia EXCEPT:
   - (A) Mekong
   - (B) Laos
   - (C) Vietnam
   - (D) Cambodia

3. Which of the following is NOT true about water laws, according to the reading?
   - (A) They must be enforced by a government.
   - (B) They can prevent water takeovers by a few powerful people.
   - (C) They make sure that everyone gets an equal share of water.
   - (D) They can prevent pollution by some users.

Self-Assessment Log

Read the lists below. Check (✓) the strategies and vocabulary that you learned in this chapter. Look through the chapter or ask your instructor about the strategies and words that you do not understand.

Reading and Vocabulary-Building Strategies

- ❏ Identifying paragraphs and whole reading topics
- ❏ Identifying the main idea by asking questions
- ❏ Using punctuation to recognize supporting details
- ❏ Skimming for topics and main ideas
- ❏ Paraphrasing
- ❏ Getting meaning from context: finding illustrations of words
- ❏ Recognizing words with similar meanings and meaning categories
- ❏ Recognizing nouns and verbs
- ❏ Finding definitions of vocabulary items

Target Vocabulary

Nouns

- ❏ body language
- ❏ directions*
- ❏ distances*
- ❏ expressions*
- ❏ fine*
- ❏ flights*
- ❏ gestures
- ❏ health*
- ❏ landmarks
- ❏ laws*
- ❏ lot*

- ❏ movements*
- ❏ murder*
- ❏ pedestrians
- ❏ procedures
- ❏ residents
- ❏ restaurants*
- ❏ robbery
- ❏ smoking*
- ❏ teenagers
- ❏ travelers

- ❏ turn
- ❏ vehicles
- ❏ wine*

Verbs

- ❏ buy*
- ❏ gesture
- ❏ measure*
- ❏ motion*
- ❏ smoke*
- ❏ turn*

Adjectives

- ❏ illegal
- ❏ serious*
- ❏ strange*

Adverbs

- ❏ rarely*
- ❏ seldom*

* These words are among the 2,000 most frequently used words in English.

Home

In This Chapter

What comes to mind when you think of a family? Is it a mother, a father, and two children (a boy and a girl)? Then the information in the first reading selection may surprise you. This reading describes different types of families, how the typical family structure has changed, and what families in the future might be like. In the second selection, you will read and give opinions about family time in the past, present, and future.

" Family faces are magic mirrors. Looking at people who belong to us, we see the past, present, and future. **"**

—Gail Lumet Buckley, African American author; daughter of singer Lena Horne (1937–   )

Connecting to the Topic

1. Look at the photo of the family below. What are they doing?

2. What kinds of activities do families in your country typically do together?

3. Do you think family life in your country or culture is changing? If so, how?

A Short History of the Changing Family

Before You Read

1 Thinking About the Topic Discuss the photos in small groups. Then answer the questions below.

1. Where and when does each scene take place? What are the people doing?

2. How are these scenes similar to situations in your family, community, or country? How are they different?

3. How do you think family life is changing these days? How might it change in the future?

▲ Modern professionals going off to work

▲ A traditional family from the 1940s or 50s

▲ Modern-day family relaxing

▲ A stay-at-home father

2 Predicting Think and talk about possible answers to these questions. When you read "A Short History of the Changing Family," look for the answers.

1. What is the difference between an extended family and a nuclear family?
2. What are some kinds of families in the world today?
3. Why and how did the structure of the family change in the twentieth century?
4. How were the 1930s and 1940s difficult years for most families?
5. How did people's ideas about marriage and family change after World War II?
6. What are the most common family forms around the world today?

 3 Previewing Vocabulary Read the vocabulary items below from the first reading. Then listen to the words and phrases. Put a check mark (✓) next to the words you know. You can learn the other words now or come back to them after you read.

Nouns

- ❏ ancestor
- ❏ biology
- ❏ birthrate
- ❏ blended families
- ❏ community
- ❏ cousins
- ❏ decade
- ❏ divorce rate
- ❏ divorces
- ❏ extended family
- ❏ future
- ❏ heads of households
- ❏ history
- ❏ millennium
- ❏ nuclear family
- ❏ relatives

- ❏ single-parent family
- ❏ social institutions
- ❏ stay-at-home mother
- ❏ stepparents
- ❏ structure
- ❏ war widows

Verbs

- ❏ adopt
- ❏ decline
- ❏ occur
- ❏ support
- ❏ take in

Adjectives

- ❏ adopted
- ❏ biological

- ❏ communal
- ❏ developing (country)
- ❏ divorced
- ❏ economic (classes)
- ❏ industrialized (country)
- ❏ loosely-related
- ❏ previous
- ❏ traditional
- ❏ widowed
- ❏ younger

Adverb

- ❏ biologically

Read

 4 Reading an Article Read the following article. Then read the explanations and do the activities after the reading.

A Short History of the Changing Family

Past Definitions of Family

A   Like the **community**, the family is a *social institution*. Long ago, human beings lived in **loosely-related** groups. Each group had a common ancestor (a family member from the distant past). But for over a millennium (a thousand years), there have been two main types of families in the world: the extended form and the nuclear form. The extended family may include grandparents, parents, and children (and sometimes aunts, uncles, and cousins)—in other words, relatives living in the same house or close together on the same street or in the same area. In contrast, the nuclear family consists of only parents and their biological (related by blood) or adopted children. Because of the industrialization in the nineteenth century, the nuclear family became the most common family structure.

Kinds of Families Today

B   Today there are many different kinds of families around the globe. Some people live in traditional families—that is to say, a stay-at-home mother, a working father, and their own biological children. Others live in two-paycheck families—that is, both parents work outside the home. There are many single-parent families; in other words, only a mother *or* a father lives with the children. Still others have adoptive or foster families (i.e., adults take care of children not biologically theirs) or blended families—in other words, divorced or widowed men and women marry again and live with the children from their previous, or earlier, marriages. Some kids have stepparents—that is, mothers or fathers related to them by marriage instead of biology. In other families, some youngsters under the age of 18 have to take care of kids—either their own or their younger siblings (brothers and sisters). In different countries around the world, there are also same-sex partnerships—with or without children—childless marriages, unmarried live-in relationships, communal living groups, and so on.

The Early 20th Century

C   What caused the structure of the family to change? Here is an example from the Western world. In the early 1900s in the United States, the divorce rate (i.e., the percent of legal endings compared to the number of marriages) began to rise, and the birthrate (i.e., the number of births per 100 or 1,000 people) began to decline; in other words, couples stayed married for fewer years, and they had fewer children. Women often chose to get an education and take jobs outside the home. Decades (ten-year periods) later, the same things began to occur in other industrialized countries—and then developing countries of the world as well.

The 1930s and 1940s

D   The decades of the 1930s and 1940s were difficult years in both industrialized and developing countries. Many families faced serious financial problems because the heads of households lost their jobs.

During World War II (1939–1945), millions of women had to take care of their homes and their children alone. Because so many men were at war, thousands of these "war widows"—that is to say, women whose husbands were away at war—had to go to work outside the home. Most women worked long hours at hard jobs. There weren't many "perfect families." They had problems. 45

After World War II

E   During the next decade the situation changed in many places. There were fewer divorces, and people married at a younger age and had more children than in the previous generation. Men made enough money to support the family, so a mother seldom worked outside the home when 50 her children were small. Children began living at home longer—that is, until an older age, usually after high school or even college. The traditional family was returning in the United States, it seemed—as in many other countries.

The End of the 20th Century

F   In the years between 1960 or so and the end of the 20th century, 55 however, there were many new changes in the structure of the family around the globe. From the 1960s to the 1990s, the divorce rate in the Western world greatly increased and the birthrate fell by half. The number of single-parent families rose, and the number of couples living together without marriage went up even more. At the end of the 20th and beginning 60 of the 21st centuries, young adults of some economic classes started staying with their parents longer, marrying later, and having kids at an older age, if at all.

The Family of the Future

G   Many people today would like the traditional two-parent family back— that is to say, they want a man and a woman to marry for life; they also 65 think the man should support the family and the woman should stay home with the children. However, few families now fall into this category. In fact, if more women decide to have children on their own, the single-parent household may become more typical than the traditional family in many countries. Also, unmarried couples may decide to have more 70 children—or they might take in foster children or adopt. And because people are staying single and living longer (often as widows), there may be more one-person households in the future. On the other hand, some people believe similar events happen again and again in history. If this is true, people may go back to the traditional extended or nuclear family of 75 the past. Others think the only certainty in history is change: in other words, the structure of the future family could begin to change faster and faster—and in more and more ways.

RECOGNIZING TOPICS IN READINGS ABOUT HISTORY

Readings about history usually begin with introductory material. These one or two paragraphs may tell the most important ideas and points of the whole selection. The several paragraphs after that may tell about various *periods* of history—probably in time order. The last paragraph may give information about the present or thoughts about the future. Each paragraph, however, still has a topic.

5 **Recognizing Topics in a Reading About History** What is the topic of each paragraph in the reading "A Short History of the Changing Family"? Read the partial topics below (one for each paragraph, A–G) and write the specific topic of each paragraph. Some items are done as examples.

A. definitions of _____

B. the _____ around the world

C. reasons for _____ *changes in the structure of the family* _____

D. the typical family _____ *in the 1930s and 1940s* _____

E. the typical family _____

F. _____ between 1960 and the beginning of the 21st century

G. family structure _____

Which phrase best tells the topic or subject of the whole reading? Give the reasons for your answer.

    (A) the advantages of the traditional family form over single-parent or adoptive relationships

    (B) the effects of World War II on jobs, home, and children in the future

    (C) reasons for divorce in a changing world community of live-in couples

    (D) changes in the structure of the family from the 20th century to the future

6 **Recognizing the Main Idea** As you learned in Chapter 4, one way to find the main idea of a reading passage is to ask one main-idea question about the information in each paragraph. Then you can ask a general question about the point of the whole reading. Read the questions that follow. Each one is about a different paragraph from the reading "A Short History of the Changing Family." Complete each question about the topic of that paragraph. Two items are done as examples.

A. _*What are the definitions*_ _____ of the two main types of families?

B. _____ the different kinds of families around the globe today?

C. _____ changes in the structure of the family?

D. _What happened to_ _____ families in industrialized countries in the 1930s and 1940s?

E. _____ family structure during the next decade?

F. _____ any changes to families after the 1960s?

G. _____ in the future?

Question About the Whole Reading: In what different ways _____ _____ in the 20th and 21st centuries?

A one- or two-sentence answer to a main-idea question can tell the point of the reading material. In order, here are some false sentences about the information in Paragraphs A–G of "A Short History of the Changing Family." The possible statement of the point of the *whole* reading is not right, either. Change the seven false sentences to true statements about the point. Then use them as correct answers to the questions above.

1. The *nuclear family* is the same as the *extended family*: it consists of many relatives (grandparents, parents, children, cousins, etc.) living in the same house.

2. There is only one kind of family on Earth today: it is the traditional nuclear family.

3. In the early 1990s in the United States (and later in other countries), the divorce rate went down and the birthrate began to rise; couples were staying married longer and having more children.

4. Before and during World War II, families faced few financial problems in the industrialized world, so women didn't have to work outside the home. Families were perfect.

5. After the war, family structure changed back in the other direction: There were more divorces and fewer stay-at-home mothers; children began to leave home earlier.

6. From the 1960s on, there were few new changes in the structure of the family around the globe.

7. People don't want the traditional two-parent nuclear family—with a working father and a mother at home; however, this structure will probably come back and all other family forms will end.

Strategy

Using a Timeline to Take Notes on Time and Time Order

In readings about history, there are often time details. These details tell when things happened. Writers indicate time in these ways:

- Naming years such as *1860* or *the year 2000*
- Centuries, decades, or time periods like *in the eighteenth century, in the early 1930s,* or *in the years between 1990 and 2001*
- A dash (–) between points of time usually means *to,* as in *1925–1955*
- Time details also appear with phrases like *long ago, since the beginning of the millennium, for a century, between the 1960s and the end of the 1900s, before the 1960s,* and many others.

7 **Identifying Time and Time Order Details** Read the list below of important events about families. Then write the number of each event in the correct box in the timeline that follows.

Events from the Reading "A Short History of the Changing Family"

1. Many families had money problems, and men were not at home, so more women began to work outside the home.
2. There have been two main types of families: the extended and the nuclear.
3. Industrialization made the nuclear family the most common form.
4. Many new family forms became common, such as single parenthood and unmarried couples living together. Young adults began taking longer to start their own families.
5. The divorce rate rose and the birthrate fell in the United States. Women began to go to school and to work outside the home.
6. People lived in loosely-related groups, not in small family units.
7. Men supported the family, and women stayed home to take care of the children. There were fewer divorces.
8. There are and will continue to be many different family structures: "traditional" two-parent families, families with two working parents, single-parent families, adoptive or foster families, blended families, and so on.

Timeline

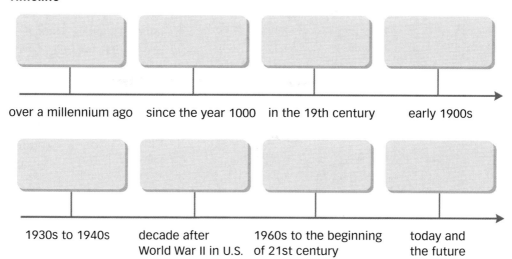

over a millennium ago   since the year 1000   in the 19th century   early 1900s

1930s to 1940s   decade after
World War II in U.S.   1960s to the beginning
of 21st century   today and
the future

 8 **Discussing the Reading** Talk about your answers to these questions.

1. What is the most common family structure in your community or culture?

2. In your opinion, what caused so many changes in the structure of the family after the middle of the 20th century? Explain your answers.

3. In your opinion, how and why might the structure of the family change in the 21st and 22nd centuries? What will cause these changes?

Part 2 Reading Skills and Strategies

Time with the Family—Past and Present

Before You Read

Strategy

Skimming to Find Time and Place in History
You learned about skimming to find the topic and main idea in Chapter 4. Now you will learn about skimming readings about history, which give information about certain periods of time. Each paragraph might be about a different year, a period of years, a decade, a century, or even a millennium. It can describe important events or changes in one or more countries or cultures—or global happenings. You can figure out the time and place in history through skimming—that is, by reading the material quickly for a purpose.

 1 **Previewing Vocabulary** Read the vocabulary items on the next page. Then listen to the words and phrases. Put a check mark (✓) next to the words you know. You can learn the other words now or come back to them after you read the next article.

Nouns			Adjectives
❑ Anglos	❑ independence	❑ date	❑ Anglicized
❑ career	❑ master	**Verbs**	❑ arranged (marriage)
❑ castle	❑ meals	❑ date	❑ asleep
❑ cooking	❑ motherhood	❑ fell (fall) in love	❑ crowded
❑ cottage	❑ protection	❑ got (get) married	❑ expected
❑ farm	❑ servants	❑ got (get) up	**Adverbs**
❑ females	❑ slaves	❑ have custody of	❑ financially
❑ fields	❑ straw mat	❑ improve	❑ modestly
❑ generations	❑ taxes	❑ pushed aside	**Preposition**
❑ goats	❑ values	❑ separated	❑ during
❑ housework	❑ waiter	❑ value	
	❑ years		

2 Skimming Read the four topics below. Then skim the four paragraphs in the article "Time with the Family—Past and Present." Match each paragraph from the article to one of the topics below. Write the paragraph letter, A, B, C, or D, in the blank.

_____ The Traditional Japanese Family in the 1900s

_____ Typical Family Structure in a Middle Eastern Country Until the End of the Twentieth Century

_____ A Simple Family in England—Around the Year 1200

_____ Possible Cultural Differences in Family Values and Customs

Read

 3 Identifying the Main Ideas Now read each paragraph a second time. Following each paragraph are three possible main-idea statements. In your opinion, which sentence or sentences best express the point of each paragraph? Fill in the letter A, B, or C. Then give the reasons for your choices.

Time with the Family—Past and Present

A   The sun was rising. A woman got up from a **straw mat** on the floor of her simple two-room family **cottage**. Her husband and their four children were still **asleep** on the mat. (There *were* five other children: the couple gave two of them to a family with too few workers; the other three died long ago.) The woman **pushed aside** the family **goats**. When she started the fire for **cooking**, the man and the children got up. While the daughter helped with the **housework**, the sons went outside to work in the **fields** with their father. They could see a castle, not far away. The family lived under the **protection** of the **master** of the castle. They weren't his **slaves** (servants), but they paid him taxes. There was no schooling, so they couldn't read or write or get jobs in cities. **During** the long workday, they took breaks only for **meals**. Occasionally, they went to the village center, where they laughed and talked and played games. At night, people of the community got together around big fires; they told stories about the past. Most families used to live this way in England over 800 **years** ago.

What is the main idea of Paragraph A?

- (A) At the beginning of the last millennium, most families lived much simpler lives than their masters. They worked on the land and in the household; they had only a little time for a social life and enjoyment.
- (B) In England in the year 1200, families used to live in castles: the daughters of the masters used to do the housework, and their sons used to work in the fields with the common people.
- (C) In the Americas of the 13th century, families didn't need masters for protection because they paid no taxes. They lived in extended family groups in the cities.

B   In the first half of the 20th century, the Japanese family was much more   15
"traditional" than the typical American family. Young people didn't even use to date; in other words, they didn't go out together as couples. Instead, they had **arranged** marriages—their parents chose their husband or wife. Maybe the couple fell in love after they got married, and maybe they didn't. Either way, the wife had children and stayed home with them while the husband supported the   20
family financially. Often the husband and wife and their children lived in an extended family situation—three generations in one **crowded** house. Today life in Japan is similar to that of many other industrialized countries in that many women work outside the home and young people choose their own mates.

What is the main idea of Paragraph B?

- (A) In Japan, the 20th century meant dating and falling in love at an early age. It also meant equal relationships in work, finances, parenting, and decision-making.
- (B) Fathers are more important than mothers in family life because they support their wives and children; they also begin businesses and buy houses for their parents and grandparents.
- (C) Until late into the 20th century, Japanese parents used to arrange their children's marriages. Some lived in the same house with the following generations; the men of the household made all the money and all the rules.

C   In the past, and in part today, much of Saudi culture has been different from   25
Western culture. Under Islam, women should behave **modestly** in public, where they are often separated from men. Women play an important role in the home and are generally expected to focus on the family. In the 1960s, the government began a national education program for girls, and soon after that, education was available to all **females**. Today, there are many more interesting   30
job opportunities for women.

What is the main idea of Paragraph C?

- (A) Saudi culture has not been influenced by Islam.
- (B) An important part of Saudi family culture after 1960 was education and career development for females.
- (C) Typical Saudi culture used to be no different from Western culture. Both parents worked outside the home and there were many single-parent families.

D   A few years ago, a sad thing happened. A young American woman left her family for career reasons; she moved far away. For this reason, a 36-year-old divorced father **has custody of** his two children, eleven and eight years old. He works long hours as a waiter, including weekends. On his days off from work, he goes to a local community college. He's studying to **improve** his job skills so he can make more money for his family. At night he does his homework at the same table as the children. But who takes care of the kids in the evenings when their father is working or going to school? His "extended family"—his mother, other relatives, and his new girlfriend—help out as much as they can. He thinks his girlfriend, who is from Mexico, his home country, is good for his family. He doesn't want to date "Anglos" or "Anglicized" women because he thinks they value their **independence** over motherhood. He wants a wife with traditional, religious values like his mother.

What is the main idea of Paragraph D?

- (A) Usually, career women leave their families for financial reasons; fathers prefer to stay home with their children and take care of them.
- (B) Life can be hard for divorced and single-parent families, and they need the help of family and friends. Some people want to marry someone from their own culture.
- (C) Community colleges are better for young adults in extended families because they allow people time for study and work.

After You Read

PARAPHRASING HISTORY TEXTS

You learned how to write a summary in Chapter 3. Here we'll look at how you can summarize information about history.

- Is there a *trend* in the history—a clear development or a change? If *yes*, then begin with that general point.

- Next, *paraphrase* (restate in other words) the important events and facts (the supporting details) in regard to that trend.

Here are possible paraphrases for important vocabulary from the reading "Time with the Family—Past and Present."

tradition: customs from the past, old rules and habits, ways that have existed a long time

typical: most common, not unusual, serving as an example

the first half of the 20th century: the earlier part of the 1900s, from about 1900 to 1950

date: go out together as couples, spend time together alone, get to know each other

schooling: an education

And here is the possible short summary of the information from Paragraph A.

The common families of England lived with their animals in small, crowded cottages; members worked hard on the farms and in their households. There were many children, but some died young. Without an education, people couldn't improve their lives financially. Even so, they had some fun in the community.

4 Writing a Summary Work in groups of four. Each student chooses a different paragraph from the reading "Time with the Family—Past and Present." Using your own words, summarize the main idea and important details. Then tell or read your summary to your group.

5 Discussing the Reading Discuss these questions about the reading with a partner.

1. In your view, were the families of long ago healthier or happier than modern families? Why or why not?

2. In your opinion, which cultures had or have the most "traditional" family forms? Explain the reasons for your answer.

3. In your opinion, should men and women lead separate lives, especially in public? At home, should they play traditional roles, especially in childcare and parenting? Describe your experiences in this regard.

4. Do you think the life of today's typical family is difficult? If so, in what ways? If not, why not?

6 Talking It Over What are your *predictions* (ideas about what will happen) for the future of the typical family around the globe?

■ In your opinion, which of the following present trends will increase, or become more common? Put a plus sign (+) on the lines before those sentences.

■ Which of the trends will decrease, or become less common? Put a minus sign (–) before those predictions.

■ Which of the trends do you think will be good for people in the 21st century? Circle the numbers of those items.

In small groups, give your answers. Explain the reasons for your predictions and views.

1. _____ Family groups will become smaller and smaller—maybe only one parent living with one or two children.

2. _____ People are going to live in extended families or large groups of relatives or friends, with all ages in the house.

3. _____ The rate of divorces will increase to almost 100 percent (%); nobody will want to marry legally anymore. Instead, couples will just live together—or apart.

4. _____ Marriage between one man and one woman might still be the most common family structure, but people are going to marry many times in their lives. Most families will be "blended," so few children will grow up with both biological parents.

5. _____ Couples will have children much later in life: the average age of first-time parents will be 40. There will be many multiple births, births of more than three babies at one time.

6. _____ Single or divorced people, unmarried couples, or same-sex partners will become foster parents to children without families, or they will adopt babies from other countries.

7. _____ Small children might spend more time in day-care centers and schools than at home. Instead of their biological parents, babysitters or relatives may care for them.

8. _____ Couples can still have children of their own, but they may choose their features before birth: their sex, color, health, and so on. Science will make this possible.

9. _____ People are going to live much longer, so they will not only have grandchildren; there will also be great-grandchildren, great-great grandchildren, and so on. All these generations will live in the same houses or neighborhoods.

10. _____ Older people are not going to live in the same communities as families with children. Because they will be busy with their own lives and friends, they won't have time for the younger generation.

Do you have any predictions of your own about the future of the family around the world? Give your ideas. Explain why you think these events or trends might happen.

Strategy

Getting Meaning from Context: Punctuation and Phrase Clues
Short definitions of new vocabulary items sometimes appear between or after certain punctuation marks such as parentheses (( )), dashes (—), or commas (,). They might also be in another sentence part after a semicolon (;) or a colon (:). The phrases *in other words* and *that is to say* or the abbreviation *i.e. (that is)* can also be clues to the meaning of vocabulary.

Example

The family is a social institution; in other words, it is an organization with a purpose inside a human community—that is, among the people living together in a certain area. (A definition of a *social institution* is "an organization with a purpose within a community." The word *community* can mean "people living together in a certain area.")

A hyphen (-) between words is another punctuation clue to the meanings of multiword adjectives before nouns, such as:

> *two-parent family*
> *loosely-related group*
> *ten-year period*

1 **Getting Meaning from Context** On the lines, finish the explanations of the words from the reading selection "A Short History of the Changing Family" on pages 87–89. (The letters in parentheses are the letters of the paragraphs.)

1. an ancestor: (A) a family member *from the distant past*

_____

2. the extended family: (A) relatives such as _____

_____

3. the nuclear family: (A) a family unit with only _____

_____

4. a stay-at-home mother: (B) a mother that _____

_____

5. single-parent families: (B) families with only _____

_____

6. blended families: (B) family groups with _____

_____

7. the divorce rate: (C) the percent of _____

_____

8. a decade: (C) a time period of _____

_____

9. war widows: (D) women whose _____

_____

For more practice, you can look for and explain other vocabulary items with meaning clues, such as a *millennium, family structure, two-paycheck families, adoptive* or *foster families, previous, birthrate,* and others.

Strategy

Recognizing Similar and Opposite Meanings

For most vocabulary items, there are words or phrases with the same or similar meanings—such as *spouse, mate,* and *marriage partner.*

For some items, there are also words or phrases with *opposite* meanings—that is, completely different, or contrasting, definitions. Examples of opposites are *adults* and *children,* or *married* and *single.*

To explain and learn new vocabulary quickly, you can learn both words with similar meanings and words with opposite meanings.

2 **Identifying Words with Similar and Opposite Meanings** In each of the following pairs of words or phrases, do the vocabulary items have the same or similar meanings? If so, write *S* for *similar* on the line. Or do the vocabulary items have *opposite* meanings? If so, write *O* on the line.

1. __S__ on the other hand / in contrast

2. __O__ even so / for this reason

3. _____ but / however

4. _____ traditional / modern

5. _____ the structure / the form

6. _____ marriage / divorce

7. _____ single-parent families / extended families

8. _____ the birthrate / the percent of deaths

9. _____ declined / went down (decreased)

10. _____ industrialized countries / developing countries

11. _____ previous or past / future or following

12. _____ occur / take place

13. _____ independence / taking care of oneself

14. _____ improve / make worse

15. _____ modestly / proudly

16. _____ stay-at-home mothers / two-income working families

17. _____ a social institution / community organization

18. _____ have custody of / be responsible for (take care of)

19. _____ a master / a slave or servant

20. _____ female or woman or girl / male or man or boy

For more practice, choose other words from the Self-Assessment Logs in Chapters 1 to 5. Tell or write similar or opposite meanings.

Strategy

Recognizing Nouns and Adjectives

A very useful vocabulary-learning strategy is to recognize parts of speech. Some words can be more than one part of speech. As examples, in the sentences that follow, the words *family*, *community*, and *ancestor* are nouns; the words *familiar*, *common*, and *ancestral* are adjectives related to those nouns:

The *family* is a basic institution *familiar* to all of us. Families usually live in a *community*. Family members have *common ancestors* and may have *ancestral* traditions.

3 **Identifying Nouns and Adjectives** Below are some sentences with related words—nouns and adjectives—on the topic of the reading material of this chapter. Within each pair of parentheses ( ), circle the correct word form. Then write the missing words in the chart that follows. (Not all of the words from the sentences are in the chart.) Some words are provided as examples.

1. Like a (community / communal), a (family / familiar) is a (society / social) institution.

2. Long ago, (humanity / human) beings lived in loosely- (relatives / related) groups with a common (ancestor / ancestral).

3. Sometimes three generations lived together in (crowd / crowded) homes.

4. Usually, only the oldest sons owned the family farmland, so the (youth / younger) children moved to cities where (education / educated) and jobs were available.

5. No longer did men and women enter into (arrangement / arranged) (marriages / married); instead, couples became partners by (choice / chosen).

6. In most of (history / historical), the (nucleus / nuclear) family form became the most common living-group arrangement.

7. Since many men went off to war in the 1930s and 40s, war (widows / widowed) took care of the children.

8. The main (reason / reasonable) for the decrease in the size of most families was (economy / economic) necessity, or need.

9. In other words, (globe / global) (industrialization / industrialized) was a major cause of the (universe / universal) changes in family size and form.

10. With so many one-parent families in the (modernization / modern) world, social (institutions / institutional) may be more in charge of the (protection / protective) of children than their biological mothers or fathers.

Noun	Related Adjective	Noun	Related Adjective
community	communal	arrangement	arranged
family			married
society			historical
relatives			nuclear (family)
ancestors			widowed
crowd			economic
youth			protective

For more practice, tell or write more nouns from Chapters 1 to 5. Which nouns have related adjective forms? What are they? Also, tell or write some adjectives with their related noun forms. (You can check your words in a dictionary.)

4 **Focusing on High-Frequency Words** Read the paragraph below and fill in each blank with a word from the box. When you finish, check your answers on page 94.

asleep	cottage	fields	housework	pushed	straw mat
cooking	during	goats	meals	slaves	years

A   The sun was rising. A woman got up from a _____ on
1
the floor of her simple two-room family _____. Her
2
husband and their four children were still _____ on
3
the mat. (There *were* five other children: the couple gave two of them to a

family with too few workers; the other three died long ago.) The woman 5

_____ aside the family _____. When
                     4   5
she started the fire for _____, the man and the children
                                           6
got up. While the daughter helped with the _____, the
                                                              7
sons went outside to work in the _____ with their father.
                                                    8
They could see a castle, not far away. The family lived under the protection 10
of the master of the castle. They weren't his _____
                                                                  9
(servants) but they paid him taxes. There was no schooling, so they couldn't
read or write or get jobs in cities. _____ the long
                                                          10
workday, they took breaks only for _____. Occasionally,
                                                        11
they went to the village center, where they laughed and talked and played 15
games. At night, people of the community got together around big fires;
they told stories about the past. Most families used to live this way in
England over 800 _____ ago.
                                  12

 5 **Making Connections** Do an Internet search about family structures in the
world today. You can type in something like *family structure in* _____ *(name
of country)*. Look up two or more places or different cultures. Take notes on the
information. How are the family structures in the two places similar? How do they seem
different? Tell a partner or the class what you learned.

Part 4   Focus on Testing

TOEFL® iBT

UNDERSTANDING DEFINITIONS AND EXPLANATIONS

The TOEFL® iBT contains a great deal of very difficult vocabulary. Part 3 of this chapter
discusses punctuation marks and phrases that signal definitions in a reading. This
strategy can be extremely useful on the TOEFL® iBT.

Readings for the TOEFL® iBT are about as difficult as textbooks in a first-year college
class. Even university students who are native speakers of English may not understand
every word in a reading. Because the vocabulary level is so high, the text often contains

definitions or explanations of unusual vocabulary. The hardest "definitions" to find are really explanations or examples, not obvious definitions.

Finding Definitions and Explanations Reread "A Short History of the Changing Family" on pages 87–89. Try to recognize definitions when you see them. Then answer the TOEFL® iBT—like questions below.

1. Which of the following is closest in meaning to *millennium,* as it is used in Paragraph A?
   - (A) the past
   - (B) a kind of family
   - (C) a long period of time
   - (D) relatives living in the same house

2. Which of the following is closest in meaning to *two-paycheck family*, as it is used in Paragraph B?
   - (A) a type of family with two children who have jobs
   - (B) a type of family in which both parents work outside the home
   - (C) a type of family in which two or more generations live together
   - (D) a type of family with biological or adopted children

3. Which of the following is closest in meaning to *siblings*, as it is used in Paragraph B?
   - (A) brothers or sisters
   - (B) husbands or wives
   - (C) sons or daughters
   - (D) parents or grandparents

4. Which of the following is closest in meaning to *developing*, as it is used in Paragraph C?
   - (A) with women in the workforce
   - (B) coming decades later
   - (C) not industrialized
   - (D) in decline

5. Which of the following is closest in meaning to *World War II*, as it is used in Paragraph D?
   - (A) something that happened in the late 1930s and early 1940s
   - (B) something that happened in the early 1900s
   - (C) something that happened from the 1960s to the 1990s
   - (D) something that happened during the 10 years after the "war widows"

Self-Assessment Log

Read the lists below. Check (✓) the strategies and vocabulary that you learned in this chapter. Look through the chapter or ask your instructor about the strategies and words that you do not understand.

Reading and Vocabulary-Building Strategies

❏ Recognizing topics in readings about history
❏ Recognizing the main idea
❏ Using a timeline to take notes on time and time order
❏ Skimming to find time and place in history
❏ Identifying the main ideas
❏ Paraphrasing in a summary
❏ Getting meaning from context: punctuation and phrase clues
❏ Identifying words with similar and opposite meanings
❏ Recognizing nouns and adjectives

Target Vocabulary

Nouns

❏ ancestor
❏ birthrate
❏ blended families
❏ community
❏ cooking*
❏ cottage*
❏ decades
❏ divorce rate
❏ divorces
❏ females*
❏ fields*
❏ future*
❏ goats*
❏ history*
❏ housework*
❏ independence*
❏ master*
❏ meals*

❏ protection*
❏ relatives*
❏ single-parent families
❏ slaves*
❏ social* institution
❏ stay-at-home mother
❏ straw mat
❏ structure
❏ widows*
❏ years*

Verbs

❏ decline
❏ has (have) custody of
❏ improve*
❏ occur
❏ pushed aside

Adjectives

❏ arranged*
❏ asleep*
❏ communal
❏ crowded*
❏ developing*
❏ economic
❏ future
❏ industrialized
❏ loosely-related
❏ previous
❏ traditional
❏ widowed*
❏ younger*

Adverb

❏ modestly*

Preposition

❏ during*

---

*These words are among the 2,000 most frequently used words in English.

Cultures of the World

In This Chapter

What does the word *culture* mean to you? In conversation form, the first reading selection gives different views on the meaning and importance of the concept. In the second selection, there are examples of typical cultural situations—happenings that led to misunderstanding or miscommunication among members of various cultures. These anecdotes or examples show how easily these types of misunderstandings can occur and why it is important to learn about the culture of places before you visit.

❝ No culture can live, if it attempts to be exclusive. **❞**

—Mahatma Gandhi,
nonviolent activist and political leader who
helped lead India to independence (1869–1948)

Connecting to the Topic

1 Look at the two groups of women in the photo below. Where do you think they are from? How are they different?

2 What is your definition of *culture*? Think of some examples of your definition.

3 Other than language, why do you think people from different cultures sometimes have misunderstandings?

Cross-Cultural Conversation

Before You Read

1 **Previewing the Topic** Discuss the picture in small groups.

1. What does the scene show? Who is taking part in a group conversation?

2. In your view, what are the cultural backgrounds of the group members? Why do you think so? Look at their clothing, the space between them, their body language, their facial expressions, and so on.

3. What do you think the people are saying about culture?

▲ People having a conversation about culture

2 **Predicting** Think about and discuss possible answers to these questions. Write down your answers. If you don't know the answers, make predictions. You can look for the answers when you read "Cross-Cultural Conversation."

1. What is a "cultural legacy" from the past? What elements might it include?

2. What are some technical or scientific achievements of ancient cultures?

3. In what ways do you think culture is universal in today's world?

4. In what ways do you think modern cultures vary around the world?

5. What are some views of the concept, or idea, of "culture"?

3 Previewing Vocabulary Read the vocabulary items below from the first reading. Then listen to the words and phrases. Put a check mark (✓) next to the words you know. You can learn the other words now or come back to them after you read.

Nouns	Verbs	Adjectives	Adverbs
❏ architecture	❏ agree	❏ amazing	❏ convincingly
❏ cathedrals	❏ contradict	❏ ancient	❏ politely
❏ civilization	❏ contributed	❏ clear	
❏ contradiction	❏ describe	❏ cultural	
❏ discoveries	❏ develop	❏ enthusiastic	
❏ legacy	❏ experience	❏ excellent	
❏ literature	❏ grinning	❏ knowing	
❏ media	❏ interrupting	❏ opposing	
❏ medicine	❏ invented	❏ pleasant	
❏ societies		❏ proud	
❏ weapons		❏ scientific	
		❏ social	
		❏ soft	

Read

 4 Reading an Article Read the following article. Then read the explanations and do the activities that follow.

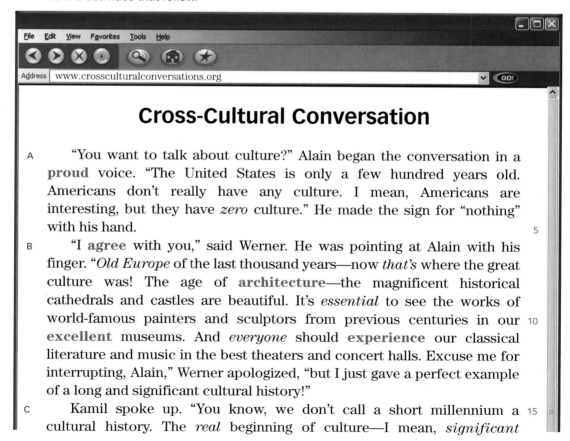

Cross-Cultural Conversation

A   "You want to talk about culture?" Alain began the conversation in a **proud** voice. "The United States is only a few hundred years old. Americans don't really have any culture. I mean, Americans are interesting, but they have *zero* culture." He made the sign for "nothing" with his hand.   5

B   "I **agree** with you," said Werner. He was pointing at Alain with his finger. "*Old Europe* of the last thousand years—now *that's* where the great culture was! The age of **architecture**—the magnificent historical cathedrals and castles are beautiful. It's *essential* to see the works of world-famous painters and sculptors from previous centuries in our 10 **excellent** museums. And *everyone* should **experience** our classical literature and music in the best theaters and concert halls. Excuse me for interrupting, Alain," Werner apologized, "but I just gave a perfect example of a long and significant cultural history!"

C   Kamil spoke up. "You know, we don't call a short millennium a 15 cultural history. The *real* beginning of culture—I mean, *significant civilization*—was in the Middle East and Africa over five thousand years ago". He continued, waving both hands in the air, "Ancient communities not only knew how to create magnificent architecture

D
▲ Historical architecture is one example of "culture"

and art; they also made **amazing scientific** and technological discoveries. They *invented* things. For instance, they figured out how to write and do mathematics; they studied astronomy— the science of the skies, the sun and the planets; they invented the calendar. They even had **medicine**; the ancient religions came from that area, too. *Their* achievements made world civilization possible. *Those* were the civilizations that gave humanity the most meaningful cultural **legacy**!"

Mei agreed with Kamil. In a **soft** but **knowing** voice, she added, "But the *really* important science and technology began to **develop** in Asia and the Americas. While the ancient Chinese were building walled cities, they organized the first governments. They invented tools for work and weapons for protection. And the native peoples of the Americas had very, very old civilizations and societies. *That* was ancient traditional culture."

E "Ancient culture? That's a **contradiction** in definitions." Grinning, Karen objected in an **enthusiastic**, friendly way. She gave a contrasting opinion. "It's *impossible* for culture to be old or traditional," she argued. The *opposite* is true! Culture isn't dead—it's *alive*. Culture is *modern*! Culture is *now*!"

F Kenji was starting to fall asleep, but suddenly he was fully awake. "I agree!" he said, interrupting Karen enthusiastically.

G "You tell them!" said Karen, appreciating the support for her point of view. For emphasis, she nodded vigorously.

H "Culture is worldwide—it's universal!" Kenji went on in his **clear** speaking style. He had a wide smile on his face. "I mean, like—take today's food culture. With our global fast food, I have to say, everyone eats the same. And because of the worldwide **media**—movies, TV, CDs (compact disks), the Internet—everybody knows the same information, plays the same music, enjoys the same stories—even the jokes! And I mean, it's like—people everywhere want to buy the same clothes—all because of advertising. A beautiful young couple in jeans and bright Hawaiian shirts anywhere in the world, eating hamburgers and French fries with their friends from many countries—*finally*, we have a global culture! And *tradition* has nothing to do with it!"

I   Nadia, however, was of another opinion. "You want to call modern movies, music, food, and clothes *culture*?" she said, sweetly but **convincingly**. "Those things don't **describe** culture. Culture isn't about the *sameness* of people in communities around the world; it's about their *differences*. Like—it's important for people to *greet* one another in various ways, and they need to use different titles and follow a variety of **social** rules in their relationships. Some **societies** are formal, while others are informal, or casual. Some groups are friendly, and others aren't. And another example is the diverse use of language—is it direct or indirect? How do communication styles include motions, gestures, facial expressions, and other body language? And *customs* are so interesting! They're what people of different national groups *do* in their everyday lives and on special occasions like holidays or celebrations. Culture means *cultural diversity*. What makes life amusing? It's the *variety* of cultures around the world, its contradictions and opposites!"   65   70   75

J   "Yeah, maybe so," contributed Alain as **politely** as possible. "On the other hand, . . ." he started to say.

K   "That *does* make some sense," interrupted Werner, beginning to smile, "as long as you don't forget the arts—architecture, painting, literature, music . . ."   80

L   "And if you also include ancient civilizations and traditions," added Kamil with a **pleasant** expression on his face. He didn't like to **contradict** Nadia or any of his female friends.

M   "Well, we can certainly have **opposing** viewpoints," concluded Karen, "and yet we still enjoy exchanging ideas." Everyone was smiling, and they wanted to talk a lot more.   85

After You Read

UNDERSTANDING READING STRUCTURE: CONVERSATION IN PARAGRAPH FORM

Explanatory material can appear in various forms. For instance, opinions and views on a topic can be in the form of a conversation—with the words of each speaker between quotation marks (" ") in a different paragraph.

5 **Understanding Reading Structure: Conversation in Paragraph Form**
In the reading "Cross-Cultural Conversation," the speakers talk about different definitions of the concept (idea) of "culture." For each section of the reading, check (✓) the topic. (The letters in parentheses ( ) refer to the paragraphs.)

1. (A, B)

_____ the long cultural legacy of the arts in European history

_____ the importance of international education through the centuries

2. (C, D)

    _____ humanity's scientific and technological discoveries and achievements

    _____ the business practices of cultural groups in Africa and the Americas

3. (E–H)

    _____ the differences among ancient cultures on various continents

    _____ the cultural sameness and similarities among modern peoples

4. (I)

    _____ cultural diversity—how groups vary in their styles and customs

    _____ attitudes toward nature in a variety of times and places

5. (J–M)

    _____ definitions of the word *society*—according to various world cultures

    _____ polite, friendly ways of discussing ideas and telling opinions

Which phrase below best tells the topic, or subject, of the whole reading "Cross-Cultural Conversation"? Give reasons for your answer.

    (A) the relationships among human beings in a variety of family structures and forms

    (B) education, food, community, family, and other subjects of interest to young people

    (C) various opinions about the meaning and importance of the concept of "culture"

    (D) variety in contrast to sameness in the global community of the Internet

6 Understanding the Point Following are some false statements about the points of the reading selection "Cross-Cultural Conversation." To make them into true statements, change the underlined words. Number 5 is about the whole reading. The first item is done as an example.

1. Some people believe that countries with ~~short~~ *long* histories have more cultural legacy than ~~old~~ *young* countries—especially in their ~~communication styles and body language~~. *technology and religion*

2. For other thinkers, civilization didn't include only old architecture and art; it also meant <u>opinions and statements</u> in mathematics, astronomy, medicine, weapons, city building, and the like.

3. Young people around the world <u>don't want</u> to think about food, media, music, or clothes as culture because those things are <u>ancient</u>, and <u>nobody</u> seems to like the same kinds.

4. According to others, diversity is <u>less significant than</u> sameness in discussions about culture; such speakers say that people should <u>decrease and forget about</u> their differences.

5. People from various <u>cathedrals and castles</u> around the world have <u>exactly the same</u> views on the meaning and importance of the concept "culture." In fact, it's common for them to express their ideas in <u>similar</u> ways.

RECOGNIZING SUPPORTING DETAIL: OPINIONS

Clearly, the speakers in "Cross-Cultural Conversation" have diverse opinions and views about the value and importance of their various concepts of culture.

- Some words in their speeches are in *italics*; this special kind of slanted print can mean the speakers think the words are important to their point, so they say them more strongly than other words.

- An exclamation point, a punctuation mark that looks like this (!), also shows strong emphasis.

---

7 **Recognizing Supporting Detail: Opinions** What did the speakers in "Cross-Cultural Conversation" value within their concepts of culture? Circle the letters of *all* the correct answers to each question.

1. Alain and Werner felt that the age of a culture added to the value of its fine arts. Which parts of culture were essential to them?
   a. fast food and junk food
   b. old painting and sculpture
   c. literature and classical music
   d. human feelings and emotions
   e. the architecture of buildings and structures
   f. things in museums, theater plays, and concerts

2. Kamil and Mei most valued the ancient civilizations of the Middle East, Africa, and the Americas. What things did they include in "a cultural legacy"?
   a. international business
   b. magnificent architecture and art
   c. scientific discoveries and invention
   d. writing and mathematics
   e. the study of astronomy
   f. protected cities and government structure

3. Kenji was happy that modern culture is worldwide and similar all over the planet. Which features did he find most important?
   a. ancient religions
   b. the historical structure of the family
   c. food from global chains
   d. Indian rock tools and weapons
   e. the media of movies, TV, and the Internet
   f. advertising for clothes and other things

4. Nadia preferred cultural diversity to sameness. What things did she include in her concept of culture?
   a. greetings, including titles and names
   b. relationships and other social rules
   c. formality in contrast to informality

d. directness and indirectness in language

e. body language and movements

f. everyday and special occasion customs

5. In what ways did the group members discuss their ideas and opinions with one another?

a. proudly and enthusiastically

b. with various hand and arm gestures

c. in a moderate or a soft voice

d. grinning or smiling—or not

e. with a clear speaking style

f. agreeing or disagreeing

 8 **Discussing the Reading** Discuss these questions in small groups.

1. In your view of the concept of culture, which parts or qualities are essential—or very important? Why?

2. According to your experience, in what ways are world cultures similar or alike? Which features are different? Explain your views.

3. Which is better for humanity and the future of the world—one global culture or cultural diversity all over the planet? Explain your reasoning or logic.

Part 2   Reading Skills and Strategies

Clues to World Cultures

Before You Read

 1 **Previewing Vocabulary** Read the vocabulary items below from the next reading. Then listen to the words and phrases. Put a check mark (✓) next to the words you know. You can learn the other words now or come back to them after you read.

Nouns	Verbs	Adjectives	Adverbs
❏ attention	❏ begged	❏ afraid	❏ backwards
❏ bite	❏ cleaned (his) plate	❏ annoyed	❏ patiently
❏ customers	❏ greet	❏ insulted	❏ loudly
❏ guest	❏ hitchhike	❏ mean	❏ rudely
❏ host	❏ ignored	❏ rude	
❏ pain	❏ serve	❏ successful	

Nouns	Verbs	Adjectives
❑ pharmacist	❑ shouted	❑ terrible
❑ pharmacy	❑ waiting on (someone)	❑ tourist (places)
❑ service	❑ whispered	❑ unwelcome

Read

UNDERSTANDING ANECDOTES

An *anecdote* is a very short story with a humorous or interesting point. Reading material on the topic of world cultures often includes anecdotes. These descriptions of cultural situations tell what happened to create cross-cultural misunderstanding or learning. Most reading of this kind is about topics such as the following:

_____ ▪ greetings and introductions; meeting new people

_____ ▪ visiting a family at home; eating and drinking with people from other cultures

_____ ▪ body language—gestures, hand movements, and facial expressions

_____ ▪ concepts of time and timing—doing things in a certain order or at the same time

_____ ▪ formality and informality, directness and indirectness in communication

_____ ▪ ideas about individual and group responsibility and rights

2 **Reading Stories with Anecdotes** Following are three short stories with the general title of "Clues to World Cultures." On the lines before *three* of the topics listed in the box above, write the story letters A, B, and C. (There are no stories about the other three topics in this part of the chapter.)

On your second reading of each story, look for "culture clues"—pieces of information that suggest differences between members of cultural groups. These possible differences in customs, attitudes, beliefs, and the like are the *point* of the material.

Following each paragraph are some questions about the "cross-cultural meaning" of the experience. Fill in the best (the most logical) answer—A, B, or C. Then give your answers and the reasons for them.

Clues to World Cultures

A   An Irish woman was visiting **tourist** places in a Latin American city when she got a **terrible** headache. She knew what medicine she needed, so she went to a local pharmacy. The **pharmacist** was waiting on another

customer when she came in. The Irish woman **patiently** waited her turn. While she was standing there, two other customers came in, then another, and then three more. Each time, the pharmacist turned his **attention** to the new people. He did not **greet** the Irish woman; he never said, "I'll be with you in a minute."

After about 20 minutes, the woman couldn't stand the **pain** in her head any longer. "Hey, I've been here a long time," she said **loudly**, very **annoyed** and insulted. "Why is everyone ignoring me? I need service, too!" she shouted **rudely** (impolitely).

1. Why didn't the pharmacist pay attention to the Irish woman when she came into his store?
  - (A) He didn't know her, and he didn't like her looks.
  - (B) She didn't greet him or ask for attention; she just stood there quietly.
  - (C) He was probably not waiting on a customer at all—just talking to a friend.

2. Why was the Irish customer insulted, angry, or hurt?
  - (A) She had a terrible headache; her pain reduced her patience.
  - (B) She expected the pharmacist to greet her and wait on her in turn (in order).
  - (C) She didn't want to buy medicine; it was too expensive at the pharmacy.

3. What is the cultural point of the story?
  - (A) In some cultures, people wait their turn for greetings and attention, but in others, they ask for these things in some clear way.
  - (B) In stores in all countries, people need to be patient: they have to stand quietly in line and wait for service—often for a long time.
  - (C) Pain is different in various parts of the world; some people can stand it better than others.

B   A Middle-Eastern businessman and his brother invited an American guest to their family home for dinner. The American got there on time and enjoyed the interesting conversation, the tea, and the attention. But as time passed, he got very, very hungry. Finally he politely whispered to his host, "Excuse me, but are we going to eat dinner?"

"Of course!" answered his host. "We usually serve the evening meal around 9:00, and when we have guests, we enjoy the long conversation before dinner."

At the dinner table everything was delicious, and the hungry American guest ate quickly. He emptied his plate, and his host put more food on it. As soon as he cleaned his plate a second time, the host gave him more. After several plates of food, he could eat no more. He was going to burst! "Please, please, please—don't give me any more food," he begged them. "I finished the food on this plate, but I can't eat another bite!"

Even then, his host insisted. The guest accepted a little more and ate it with difficulty. Finally, the supper dishes were removed. There was more conversation—with more tea and coffee. At about midnight, the server brought a pitcher of ice water. The tired American knew it was OK to thank his hosts and leave. 30

1. Why did the host family serve the evening meal so late?

- (A) They were waiting for the guest to say he was hungry.
- (B) After an hour or two of conversation with guests, supper is usually served around 9:00.
- (C) The hosts were busy talking to the guest, so dinner wasn't ready yet.

2. Why did the American guest eat more food than he wanted?

- (A) He was very, very hungry because there was no food in his house and he never went to restaurants.
- (B) In the dinner conversation, his hosts talked and talked; he didn't get a chance to answer, so he paid attention only to the food.
- (C) His host kept putting food on his plate; he didn't want to leave food or seem impolite, so he ate it all.

3. What is the cultural point of the story?

- (A) In some cultures, there is a lot of social conversation before and after the evening meal with guests; also, servers put food on guests' plates every time they are empty.
- (B) All over the world, dinner guests should eat a lot; if they leave anything on their plates, their hosts will think they don't like the food.
- (C) In some cultures, guests eat more than their hosts; in others, it is impolite to eat a lot at other people's houses.

c   A group of international students were attending college in Europe. They had a long time between semesters for travel, so they decided  to hitchhike as far as they could in other countries. In many places, they were 35 **successful**. They put their thumbs out or pointed them backwards and smiled; friendly drivers stopped. As soon as the first traveler got a "yes" answer from a driver, he motioned with his hand or fingers for his friends to 40 come—or he held both thumbs up in an "OK" sign or made a circle with the thumb and the next finger of one hand. The young tourists saved money, saw a lot of the countryside, and had interesting conversations and experiences. 45

▲ A student hitchhiking

On the other hand, in Greece and Turkey, the visitors were not so lucky. Few drivers stopped to give them rides; instead, most people ignored them. Others gave them mean looks from their cars; they seemed almost insulted that the visitors were begging for rides. A few drivers shouted terrible words at the travelers; two even got out of their truck and started a fight. The students thought the drivers were very **rude**. They felt confused, afraid, and unwelcome. After a few days the students took the bus back to the countries where they were studying.

50

1. Why did the young travelers get rides successfully in many places in Europe?
   - (A) Drivers knew they were trying to "thumb rides" because they recognized the meanings of their hand gestures.
   - (B) All the travelers were good-looking young men, and the drivers that stopped were single women.
   - (C) Most people knew the students had money; they expected payment for the rides in their cars and trucks.

2. Why weren't the student tourists so lucky in Greece and Turkey?
   - (A) In those countries, there are laws against hitchhiking, so drivers aren't allowed to give rides to travelers.
   - (B) In certain places, the custom is to ask for rides with printed signs: the signs should tell the place the travelers want to go.
   - (C) The "hitchhiking" thumb gesture has an insulting meaning in those cultures: drivers thought the young people were being rude and disrespectful.

3. What is the cultural point of the story?
   - (A) Hand gestures are rude because they are kinds of body language: visitors to other cultures should always ask for things with words.
   - (B) Travelers should hitchhike only in their home cultures: drivers are afraid to give rides to foreigners.
   - (C) The same gestures (hand positions and movements) can have very different meanings in various cultures—even opposite meanings.

After You Read

3 **Summarizing an Anecdote** Work in groups of three. Choose an anecdote from the reading selection "Clues to World Cultures." Read it carefully. Begin with the cultural point or "message" of the material. Paraphrase or retell the story in your own words. Then tell or read your summary to your group.

4 Discussing the Reading In small groups, talk about your answers to these questions. Be prepared to tell the class some of the highlights from your discussion.

1. In your community, city, or country, do people pay attention to others one at a time or all at the same time? Who gets attention first—the people already in conversation or the new people?

2. At dinner parties in your culture, what are some of the "rules" or customs? How do hosts offer or serve food? How do guests ask for food—or ask for more?

3. What are some hand, finger, or thumb positions or movements in your culture? What do they mean—and do they have the same meanings in all situations? Do people from other communities or countries use the same gestures in the same ways? Explain.

4. What is a "cross-cultural situation"? What kinds of things might cause misunderstandings between members of two different cultures?

5 Talking It Over Below are some statements about cultural attitudes and customs. In your opinion or experience, which sentences are true for typical situations in your social group, your community, your country, or your culture? Check (✓) those items and explain your choices. Where do you think the other statements might be true? Why do you think so?

1. _____ To greet each other, people bow the head or bend the body forward. This body movement shows respect. Shaking hands or kissing and hugging are not common forms of greeting.

2. _____ Young people usually dress informally. Even for business or special occasions, they can wear comfortable clothes, like jeans and bright Hawaiian shirts.

3. _____ Families invite guests to their homes for dinner parties; they prepare special meals. They rarely meet guests in restaurants.

4. _____ Guests come on time for dinner parties, but hosts don't usually serve food right away. Instead, people enjoy drinks and conversation for a long time before the meal.

5. _____ People give gifts of money for special occasions, like birthdays, weddings, and holidays. They bring food or wine gifts to dinner parties.

6. _____ On social occasions, people smile a lot. They give compliments; that is, they say nice things to others about their clothes, their appearance, their houses, and so on.

7. _____ On the street and in public places like stores, people are not usually very polite; they try to be first and to get what they want. They may shout or use rude gestures.

8. _____ In classes at schools and colleges, students try to be first to answer questions. They tell their ideas and say their opinions on many topics. They may contradict the teacher.

9. _____ The individual is more important than the group or the community. Each person is responsible for his or her own needs, achievements, and successes.

10. _____ Time is very important in society because time means money; most people are in a hurry all the time.

Do you have any statements of your own about cultural customs, habits, attitudes, and actions? Give your ideas. Others can give their opinions about your statements. They can name the cultures where your statements are most often true.

Part 3 | Vocabulary and Language-Learning Skills

Strategy

Understanding New Vocabulary in Context
In the reading "Cross-Cultural Conversation" on pages 109–111, the speakers talk about two kinds of culture. One meaning of *culture* is "a society's achievements in the arts, science, or government." Werner has that meaning in mind when he talks about the cathedrals, castles, and museums of Europe. Another meaning of *culture* is "the values, beliefs, and customs of a society." Nadia has that meaning in mind when she talks about greetings, titles, and social rules. Look back at the reading and determine what meaning of *culture* the speaker has in mind based on the context.

1 **Understanding New Vocabulary in Context** Below are some sentences with important vocabulary from the reading selection on pages 109–111. From the context, answer the questions about the underlined items. Then choose the meaning that seems the most logical in the context. To practice what you've learned about getting meaning from context, figure out the meanings of words from the clues in the paragraph.

1. Some examples of the architecture of old Europe are the magnificent cathedrals and castles. The design and building styles of modern architecture are excellent too.

What are some examples of old *architecture*?

_____

What are some examples of modern *architecture*?

_____

What does the noun *architecture* mean in these sentences?
- (A) the form and plan of buildings and other structures
- (B) the art and science of designing the study of classical literature
- (C) people that study the culture of old Europe and other societies

2. Perhaps the real beginning of civilization—with its scientific and technological discoveries and inventions—was in the Middle East and Africa. Over five thousand years ago, those ancient civilizations had astronomy, mathematics, medicine, government, and so on.

Where and when did *civilization* begin?

_____

What kinds of things did ancient *civilizations* have?

_____

Which word is a synonym of the word *civilization*?

- (A) astronomy
- (B) technology
- (C) culture

3. The cultural legacy of ancient Chinese and Indian peoples included walled cities, the first governments, tools for work, and weapons for protection. Modern peoples built on this legacy.

Does a *legacy* come from the past, the present, or the future?

_____

What kinds of things might a *legacy* include?

_____

What is a possible explanation of the word *legacy*?

- (A) a gift of money that somebody gives to another person
- (B) ideas and achievements passed from earlier generations to modern society
- (C) the state or condition of being legal; not against the law

4. "For me, the idea of ancient culture creates a contradiction in definitions," said Karen, going against Mei's views. "Only modern things can be part of culture. Of course, people that like classical art and music will contradict me."

According to Karen, what kinds of things are part of culture?

_____

Does Karen think that people who like classical art and music agree with her?

_____

Do Karen and Mei have the same or different opinions?

_____

What might the noun *contradiction* and the verb *contradict* mean?

- (A) (noun) the opposition of two opinions; (verb) to say that someone's ideas are wrong or not true
- (B) (noun) the short forms of two words together; (verb) to put words together
- (C) (noun) wearing a Hawaiian shirt in an ancient culture; (verb) to eat hamburgers with French fries

5. Because of the worldwide <u>media</u>—movies, TV, CDs, the Internet, newspapers, magazines—everybody knows the same information, plays the same music, and enjoys the same jokes.

What are some examples of "the worldwide media"?

_____

What are some things that *the media* give to people around the world?

_____

How might you define the phrase *the media*?

Ⓐ events that appear in the daily news and that everyone knows about
Ⓑ the tradition of being in the middle—not on the extremes of possible views
Ⓒ the combination of visual, sound, and printed ways to send ideas around the world

Strategy

Recognizing Nouns, Verbs, and Adjectives

If you don't know the meaning of a new vocabulary item, it helps to figure out its part of speech.

- Is the word a noun (a person, place, thing, or concept)?
- Is it a verb—a word for an action or a condition?
- Maybe the word is an adjective; in other words, its function might be to describe a noun or pronoun.

One way to tell the part of speech of an item is to recognize its function or purpose in the sentence—what does the word *do* or *serve as*? Another is to figure out what question the item answers. Below is a summary of these clues to parts of speech.

Part of Speech	Function or Purpose	Question the Word Answers	Examples
A noun	serves as the subject of the sentence is the object or complement of a verb or is the object of a preposition	Who? (What person?) What? (What thing, place, or concept?)	Karen writes long letters to a good <u>friend</u> in <u>France</u>.
A verb	names an action, an activity, or a condition (a state of being)	What does the subject of the sentence do?	Karen <u>writes</u> long letters to a good friend in France.
An adjective	describes a noun or pronoun	How is it?	Karen writes <u>long</u> letters to a <u>good</u> friend in France.

2 **Recognizing Nouns, Verbs, and Adjectives** In the blanks of the sentences on the left, write the missing noun, verb, and adjective from the parts of speech chart. Then give the parts of speech of the words. The first item is done as an example.

1. Our class discussed the definition of modern culture, but there were a lot of ___opposing___ (adjective) views. The main ___opposition___ (noun) came from Carmel. She _____d (verb) everything we said!

Noun	Verb	Adjective
opposition	oppose	opposing

2. Can you _____ a typical cross-cultural situation? In your _____, use as many _____ words as you can.

Noun	Verb	Adjective
description	describe	descriptive

3. To attract tourists, cities advertise the _____ of their architecture. They say that the buildings _____ in their beauty. They talk about the _____ artwork, too.

Noun	Verb	Adjective
excellence	excel	excellent

4. Are you an _____ traveler? Do you like to _____ the customs and habits of people in other cultures? Do you enjoy new _____?

Noun	Verb	Adjective
experiences	experience	experienced

5. One definition of the word _____ is "a high level of culture." Does a good education _____ people? Does it make them more _____?

Noun	Verb	Adjective
civilization	civilize	civilized

6. When did ancient civilizations _____ the calendar? Which _____ people figured it out? What were some of their other _____?

Noun	Verb	Adjective
inventions	invent	inventive

7. People of the same cultural background don't always _____ on the values of society. Even _____ people aren't in _____ all the time.

Noun	Verb	Adjective
agreement	agree	agreeable

8. Every _____ (group of people of the same culture) has _____ problems to solve. It also has to _____ its young people.

Noun	Verb	Adjective
society	socialize	social

9. Sometimes two cultural values seem to _____ each other. For instance, individual achievement may be _____ to the interests of families. It may create _____.

Noun	Verb	Adjective
contradictions	contradict	contradictory

10. When did global advertising begin to _____ through the Internet? The _____ of the Internet is a significant achievement all over the globe, including in _____ nations.

Noun	Verb	Adjective
development	develop	developing

UNDERSTANDING ADVERBS OF MANNER

Adverbs are parts of speech that answer the question "how?" or "when?" or "where?" "Adverbs of manner" tell *how* or in *what way* something happens.

- Most often, adverbs of manner are closely related to adjectives. Some examples of adjectives are *easy* and *loud*.

- Adverbs of manner usually end in the letters *–ly*. For example, the adverb *easily* means "in an easy way." *Loudly* is an adverb of manner with the meaning "in a loud voice."

- Adverbs for adjectives with the *–ly* ending, like *friendly*, can be difficult to pronounce. More often, such adjectives appear in noun phrases, such as *in a friendly tone*.

3 **Using Adverbs and Adjectives of Manner** Below are some sentences with pairs of related words—one adjective and one adverb of manner in each pair. In each blank, write the missing word—the adjective related to the underlined adverb or the adverb related to the underlined adjective. The first item is done as an example.

1. A proud Frenchman began the conversation about culture _proudly_. His friend was very _patient_, so he responded patiently.

2. A German student answered him in a _____ and _____ voice. She spoke clearly and pleasantly.

3. An American member of the group had a _____ way about her. She answered questions knowingly. She didn't find the questions rude so she didn't respond _____.

4. A Middle-Eastern woman with an _____ voice said she found ancient civilizations amazing. "_____, the ancients studied astronomy thousands of years ago," she explained enthusiastically.

5. An angry man stated his opinions _____. He was so loud that students in the next room heard him!

6. "The _____ mind looks at problems and situations scientifically," said someone from a well-developed Asian culture.

7. "But _____ scientists don't always know how to communicate successfully."

8. "I'm afraid I have to disagree with you," a nice African man answered _____. "According to the rules of their culture, most people try to be <u>polite</u>."

9. In a _____ voice, a young Chinese student said his opinion; but he said it too <u>softly</u> for the others to hear.

10. Finally, the most _____ and <u>convincing</u> member of the group ended the discussion <u>enthusiastically</u> and _____.

4 Focusing on High-Frequency Words Read the paragraphs below and fill in each blank with a word from the box. When you finish, check your answers on pages 115–116.

annoyed	customer	loudly	pain	rudely	tourist
attention	greet	medicine	patiently	terrible	

A   An Irish woman was visiting _____ places in a Latin
                                          1
American city when she got a _____ headache. She knew
                                          2
what _____ she needed, so she went to a local pharmacy.
              3
The pharmacist was waiting on another _____ when
                                                      4
she came in. The Irish woman _____ waited her turn.   5
                                          5
While she was standing there, two other customers came in, then
another, and then three more. Each time, the pharmacist turned
his _____ to the new people. He did not
              6
_____ the Irish woman; he never said, "I'll be with you
        7
in a minute."   10

After about 20 minutes, the woman couldn't stand the
_____ in her head any longer. "Hey, I've been here a long
        8
time," she said _____, very _____ and
                          9   10
insulted. "Why is everyone ignoring me? I need service, too!" she
shouted _____ (impolitely).
              11

5 **Making Connections** Do an Internet search about a culture that you don't know well. You can use a search engine and type in the country's name and the word *culture*, for example, *Mexican culture*.

Identify at least five things that you learn about that culture. It can be anything like food, language, sports, music, types of greetings, gestures, money, architecture.

Tell your classmates what you learned about that culture. What do these things indicate about cultural norms or customs in that country? Are these things similar to or different from things in your culture?

Culture: _____

Website(s): _____

Five things I learned about this culture:

_____

_____

_____

_____

_____

Similarities to my culture: _____

_____

Differences from my culture: _____

_____

Part 4 Focus on Testing

TOEFL® iBT   PRACTICING VOCABULARY QUESTIONS

A well-developed English vocabulary is one of your best tools for doing well on the TOEFL® iBT. For each passage in the reading section, there will be two or three direct vocabulary questions.

Each direct vocabulary question on the TOEFL® iBT is asked in the following way: "Which of the following is closest in meaning to _____ (vocabulary item) used in Paragraph X?" Part 3 of this chapter discusses getting meaning from context.

Notice that the question emphasizes a context (". . . in Paragraph X"). In some cases, the word you are considering has several meanings. You must choose the meaning that fits the context specified in the question.

Practicing Vocabulary Questions Below is a new reading, "Cultural Anthropology." Using the skills you practiced in Part 3 of this chapter, try to answer the TOEFL® iBT—like questions that follow. The target vocabulary words—those asked about in the questions—are highlighted in the reading and the question.

Cultural Anthropology

A   The science of anthropology is divided into several branches, one of which is cultural anthropology. This branch looks at the basic beliefs, possessions, and behavior common within a society. For example, the crops a group plants or the ways in which a society catches and cooks fish are concerns of the cultural anthropologist.

B   One of the main goals of cultural anthropology is to discover relationships among groups that presently seem very distant from each other. Such discoveries, along with other evidence, may show that such disparate cultures come from the same origins. A cultural anthropologist may see, for example, that owning cattle has a huge significance in two African societies that are now separated by thousands of miles. This fact, together with other evidence, could indicate that both cultures came from the same Bantu ancestor in the past.

C   Cultural anthropologists and linguists each contributed evidence in determining the origin of a large group of cultures—the Malayo-Polynesian. Since the late 18th century, scholars knew of similarities among peoples from Madagascar (off the east coast of Africa), through Southeast Asia and New Zealand, to Easter Island just west of South America. There were some similarities in appearance but, more importantly, also similarities in beliefs and practices. Still, it seemed hard to believe that one culture was the ancestor to so many people in different parts of the world. And even if they were all related, where did they come from?

D   Linguists (who study language patterns and structure) used research and reasoning to pinpoint the island of Formosa (present-day Taiwan) as the origin of Malayo-Polynesian languages. It is there that such languages exist in the greatest number in relatively small areas. This means that the peoples of Formosa have had the longest time of all the Malayo-Polynesians to develop distinct local languages.

E   Cultural anthropologists were interested, but they needed more evidence. They found it in two items of food—millet and pork. Millet, a kind of cereal grain, is part of an agricultural tradition carried from Formosa to vastly different climates, where it remains a cultural staple of traditional Malayo-

Polynesian societies. The same goes for domesticated pigs. Malayo-Polynesians continue to raise and eat pigs even in areas that probably had no native pig species until the arrival of humans came from the Formosans.

F Current customs might seem to cast doubt on this theory. Modern Malays, for example, usually avoid any contact with pigs or their meat. The Malayo-Polynesians, however, arrived in Malay lands thousands of years ago, before Muslim missionaries brought their religion's rules. The strongest evidence comes from small, traditional cultures in these regions, not from the Islamized or Westernized larger societies.

1. Which of the following is closest in meaning to concerns as it is used in Paragraph A?
   - (A) worries
   - (B) goals
   - (C) interests
   - (D) branches

2. Why does the author twice use the phrase with other evidence (Paragraph B)?
   - (A) to show that other evidence tells cultural anthropologists what to study
   - (B) to show the relationship between two widely separate cultures
   - (C) to show an important tradition among anthropologists
   - (D) to show that cultural anthropologists do not draw conclusions from one fact alone

3. Which of the following is closest in meaning to disparate as it is used in Paragraph B?
   - (A) different
   - (B) similar
   - (C) distant
   - (D) nearby

4. Which of the following is closest in meaning to practices as it is used in Paragraph C?
   - (A) exercises
   - (B) workplaces
   - (C) activities
   - (D) ideas

5. Which of the following is closest in meaning to cast doubt on as it is used in Paragraph F?
   - (A) make clear
   - (B) cause some questioning of
   - (C) say terrible things about
   - (D) make unclear

Self-Assessment Log

Read the lists below. Check (✓) the strategies and vocabulary that you learned in this chapter. Look through the chapter or ask your instructor about the strategies and words that you do not understand.

Reading and Vocabulary-Building Strategies

❑ Understanding reading structure: conversation in paragraph form
❑ Recognizing supporting detail: opinions
❑ Understanding anecdotes
❑ Summarizing an anecdote
❑ Understanding new vocabulary in context
❑ Recognizing nouns, verbs, and adjectives
❑ Understanding adverbs of manner

Target Vocabulary

Nouns
❑ architecture
❑ attention*
❑ civilization
❑ contradiction
❑ customer*
❑ legacy
❑ media
❑ medicine*
❑ pain*
❑ societies*

Verbs
❑ agree*
❑ contradict
❑ describe*
❑ develop*
❑ experience*
❑ greet*
❑ invented*

Adjectives
❑ amazing
❑ annoyed*

❑ clear*
❑ enthusiastic
❑ excellent*
❑ knowing*
❑ opposing*
❑ pleasant*
❑ proud*
❑ rude*
❑ scientific*
❑ social*
❑ soft*

❑ successful*
❑ terrible*
❑ tourist*

Adverbs
❑ convincingly
❑ loudly*
❑ patiently*
❑ politely*
❑ rudely*

---

*These words are among the 2,000 most frequently used words in English.

Health

In This Chapter

What age do you think of as old? Sixty? Seventy? Eighty? The first reading selection is about some places in the world where eighty-year-olds still have many years ahead of them. You will read about where these people live and ideas on why they live so long. In the second reading selection, you will learn about some exciting technological changes and trends in modern medicine. You will also learn about some theories on the causes and cures of certain diseases.

" He who has health has hope, and he who has hope has everything. **"**

—Arabian proverb

Connecting to the Topic

1 What do you think the secret is to a long and healthy life?

2 Would you want to live to be over 100 years old or older? Why? Why not?

3 Eating nutritiously is important for good health. What are five other things people can do to stay healthy?

The Secrets of a Very Long Life

Before You Read

1 Previewing the Topic Look at the photo and read the questions below. Discuss them in your groups.

1. What is the relationship of the two people? What are they doing?

2. Describe the lifestyle of the couple. What do they probably do all day? Do you think they are healthy? Why or why not?

3. Do you know any very old people? Do they have any "secrets" of a long life?

▲ An elderly couple taking a walk

2 Predicting Talk about these questions with a partner. When you read "The Secrets of a Very Long Life," look for the answers.

1. What places in the world are famous for people who live a very long time?

2. What is the environment like in places where people live a long time?

3. What kind of diet do you think people in these places have?

3 Previewing Vocabulary Read the vocabulary items on the next page from the first reading. Then listen to the words and phrases. Put a check mark (✓) next to the words you know. You can learn the other words now or come back to them after you read.

Nouns	Verbs	Connectors
❏ altitude	❏ consume	❏ as a result
❏ an average	❏ cure	❏ furthermore
❏ benefits	❏ prevent	❏ however
❏ claims	❏ solve	❏ in addition
❏ disease	❏ theorize	❏ moreover
❏ environment		❏ nevertheless
❏ inhabitants	**Adjectives**	❏ therefore
❏ longevity	❏ active	❏ thus
❏ populations	❏ available	
❏ preservatives	❏ different	
❏ streams	❏ famous	
❏ stress	❏ long-lived	
❏ theories	❏ moderate	
❏ validity	❏ unpolluted	
	❏ valid	

Read

4 **Reading an Article** Read the following article. Then read the explanations and do the activities that follow.

The Secrets of a Very Long Life

Introduction

A   There are several places in the world that are **famous** for people who live a very long time. These places are usually in mountainous areas, far away from modern cities. Even so, doctors, scientists, and public health experts often travel to these regions to **solve** the mystery of a long, healthy life. In this way, the experts hope to bring to the modern world the secrets of   5
longevity.

Hunza in the Himalayan Mountains

B   Hunza is at a very high altitude in the Himalayan Mountains of Asia. There, many people over 100 years of age are still in good physical health. Additionally, men of 90 are new fathers, and women of 50 still have babies. What are the reasons for this good health? Scientists believe that the   10
people of Hunza have these three main advantages or benefits: (1) a healthful **unpolluted environment** with clean air and water; (2) a simple diet high in vitamins, fiber, and nutrition but low in fat, cholesterol, sugar, and unnatural chemicals; and (3) physical work and other activities, usually in the fields or with animals.   15

The Russian Caucasians and Vilcabamba

C   People in the Caucasus Mountains in Russia are also famous for their longevity. Official birth records were not available, but the community says a woman called Tsurba lived until age 160. Similarly, a man called Shirali probably lived until 168; moreover, his widow was 120 years old. In general, the people not only live a long time, but they also live well. In other words, they are almost never sick. Furthermore, when they die, they not only have their own teeth but also a full head of hair, and good eyesight too. Vilcabamba, Ecuador, is another area famous for the longevity of its **inhabitants**. This mountain region—like Hunza and the Caucasus—is also at a very high altitude, far away from cities. In Vilcabamba, too, there is very little serious **disease**. One reason for the good health of the people might be the clean, beautiful environment; another advantage is the **moderate** climate. The temperature is about 70° Fahrenheit all year long; furthermore, the wind always comes from the same direction. In addition, the water comes from mountain **streams** and is high in minerals: perhaps as a result of this valuable resource, the region is rich in flowers, fruits, vegetables, and wildlife.

▲ An inhabitant of the Caucasus mountains

Differences in the Diets of People with Unusual Longevity

D   In some ways, the diets of the inhabitants in the three regions are quite different. Hunzukuts eat mainly raw vegetables, fruit (especially apricots), and chapatis—a kind of pancake; they eat meat only a few times a year. In contrast, the Caucasian diet consists mainly of milk, cheese, vegetables, fruit, and meat; also, most people there drink the local red wine daily. In Vilcabamba, people eat only a small amount of meat each week; their diet consists mostly of grain, corn, beans, potatoes, and fruit. Even so, experts found one surprising fact in the mountains of Ecuador: most people there, even the very old, consume a lot of coffee, drink large amounts of alcohol, and smoke 40 to 60 cigarettes daily!

Similarities in Diet

E   However, the typical diets of the three areas are similar in three general ways: (1) The fruits and vegetables are all natural; that is, they contain no preservatives or other chemicals. (2) Furthermore, the **population** uses traditional herbs and medicines to **prevent** and cure disease. (3) The inhabitants consume fewer calories than people do in other parts of the world. A typical North American eats and drinks an average of 3,300 calories every day, while a typical inhabitant of these mountainous areas takes in between 1,700 and 2,000 calories.

Other Possible Reasons for Healthy Longevity

F Inhabitants in the three regions have more in common than their mountain environment, their distance from modern cities, and their low-calorie natural diets. Because they live in the countryside and are mostly farmers, their lives are physically hard and extremely active. Therefore, they do not need to try to exercise. In addition, the population does not seem to have the stress of fast city work and recreation. As a result, people's lives are relatively free from worry—and therefore, illness or other health problems. Thus, some experts believe that physical movement and a stress-free environment might be the two most important secrets of longevity. An additional health advantage of life in these long-lived communities may be the extended family structure: the group takes care of its members from birth to death.

The Validity of Longevity Claims

G Nevertheless, some doctors theorize that members of especially long-lived populations have only one thing in common: they don't have valid official government birth records. These health scientists think there is a natural limit to the length of human life; in their theories, it is impossible to reach an age of more than 110 years or so. Therefore, they say, claims of unusual longevity in certain groups are probably false.

After You Read

Strategy

Recognizing Reading Structure Using a Mind Map
You can organize the topics and main ideas of a reading by using a mind map. It can be used to review and recall material.

- A mind map shows the relationship of the topics, main ideas, and supporting details.
- The main topic is placed in the center of the map.
- The most general parts of the reading can appear in big circles connected to the central topic.
- The main idea for each paragraph can appear in smaller circles connected to these general parts.
- Supporting details are connected to the main ideas.
- You can use color to help organize the material.

5 **Recognizing Reading Structure Using a Mind Map** Look at the example of a mind map for the material in Paragraph B of the reading "The Secrets of a Very Long Life." Then answer the questions that follow the mind map below.

A Mind Map of Paragraph B

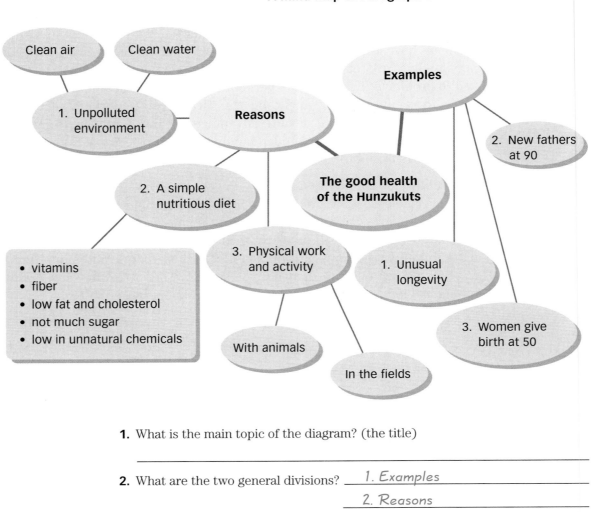

1. What is the main topic of the diagram? (the title)

   _____

2. What are the two general divisions? ___*1. Examples*___

   ___*2. Reasons*___

3. What are the three examples given?

   _____

   _____

   _____

4. How many main reasons are there for the good health of the people of Hunza?

   _____

   What are these reasons?_____

   _____

   _____

5. What are two characteristics or elements of an unpolluted environment?

_____

_____

6. How many characteristics of a simple nutritious diet are there in the diagram?

_____

List three of them:

_____

7. "In the fields" and "with animals" are two details of what reason for good health?

_____

6 **Completing a Mind Map** Read and complete the mind map below about "The Secrets of a Very Long Life." Choose your answers from the phrases in the box after the diagram. Then answer the question about the main idea.

A Mind Map of "The Secrets of a Very Long Life"

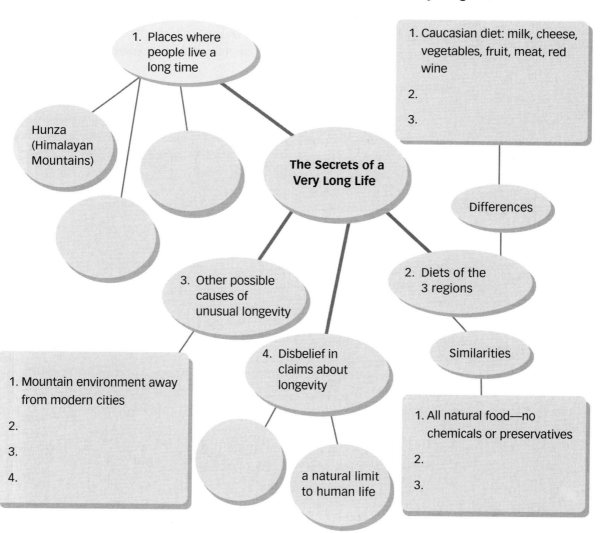

Hunzukut diet: raw vegetables, fruit, *chapatis*	Ecuadorian diet: grain, vegetables, fruit, coffee, alcohol, cigarettes
The Caucasus Mountains in Russia	no valid birth certificates
fewer calories	hard physical activity
stress-free lives	extended family structure
Vilcabamba, Ecuador	traditional herbs as medicine

Answer the question.

What is the main (the most general) topic of the reading?

- (A) places in the world where people live a long time
- (B) some possible secrets of the mystery of longevity
- (C) a comparison of the health of people in the Caucasus Mountains and Ecuador
- (D) the typical diet of the inhabitants of mountain regions

7 Understanding the Main Idea Finish the possible main-idea question about the reading selection "The Secrets of a Very Long Life." Then in the paragraph that follows, change the underlined words so that the paragraph answers the question.

Main-idea question:

Why do people in some areas of the world —————————————*?*

According to health specialists that <u>have</u> longevity, there are <u>no</u> possible reasons for a <u>short</u> and <u>unhealthy</u> life. The first requirement might be a high level of hard <u>mental</u> work and activity <u>without</u> freedom from modern worries. Second, the physical environment makes <u>no</u> difference: people seem to live longer in a <u>low desert or jungle</u> region with <u>a changing</u> climate of <u>very hot and very cold</u> air temperatures. And finally, diet <u>doesn't</u> <u>matter</u>: long-lived people seem to eat mostly foods high in <u>fat, cholesterol, and sugar</u> but low in <u>vitamins and nutrition.</u>

Recognizing Supporting Details After Punctuation, Numbers, and Connecting Words

Punctuation, numbers, and connecting words can show the relationship of main ideas to supporting details. They also show the relationship of general points to more specific ones.

- A colon (:) before a list often indicates the relationship of the following material to the previous point.

- Numbers in parentheses within a paragraph, like (1), (2), and so on, come before separate items that all relate to the same main point.

- Connecting words and phrases also give clues to the relationships among points. The phrase *for instance* means that the following sentence part will give instances, or examples, of a previous statement.

- There are connecting words such as *and* or *furthermore* that show addition. They introduce similar facts or concepts or give additional evidence or arguments.

- Some connecting words, such as *but* or *however*, mean that differences, opposites, or contradictions will follow. Still other vocabulary of this kind indicates causes, reasons, or results. Examples include *thus* and *therefore*.

Read the commonly used connecting adverbs and phrases below.

Addition or Similarity	Contrast or Contradiction	Causes, Reasons, or Result
and	but	thus
also	while	therefore
too	instead	for this reason
in addition	even so	as a result
additionally	however	because of this
furthermore	nevertheless	
moreover	in contrast	
in the same way	on the other hand	
similarly		

8 **Recognizing Supporting Details After Punctuation, Numbers, and Connecting Words** Use punctuation clues, numbers in parentheses, and connecting words to help you find the answers to these questions. You will find the answers in the reading selection "The Secrets of a very Long Life." On the lines, write the answers in your own words.

1. High mountain regions where people live to a very old age are far away from modern cities. For what two reasons might medical scientists and health specialists travel there?

   _____

   _____

2. According to scientists, what are three reasons for the good physical health of the people of Hunza?

   _____

   _____

3. Who were two people similar in their longevity to the Caucasian woman Tsurba?

   _____

   _____

4. In what ways do the people of the Caucasian region live well even in old age?

   _____

   _____

   _____

5. What are four or five healthful elements or features of the environment in Vilcabamba, Ecuador?

   _____

   _____

   _____

6. In what three general ways are the diets of inhabitants of the Hunza, the Caucasus, and Vilcabamba similar?

   _____

   _____

   _____

7. In addition to diet, what are three other possible reasons for the healthy longevity of the populations discussed in the reading?

   _____

   _____

   _____

8. Why don't all doctors believe the longevity claims of these groups of people?

   _____

   _____

   _____

9 **Discussing the Reading** In groups of three, talk about your answers to the following questions.

1. Do you believe that the people discussed in the reading selection *really* lived to over 150 years of age? Why or why not?

2. Do you hope or plan to live to a very old age? Why or why not?

3. Can you suggest any other things that might lead to a long, healthy old age?

Part 2 Reading Skills and Strategies

Claims to Amazing Health

Before You Read

1 **Previewing Vocabulary** Read the vocabulary items below from the next reading. Then listen to the words and phrases. Put a check mark (✓) next to the words you know. You can learn the other words now or come back to them after you read.

Nouns
- ❑ advice
- ❑ bacteria
- ❑ birth defects
- ❑ characteristics
- ❑ cherry juice
- ❑ combination
- ❑ cure
- ❑ damage
- ❑ decisions
- ❑ engineering
- ❑ folk medicine

- ❑ genes
- ❑ geneticists
- ❑ joints
- ❑ length
- ❑ parasites
- ❑ patients
- ❑ physiologist
- ❑ senior citizens
- ❑ specialists
- ❑ viruses

Verbs
- ❑ color
- ❑ correct
- ❑ determine
- ❑ oppose
- ❑ recommend
- ❑ take advantage of

Adjectives
- ❑ accurate
- ❑ dishonest
- ❑ elderly
- ❑ fraudulent
- ❑ genetic
- ❑ proven
- ❑ sour

Connector
- ❑ as opposed to

Read

2 **Understanding Facts and Opinions** With a topic like healthcare or medicine, personal beliefs may contradict proven scientific fact. In fact, a definition of the word *fact* might be "reality as opposed to opinion."

Following are four readings on the general topic of "Claims to Amazing Health." They tell the views of some healthcare and medical experts; all of these opinions come from a combination of proven fact and personal belief.

Skim each paragraph. Then answer the question above each paragraph about the topic. Choose A, B, or C. Then read each paragraph a second time. Read the question below the paragraph and fill in the letter of the statement that best tells the point.

Claims to Amazing Health

Which title best expresses the topic of Paragraph A?
- (A) The Value of a Variety of Valid Views
- (B) Long on Longevity: Free but False
- (C) Internet Help and Hope: Health Benefits vs. Costs

A   On the subject of physical health and medical research, there are thousands of amazing websites where people can get information. However,

▲ Many people use the Internet to find health-related information.

when does the *amount* of available information affect its validity and health benefit? The Internet is greatly influencing people's attitudes about their own healthcare: probably, this worldwide cultural trend improves global health. Because computer users can look up almost any topic of interest to them, they become their own researchers. In the busy modern world, doctors don't always take the time to explain illnesses and possible remedies to their **patients**; they may not give scientific details in words that are easy to understand, either. For this reason, many hopeful people take advantage of Internet resources to find the facts they need for good medical **decisions**. But are the beliefs of "experts" always completely **accurate** or real? Are they helpful to *everyone* that needs advice on a specific medical condition? The health products or books that seem the most wonderful are often the most fraudulent—that is **dishonest** or false. Do sick or worried people expect too much when they look for clear, easy answers to difficult health questions or problems on the computer?

Which sentence best states the point of the facts and beliefs in Paragraph A?
- (A) The great amount of medical information (facts and opinions) available on the Internet may improve people's attitudes about health; on the other hand, some claims might be inaccurate or dishonest—and therefore dangerous.
- (B) To find out the easiest and best ways to solve difficult health problems and cure diseases, everyone should go online—that is, people ought to look up the topics that interest them on the Internet.
- (C) Doctors are too busy to help their patients, especially the people that are the oldest or the sickest; therefore, these people have to take advantage of the Internet to find help.

Which title best tells the topic of Paragraph B?

    (A) The Cure for All Cancers: Causes and Cases

    (B) Theories and Advice from Medical Specialists

    (C) The Personal Problem of Parasites in Patients

B   Many specialists have their own theories about illness and health. As an [25] example, a California physiologist (someone who studies biology) has written books with the titles *The Cure for All Diseases* and *The Cure for All Cancers*. She says there are only two causes of disease: (1) pollution of the environment and (2) parasites (harmful plants and animals that feed on living things) inside the human body. To prevent or cure the illnesses that [30] these parasitic bacteria and viruses cause, she offers (tries to sell) two kinds of health products on the Internet and in other places: electronic machines and herbal medicines. The two beneficial effects of these items in humans and animals, this scientist claims, are (1) to clean out the body, freeing it of parasites and (2) to rebuild new healthy living cells. According [35] to her theories, people will feel better and live longer as a result. In addition, other medical experts recommend kinds of natural, nontraditional, or non-Western remedies for modern health disorders such as heart disease, cancer, asthma, nervousness, depression, and so on. Their advice might include (1) special diet plans with added vitamins and [40] minerals, (2) folk medicine, (3) environmental changes, or (4) unusual therapies that patients don't get from traditional doctors.

Which sentence best states the point of the facts and beliefs in Paragraph B?

    (A) In the human body, parasites are dangerous viruses and bacteria; for this reason, everyone must use electronic machines and herbal medicines to fight against them.

    (B) Nontraditional and non-Western remedies are more effective cures and remedies for health problems than the methods of doctors that offer information over the Internet.

    (C) Many medical specialists have their own theories about illness and health, including the causes of disease and the beneficial effects of certain products and therapies.

Which title best tells the topic of Paragraph C?

    (A) Colorful Cures for Continuing Care: Natural Food Remedies

    (B) A Variety of Theories vs. Advice from Medical Experts

    (C) Family and Folk Falsehoods—Physical Facts and Figures

C   In a small-town farm market, hundreds of **elderly** people drink a glass of **sour** dark cherry juice every day. These happy senior citizens, some of them over the age of 90, claim that the natural fruit juice cures—or at least [45] decreases—the pain of their arthritis, a disease of the joints of the aging body. It's a folk remedy, not a **proven** medical therapy. Nevertheless, science is beginning to figure out why sour cherry juice might work to improve the health of patients with arthritis. The secret is in the substance that gives the cherries their dark red color. It belongs to a classification of 50 natural nutrients that color blueberries, strawberries, plums, and other fruits—and vegetables too. Moreover, these coloring substances may help to prevent serious health disorders like heart disease and cancer. In other words, vitamins and fiber are not the only reasons to eat fruits and vegetables. "To take advantage of natural whole foods," advise nutritionists 55 and health researchers, "think variety and color."

Which sentence best states the point of the facts and beliefs in Paragraph C?

    (A) Color makes people happy, so it improves their health and state of mind; therefore, families should wear colorful clothes at meals.

    (B) Like vitamins and fiber, the substances in foods that give them color may offer an important health advantage.

    (C) Dark red foods are the best for nutrition, but bright yellow and green vegetables are more effective for elderly people that have arthritis pain.

Which title best tells the topic of Paragraph D?

    (A) Claims of the Advantages of Genetic Research and Engineering

    (B) Defects in Gene Structure and Insect Damage to Foods

    (C) Characteristics of Folk Remedies vs. Beliefs of Geneticists

D   What are *genes* and why are medical researchers always trying to find out more about them? Genes are part of the center (that is, the *nucleus*) of every living cell; in the form of DNA (deoxyribonucleic acid), this biological **genetic** material determines the characteristics (features) of 60 every living thing—every plant, animal, and human being—on Earth.

Medical *geneticists* are scientists that study DNA and genes for many purposes: (1) to learn how living things such as parasites, viruses, and bacteria cause illness; (2) to 65 find the gene or **combination** of genes that cause certain diseases to pass from parents to their children; (3) to prevent or **correct** (repair) birth defects; (4) to change gene structure to improve health and increase the 70 length of human life (longevity); and (5) to change the biological characteristics of animals and humans in ways that are beneficial to society. Another use of genetic technology that some scientists support is 75

▲ A DNA strand

changing the genes of the food farmers grow. Genetic engineers claim that these differences in DNA structure will increase food production, prevent **damage** from insects, and improve world health; in contrast, others **oppose** the use of genetic **engineering** not only in plants but also in animals and humans.

80

Which sentence best states the point of the facts and beliefs in Paragraph D?

(A) Deoxyribonucleic acid is not as beneficial as DNA—the biological material related to genetics—in research on the causes of birth defects.

(B) Genetic engineers and other specialists claim that research into the gene structure of living things can improve human health in many ways.

(C) Because there is a natural limit to the length of human life, only changes in gene structure can increase longevity in senior citizens that drink cherry juice.

After You Read

Strategy

Summarizing Using a Mind Map

You learned how to summarize in previous chapters. Another way to summarize is to use a mind map.

■ First, figure out the topic, the main ideas, and the supporting details. You can make a mind map showing the relationship of the points to one another.

■ Then create a short summary from the items in the map.

Below is an example of a mind map of Paragraph A from the reading "Claims to Amazing Health." A summary based on the mind map follows.

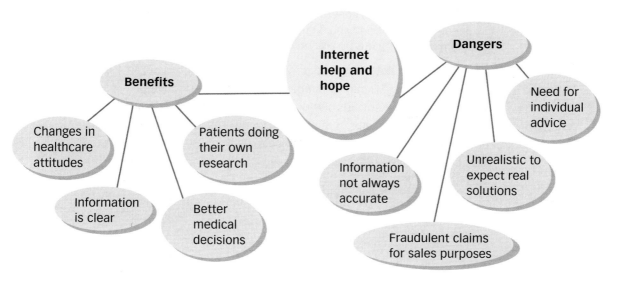

Benefits vs. Limits of Internet Health Information

On the Internet, people can find many medical facts and beliefs. Their availability can improve world health: people may change their attitudes about healthcare when they get information in clear language through their own research. Then they can make better medical decisions. However, the information on the Internet may not always be accurate or helpful to all individuals. There may even be fraudulent claims about products to increase sales. Is it realistic to expect real solutions to difficult health problems from a computer? Maybe it is; maybe it isn't.

3 **Summarizing Using a Mind Map** Work in groups of three. Each person chooses a different paragraph (B, C, or D) from the reading "Claims to Amazing Health." Read your paragraph carefully. Make a mind map about your paragraph. Place the topic in the middle of the mind map. Then complete the map.

Next, from your mind map, summarize the information in as few sentences as possible, paraphrasing the important points in your own words.

Then tell or read your summary to your group.

4 **Discussing the Reading** In small groups, talk about your answers to these questions. Then tell the class the most interesting information or ideas.

1. Do you, or do you want to go to the Internet for information about health and medicine? Why or why not? In your view, what are the benefits and limits of this kind of research?

2. What natural, nontraditional, or non-Western remedies for modern health disorders have you heard about? What do the experts that offer these cures claim? Do you believe their claims? Why or why not?

3. Do you believe that natural chemicals in food, including substances that give color, can decrease pain or help prevent serious disease? Why or why not? If so, which foods do you recommend for these reasons?

4. In your opinion, is genetic research beneficial for global health? How about genetic engineering (changing the gene structure of plants, animals, and humans)? Explain the reasons for your views.

5 **Talking It Over** Many sick or worried people want useful advice about health or medicine; "experts" like to recommend beneficial foods and other substances, helpful kinds of activity, other kinds of therapy, or health books and products. Below are some common health problems in the modern world. Check (✓) the situations that you know or want to know about. Then give advice to help solve the problem or tell your opinions. (You can do your own research, of course.)

1. _____ An international student is homesick for his country; in addition, he worries about his finances and grades. For these reasons, he sleeps a lot but still feels tired; he is also nervous.

2. _____ A young man in a cold northern climate gets depressed during the long, dark winter months. He is irritable and moody. He thinks he has SAD (Seasonal Affective Disorder).

3. _____ During times of forceful winds from the mountains, a Japanese woman seems to have more asthma attacks. She can't breathe very well, and she feels afraid.

4. _____ The members of a family often get colds or the flu (influenza)—not only during the winter but also during changes in the seasons. Occasionally, someone gets pneumonia.

5. _____ A professor is having memory problems. From the Internet, she learned that foods with the substance lecithin and B-vitamins can help, so she eats a lot of broccoli, soybeans, and nuts. Even so, she often forgets what she is doing.

6. _____ A brother and sister disagree on the best kinds of foods to eat for good health. He follows a famous high-protein diet plan that allows only certain foods at certain times. She wants to eat what tastes good.

7. _____ A Czech woman serves nutritious salads and other vegetables to her family, but her husband won't eat them. He prefers high-calorie meat and dairy dishes with rich desserts, and he is getting very fat. She is afraid he will die of a heart attack.

8. _____ A young male athlete *feels* strong and healthy, but he is worried about his longevity because of his relatives' diseases. For this reason, he welcomes research into genetic engineering.

9. _____ A 70-year-old man drinks a lot of coffee and smokes cigarettes; he also enjoys alcoholic drinks. He likes to go walking in his mountain community; however, he is often in pain from his arthritis.

10. _____ A couple is going to have a baby. Because there is a history of genetic defects in several generations of their extended families, they are worried about the child's chances for good health and long life.

Part 3 Vocabulary and Language-Learning Skills

Strategy

Getting Meaning from Context

As you learned in Chapter 6, even without definitions or explanations in the same sentence or paragraph, you can figure out new vocabulary. There may not be definitions, words with similar or opposite meanings, illustrations, or punctuation clues to help. Even so, the message or meaning of the reading may lead to useful guesses about the meaning of unfamiliar or difficult vocabulary.

1 **Figuring Out New or Difficult Vocabulary** Read the following sentences with vocabulary from the reading selection. From the context, answer the questions that follow. Then use logic to figure out a definition of each word. Fill in the letter of the explanation closest to yours.

1. To discover the secrets of <u>longevity,</u> health specialists are studying people that reach ages well over 100. These <u>long-lived</u> individuals enjoy good health all their lives, too.

Who is trying to find out about *longevity*? _____

_____

Why might these scientists want to know such "secrets"? _____

_____

Whom are these researchers studying?

_____

_____

What does the noun *longevity* mean?
- (A) health researchers
- (B) a hundred different ages
- (C) many years between birth and death
- (D) old people in the mountains

What is the meaning of the adjective *long-lived*?
- (A) living a long time
- (B) dying at an early age
- (C) the altitude of the Himalayan Mountains
- (D) having a full head of hair and healthy teeth

2. Scientists believe the people of certain high mountain regions have the benefit of a healthful <u>environment</u> with clean air and water and <u>moderate</u> temperatures—not very hot or very cold.

What is an *environment* in this sentence?
- (A) clean air and water
- (B) a healthful place in the desert
- (C) unnatural or extreme atmospheric conditions
- (D) the conditions of a place that influence people

What two things can an *environment* have? _____

Where might an *environment* be? _____

What kinds of temperatures are not *moderate*? _____

What is the meaning of the adjective *moderate*?
- (A) very hot and very cold
- (B) not extreme; in the middle
- (C) related to the air and water of a region
- (D) of the modern world

3. A woman named Tsurba and a man named Shirali were among the long-lived inhabitants of the Caucasus Mountain region of Russia. Other people that inhabit the area don't seem to get sick often either.

Were Tsurba and Shirali *inhabitants* of or visitors to the mountains?

_____

Are *inhabitants* people, places, things, or actions? _____

_____

Who are the *inhabitants* of a place?

    Ⓐ people that live there

    Ⓑ people that live there in summer

    Ⓒ people that study the environment in that region

    Ⓓ hardworking, physically active farmers

What is the meaning of the verb *inhabit*?

    Ⓐ to make an action difficult

    Ⓑ to work during the day in a place

    Ⓒ to have scientific interests in common

    Ⓓ to live in (a region or area)

4. A healthful environment includes unpolluted clean water; the water might come from high mountain streams and contain a lot of minerals.

If an environment has clean water, is the water *polluted*? _____

_____

What do high mountain *streams* bring to a healthful environment? _____

_____

What is high in minerals? _____

_____

What does the adjective *unpolluted* mean?

    Ⓐ dirtying of the earth and air

    Ⓑ high in preservatives and chemicals

    Ⓒ having a lot of vitamins and minerals

    Ⓓ not containing unhealthful substances

What are high mountain *streams*?

    Ⓐ small rivers of moving water

    Ⓑ regions with little serious disease

    Ⓒ widows that keep birth records for communities

    Ⓓ to move a lot from one place to another

5. According to some doctors, long-lived populations have only one thing in common: Their members don't have valid birth records. Because the government didn't write down when these people were born, their claims of unusual longevity are false.

What do *populations* contain? _____

What are *populations*?

- (A) members of government
- (B) ideas that are widespread
- (C) all of the people living in specific areas
- (D) kinds of freedom from worry

Do *all* health experts believe that certain populations have unusual longevity?

_____

What don't these long-lived people have? _____

What does the adjective *valid* mean?

- (A) officially legal or accepted
- (B) of high value in the community
- (C) to prove something is correct
- (D) of the region of Vilcabamba

Do certain populations make *claims* about unusual longevity? _____

Do people in these communities believe the *claims*? _____

What is the meaning of the noun *claims* in this context?

- (A) to state something is right and real
- (B) attempts to get money that is legally yours
- (C) something important about a person
- (D) statements of the truth of information

For more practice, you can look for and figure out the general meanings of other vocabulary items, such as *benefits, preservatives, an average,* and *stress*. For each item, explain the logical reasoning for your guesses at the definition.

2 Identifying Synonyms Read the vocabulary words in Column A. Select the word in Column B that has the same or a similar meaning as the vocabulary word.

Column A

1. _d_ cure
2. ____ length
3. ____ patients
4. ____ solve
5. ____ oppose
6. ____ accurate
7. ____ dishonest
8. ____ elderly
9. ____ proven
10. ____ sour
11. ____ prevent

Column B

a. measured distance
b. verified
c. disagree with
d. remedy
e. not allow
f. not truthful
g. find an answer
h. not sweet, tart
i. sick people
j. correct
k. old

RECOGNIZING PARTS OF SPEECH
FROM WORD ENDINGS: SUFFIXES

One way to tell the part of speech of a vocabulary item is to recognize its function or purpose. (Remember: nouns serve as sentence subjects or objects; verbs name actions; adjectives modify nouns; adverbs modify verbs.)

Another useful clue to the part of speech of a word is its ending, or *suffix*. Below are a few of the common word endings that may indicate if a word is a noun, an adjective, or an adverb.

Nouns			Adjectives			Adverbs	
Suffixes	*Examples*		*Suffixes*	*Examples*		*Suffixes*	*Examples*
-ance	ignorance		-ant	ignorant		-ly	slowly
-ence	differences		-ent	different		-ward	backward
-ity	availability		-able	available			
-ment	amusement		-ible	responsible			
-ness	happiness		-ive	active			
-sion	decision		-ic(al)	economical			
-tion	vacation		-ous	famous			

3 **Identifying Parts of Speech from Suffixes** Read some important nouns, adjectives, and adverbs (or related words) below from the reading selections in Chapters 1 to 7. On the line before each item, indicate the part of speech: Write *n* for noun, *adj* for adjective, or *adv* for adverb. You might want to <u>underline</u> the ending (suffix) that indicates the part of speech. A few words are done as examples.

1. __*n*__ ability
2. __*adj*__ active
3. __*adv*__ actively
4. ____ activity
5. ____ agreement
6. ____ agreeable
7. ____ agreeably
8. ____ biological
9. ____ believable
10. ____ beneficial

11. ____ changeable
12. ____ convenient
13. ____ disappearance
14. ____ forward
15. ____ longevity
16. ____ magnificent
17. ____ politeness
18. ____ prevention
19. ____ preventive
20. ____ production

21. ____ religious
22. ____ requirements
23. ____ residence
24. ____ returnable
25. ____ sensible
26. ____ similarly
27. ____ supportive
28. ____ television
29. ____ theoretical
30. ____ visual

4 **Choosing Word Forms with Suffixes** Read the sentences below from the readings in Chapter 7. Circle the correct word form in parentheses ( ). Then write the missing words in the *Parts of Speech Chart* that follows—except for the boxes with Xs. Some of the items are done as examples. Not all of the words from this activity appear in the chart.

1. Three (mountains /(mountainous)) regions of the globe are (fame /(famous)) for the (longevity / long) of their inhabitants. There may be (variety /various) reasons for their long lives.

2. According to (science / scientific) research, many elderly inhabitants of the Himalayan Mountains are still in good (physics / physical) health. One (reason / reasonable) for their amazing condition might be the low level of (pollution / polluted) in their (environment / environmental).

3. Is a simple, (nature / naturally) (nutrition / nutritious) diet (benefits / beneficial) to human health? Is physical work also (advantages / advantageous)?

4. Farmers in the countryside (usual / usually) lead (action / active) lives—that is to say, they fill their days with (activity / actively) and physical (move / movement).

5. Official birth records of (special / especially) long-lived people are seldom (availability / available). Nevertheless, health specialists are in (agreement / agreeable): These amazing people are (general / generally) in good health in their old age.

6. In some regions, the (types / typical) diet of the inhabitants consists of (most / mostly) meat and dairy products; in contrast, other groups consume (main / mainly) fruits and vegetables and use (tradition / traditional) herbs as medicine.

7. How (importance / important) is the (environment / environmentally) to human health? There is some (confusion / confused) about the (validity / valid) of the research into the matter.

8. The amount of (availability / available) medical (information / informative) on the Internet is amazing. This (combination / combined) of proven fact and opinion is changing (culture / cultural) attitudes of people about their own healthcare.

9. Some patients are (ignorance / ignorant) of the facts they need to make the best (medicine / medical) (decisions / decisive). These people may benefit from the (recommendations / recommend) of a number of health experts.

10. Many scientists believe in the (value / valuable) of (genes / genetic) research and engineering. They hope they can make (defects / defective) genes healthy and prevent (biology / biological) diseases.

Parts of Speech		
Noun	Adjective	Adverb
advantages	advantageous	X
availability	*available*	X
activity	active	_____
biology	_____	biologically
_____	confused	X
culture	_____	culturally
defects	_____	X
decisions	decisive	_____
fame	_____	famously
genes	_____	genetically
generalities	_____	_____
humanity	_____	_____
_____	_____	ignorantly
importance	_____	importantly
_____	natural	_____
mountains	_____	X
_____	typical	*typically*
_____	_____	traditionally

5 **Focusing on High-Frequency Words** Read the paragraph below and fill in each blank with a word from the box. One of the words is used twice. When you finish, check your answers on pages 144–145.

combination	damage	engineering	parents
correct	diseases	improve	oppose

D   What are *genes* and why are medical researchers always trying to find out more about them? Genes are part of the center (that is, the *nucleus*) of every living cell; in the form of DNA (deoxyribonucleic acid), this biological genetic material determines the characteristics (features) of every living

thing—every plant, animal, and human being—on Earth. Medical *geneticists* 5
are scientists that study DNA and genes for many purposes: (1) to
learn how living things such as parasites, viruses, and bacteria cause
illness; (2) to find the gene or _____ of genes that cause

1
certain _____ to pass from _____ to

2   3
their children; (3) to prevent or _____ (repair) birth 10

4
defects; (4) to change gene structure to _____ health and

5
increase the length of human life (longevity); and (5) to change the biological
characteristics of animals and humans in ways that are beneficial to society.
Another use of genetic technology that some scientists support is
changing the genes of the food farmers grow. Genetic engineers claim that 15
these differences in DNA structure will increase food production, prevent
_____ from insects, and _____ world

6   7
health; in contrast, others _____ the use of genetic

8
_____ not only in plants but also in animals and humans.

9

6 **Making Connections** Find advice about health on the Internet. Look for tips on
one aspect of health. You can look for tips on healthy eating running, walking, dieting,
doing yoga, living a long life, quitting smoking, or anything else that interests you.

Type in *tips on* _____. Look at a couple of websites. Write down at least five
tips that you agree with. Write down at least three that you disagree with or question.
Tell the whole class what you have learned.

Topic: _____

Tips I agree with	Tips I disagree with

FOCUSING ON TIMED READINGS AND NOTE-TAKING

In the reading section of the TOEFL® iBT, you have 20 minutes to read and answer the questions for each reading. During that time, you can reread parts of the passage if you need to. You can check your answers by looking back at the text. You can skip difficult questions and come back to them later. All this is possible only in the reading section.

The best note-taking strategy is to concentrate on main ideas. Also, if you have time, list supporting details under them. Use lots of abbreviations and don't worry about spelling in your notes.

Taking Notes on a Timed Reading Read the following passage and answer the questions. Before you begin, set a timer for 20 minutes. You have that much time to read the essay, take notes, and respond to all the questions. If you have time at the end, go back and check answers to any questions you were unsure about.

Calorie Counting

A   In discussions about healthy eating, there are not many points of agreement. Almost everyone, however, recognizes that people should take in about as many calories as they use up. A calorie is not a substance but a measure of heat. In the context of eating, calories tell how much energy the body can get by burning up a certain food item. Balancing the calories in food with the body's energy needs is the central goal of any long-term diet program.

B   It should be clear that calories in food are not a bad thing. In fact, we would die without them. Archaeologists suspect that many healthy civilizations either died or relocated because they could no longer get enough calories from their food. The Anasazi of the American southwest, for example, probably suffered a huge loss in their calorie intake, and their health, when deforestation slowly removed deer and pine nuts from their diet. Our appetite for food, a problem for many modern humans, is a natural drive for survival. In fact, some of the most irresistible foods—those high in fat or sugar—have a special hold on humans because ancient impulses tell us to consume them. Our bodies see them as a calorie bonus, as a survival resource.

C   Modern humans have trouble with weight mostly because the body has not adapted to the constant food supply much of the world enjoys. In humans, physical evolution takes a lot more time than social evolution. Pre-historic Europeans or North Americans had to worry about hunting down enough deer, or catching enough fish, or raising enough beans. Modern humans in prosperous nations have a ready supply of affordable calories at the nearest grocery store. Nevertheless, our bodies tell us to store up extra calories, just in case.

D   Responding to that urge causes no problems if a person uses those extra calories. Our ancient ancestors probably did. The walking, hunting, tree-felling, clothes-washing, and other physical activities of a low-tech civilization used up a lot of calories. Modern life is far less active. Even a moderately active person in a wealthy society today has to deliberately exercise to even come close to such a level of activity.

E   So how many calories does an average person need? That question cannot be answered. There is no average person. Calorie needs vary because each person processes food in a slightly different way, depending on body chemistry. And calorie needs are greatly influenced by height, weight, age, and other factors. Still some estimates can be made if we put certain numbers into a long formula from the U.S. Department of Agriculture (USDA). Let's assume two healthy, moderately active young people, each 20 years old. The man is 6 feet tall and weighs 160 pounds. The woman is 5 feet, 6 inches tall and weighs 120 pounds. According to the USDA formula, the man would need to take in about 2,750 calories each day. The woman should take in about 2,002 calories each day.

F   These target levels include the energy it takes simply to operate the body—breathing, pumping blood, raising one's arms, etc. They also include the energy needed for moderate activity (such as walking one or two miles each day, cutting the grass, or walking up and down stairs). Each of these activities uses few calories. Walking for about 30 minutes, for example, burns up only about 140 calories. Running for 30 minutes burns up twice as many calories, but that's still under 300. Compare that to the energy in a good-sized turkey sandwich with mayonnaise—about 450 calories. And that's just lunch.

1. Which of the following best expresses the main idea of the reading as a whole?
   - (A) A healthy diet should balance the number of calories the body takes in with the number it uses.
   - (B) Early humans had a healthier way of living than modern people do.
   - (C) Modern humans are healthier than their ancient ancestors.
   - (D) People do not agree about which foods should be part of healthy eating.

2. Which of the following best expresses the main idea of Paragraph B?
   - (A) The Anasazi civilization lost two important sources of calories.
   - (B) Humans cannot survive unless they take in enough calories.
   - (C) Civilizations have died because they depended on fats and sugars.
   - (D) Humans naturally seek high-calorie foods.

3. Which of the following best expresses the main idea of Paragraph C?
   - (A) Some of the body's survival techniques do not fit in with modern society.
   - (B) The human body cannot evolve in ways that keep it healthy.
   - (C) The human body has stopped evolving, but societies continue to evolve.
   - (D) The food-supply system in modern societies is better than that in earlier societies.

4. Why does the author mention walking in Paragraph D?
   - (A) It is the most important activity of humans in low-tech societies.
   - (B) It is the most important source of exercise for modern humans.
   - (C) As an example of the activities common in low-tech societies.
   - (D) As an example of the activities that are not part of life in modern societies.

5. Which of the following best expresses the main idea of Paragraph E?
   - (A) There is no way to estimate how many calories a person should take in.
   - (B) Personal traits like weight, height, and age have to be considered in any calculation of calorie needs.
   - (C) Men need to take in more calories each day than women need to take in.
   - (D) The USDA has a formula for figuring out how many calories a person should take in every day.

6. Which of the following best expresses the main idea of Paragraph F?
   - (A) Most people get all of their calories by eating lunch.
   - (B) Moderate activity burns up most of the calories a person takes in.
   - (C) The energy needed for breathing and other basic body functions is greater than the energy needed for moderate exercise.
   - (D) Food contains so many calories that it is hard to burn them all up.

Self-Assessment Log

Read the lists below. Check (✓) the strategies and vocabulary that you learned in this chapter. Look through the chapter or ask your instructor about the strategies and words that you do not understand.

Reading and Vocabulary-Building Strategies
- ❏ Recognizing reading structure using a mind map
- ❏ Understanding the main idea
- ❏ Recognizing supporting details after punctuation, numbers, and connecting words
- ❏ Understanding facts and opinions
- ❏ Summarizing using a mind map
- ❏ Figuring out new or difficult vocabulary
- ❏ Identifying synonyms
- ❏ Identifying parts of speech from suffixes
- ❏ Choosing word forms with suffixes

Target Vocabulary

Nouns		Verbs	Adjectives	
❏ claims*	❏ environment	❏ correct*	❏ accurate	❏ proven*
❏ combination*	❏ genes	❏ oppose*	❏ dishonest*	❏ sour*
❏ cure*	❏ inhabitants	❏ prevent*	❏ elderly*	❏ unpolluted
❏ damage*	❏ length*	❏ solve*	❏ famous*	❏ valid
❏ decisions*	❏ longevity		❏ genetic	
❏ disease*	❏ patients		❏ long-lived	
❏ engineering*	❏ population*		❏ moderate*	
	❏ streams*			

*These words are among the 2,000 most frequently used words in English.

Entertainment and the Media

In This Chapter

Do the visual media—television, movies, computers—damage the human brain? Is watching TV really addictive—like smoking cigarettes, taking drugs, or drinking alcohol? Does it contribute to the decline of the traditional family and of moral values in society? The first reading looks at the positive and negative effects of TV and video on viewers around the world. The second reading is about entertainment in other forms and the typical plots of media stories.

❝ In the age of television, image becomes more important than substance. **❞**

—Samuel I. Hayakawa
semanticist, educator, and U.S. senator (1906–1992)

1 How do you think watching TV can be helpful? How can it be harmful?

2 Do you think watching TV can influence the way people act and feel? If so, how?

3 What are some popular TV shows? Why do you think they are popular? What type of show do you think is being filmed in the photo below?

How the Visual Media Affect People

Before You Read

1 Previewing the Topic Look at the photos and read the questions below. Discuss them in small groups.

1. What are the people doing?
2. How are the photos similar? How are they different?
3. Are any of the scenes similar to a scene in your home? Why or why not?

▲ A family watching TV

▲ A family reading

2 Predicting Discuss possible answers to these questions. If you don't know the answers, make predictions. You can look for the answers when you read "How the Visual Media Affect People."

1. What are some examples of visual media?
2. How might the amount of time spent in front of a TV or computer have a negative effect on family life? In what ways can watching television be helpful in people's lives?
3. What might low-quality programming do to the human brain? What might it do to people's lives?
4. What are some possible effects of violent movies or TV programs on people's personalities and behavior?
5. What are some signs of possible addiction to visual media like TV and computers?

3 **Previewing Vocabulary** Read the vocabulary items below from the first reading. Then listen to the words and phrases. Put a check mark (✓) next to the words you know. You can learn the other words now or come back to them after you read.

Nouns	Verbs	Adjectives
❏ addiction	❏ concentrate	❏ addicted
❏ behavior	❏ envy	❏ aural
❏ disadvantages	❏ focus	❏ average
❏ hospitals	❏ improve	❏ boring
❏ images	❏ practice	❏ dissatisfied
❏ personalities	❏ reduce	❏ elderly
❏ programming	❏ replace	❏ envious
❏ reality	❏ scares	❏ exciting
❏ stars	❏ shout	❏ immoral
❏ tension		❏ nursing
❏ viewers		❏ unlimited
❏ violence		
❏ visual media		

Read

4 **Reading an Article** Read the following article. Then read the explanations and do the activities that follow.

How the Visual Media Affect People

Introduction: Benefits of the Visual Media

A   How do television and the other **visual media** affect the lives of individuals and families around the globe? The media can be very helpful to people (and their children) who carefully choose what they watch. With high-quality **programming** in various fields of study—science, medicine, nature, history, the arts, and so on—TV, videotapes, and DVDs increase the knowledge of the average *and* the well-educated person; they can also **improve** thinking ability. Moreover, television and other visual media benefit **elderly** people who can't go out often, as well as patients in **hospitals** and residents of **nursing** facilities. Additionally, it offers language learners the advantage of "real-life" audiovisual instruction and **aural** comprehension practice at any time of day or night. And of course, visual media can provide almost everyone with good entertainment—a pleasant way to relax and spend free time at home.

Media Replaces Other Activities

B   Nevertheless, there are several serious disadvantages to the visual media. First of all, some people watch the "tube" for more hours in a day than they do anything else. In a large number of homes, TV sets—as many as five or more in a single household—are always on. Many people watch TV for many hours a day or spend hours playing games or surfing on their computers; they download music, movies, and other forms of entertainment. Instead of spending time taking care of their kids, parents often use a video screen as an "electronic baby-sitter." As a result, television and video can easily **replace** family communication as well as physical activity and other interests.

The Effects of TV on the Mind

C   Second, too much TV—especially programming of low educational value—can reduce people's ability to **concentrate** or reason. In fact, studies show that after only a minute or two of visual media, a person's mind "relaxes" as it does during light sleep. Another possible effect of television and videotapes on the human brain is poor communication. Children who watch a lot of TV may lose their ability to focus on a subject or an educational activity for more than 10 to 15 minutes. Maybe it is because of the visual media that some kids—and **adults** too—develop attention deficit disorder (ADD), a modern condition in which people are unable to pay attention, listen well, follow instructions, or remember everyday things.

The Effects of Violence in the Media

D   A third negative feature of the media is the amount of **violence** on the screen—both in real events in the news and movies or in TV programs. It **scares** people and gives them terrible nightmares; the fear created by media images and language can last for a long time. On the other hand, frequent **viewers** of "action programming" get used to its messages: they might begin to believe there is nothing strange or unusual about violent crime, fights, killing, and other terrible events and **behavior**. Studies show that certain personality types are likely to have strong **emotional** reactions or dangerous thoughts after some kinds of "entertainment." They may even copy the acts that they see on violent shows—start fires, carry and use weapons, attack people in angry or dangerous ways, and even worse.

Dissatisfaction with Normal Living

E   Because of the visual media, some people may become **dissatisfied** with the reality of their own lives. To these viewers, everyday life does not seem as exciting as the roles actors play in movies or TV dramas. They realize they aren't having as much fun as the **stars** of comedy shows. Furthermore, average people with normal lives may **envy** famous media personalities, who seem to get **unlimited** amounts of money and attention.

Also, media watchers might get depressed when they can't take care of situations in real life as well as TV stars seem to. On the screen, they notice actors solve serious problems in hour or half-hour programs—or in twenty-second commercials.

Boredom with Real Life

F   Yet another negative feature of modern television is called "trash TV." These daily talk shows bring real people with strange or **immoral** lives, **personalities**, or behavior to the screen. Millions of viewers—including children—watch as these "instant stars" tell their most personal secrets, shout out their angry feelings and opinions, and attack one another. TV watchers seem to like the emotional atmosphere and excitement of this kind of programming—as well as the tension of the real but terrible stories on TV "news magazine" shows. A newer version of this kind of entertainment is called "**reality** TV." In shows like *Survivor*, *The Amazing Race*, *American Idol*, and *The Apprentice*, "real people" compete for attention, fame, and other rewards. What effect does frequent viewing of such programs have on people's lives? It makes television more real than **reality**, and normal living begins to seem **boring**.

▲ Watching certain types of programs can make normal living seem boring.

Disadvantage of the Media: Addiction

G   Finally, the most negative effect of all of these kinds of visual media might be **addiction**. People often feel a strange and powerful need to watch TV, download visual material, or play a DVD even when they don't enjoy it or have the free time for entertainment. Addiction to a TV or computer screen is similar to drug or alcohol dependence: addicts almost never believe they are **addicted**. Even so, truthful media addicts have to answer *yes* to many of these questions:

- Do you immediately turn on the TV set or computer when you arrive home from school or work?
- Do you watch a lot of programming that requires little focus or thinking ability?
- Can you concentrate on another topic or activity for only ten to 15 minutes at a time?
- Do you enjoy the action and violence of the media more than activity in your own life?

- Do you feel **envious** of the lives of well-known TV or screen personalities or the participants in "reality TV" shows?
- Do you feel closer to the people on TV than to your own family members and friends?
- For you, is TV or video the easiest—and, therefore, the best—form of relaxation or fun? 95
- Would you refuse to give up your TV viewing and Internet connection for a million dollars?
- Would you like to compete on a TV reality show more than do anything else? 100

After You Read

Strategy

Recognizing Reading Structure: Using an Outline

We learned in Chapter 7 how to use a mind map to help review and organize information in a reading. Here we're going to learn how to use an outline.

- An outline shows the relationship of the topics, main ideas, and supporting details or examples.
- The topic is usually the title of the outline.
- The main ideas and subtopics of the reading can appear after numbers like this: I, II, III, IV.
- The supporting details or examples are written under the main ideas after capital letters like this: A, B, C.
- Sometimes the supporting details have more details. Those can be written after numbers like this: 1, 2, 3.

5 Completing an Outline On the next page is an incomplete outline for the reading "How the Visual Media Affect People." The reading gives two opinions about the visual media. Look at the outline and first answer these questions:

What is the topic? _____

What are the two main subtopics about the topic? _____

_____

Now read the phrases below that will complete the outline. They are the positive and negative effects of the visual media. Read each phrase and scan the article to find the one or two paragraphs where the information appears. Write the letter(s) of the paragraph in the parentheses ( ). Then write the phrases in the outline below.

- Increase people's knowledge and thinking ability   (A)
- Benefit the elderly and the sick   ( )
- Take too much time from family life and other activities   (B)
- Reduce people's ability to concentrate, focus, or reason   ( )
- Scare people or get them used to violence   ( )
- Provide language learners instruction and practice   (A)
- Offer good entertainment during free time   ( )
- Cause dissatisfaction in normal people's lives   ( ) and ( )
- Addict people to TV and video   ( )

Effects of the Visual Media

I. _____ *Advantages* _____

   A. _____

   B. _____

   C. _____

   D. _____

II. _____ *Disadvantages* _____

   A. _____

   B. _____

   C. _____

   D. _____

   E. _____

6 Understanding the Point and Recognizing Supporting Details

Finish the possible main-idea question about the material of the reading selection "How the Visual Media Affect People." In the paragraphs that follow, change the underlined words so that the paragraphs accurately answer the question.

Main-idea question:

What are some positive and negative features of _____?

A   Television and other visual media probably influence people's lives in <u>positive but not negative</u> ways. Here are examples of their possible benefits: (1) <u>Low-quality</u> programming in various fields provides education value to <u>only scientists, doctors, naturalists, historians, and artists.</u> It can <u>damage</u> thinking ability. (2) Also, elderly and sick people who rarely go out 5 <u>can't ever</u> enjoy TV, videotapes, or DVDs. (3) <u>In contrast</u>, students get <u>no</u> educational benefit from shows in the languages they are trying to learn. (4) Another advantage is that TV can help people to <u>get nervous and tense</u> in their free time at home.

B   <u>In exactly the same way</u>, there are serious disadvantages to the visual 10 media: (1) An "electronic baby-sitter" is likely to <u>bring children and their parents closer together</u> and <u>increase</u> the amount of time they spend on other activities. (2) Second, too much television or work on a computer may make it <u>easier</u> for the overly relaxed brain to pay attention, concentrate, or reason. (3) Third, violent or horrible TV images and 15 language can give frequent viewers <u>beautiful dreams</u>, making them fearful of <u>technology, medicine, or the arts</u>; or people may begin to think of terrible events or acts as <u>very strange or unusual</u>. (4) A fourth possible disadvantage of too much television, video, and other kinds of visual media is that people may become <u>too satisfied</u> with the reality of their <u>exciting</u> 20 <u>and fun</u> lives. (5) And finally, the most negative effect of the visual media is probably viewer <u>independence</u>. TV and video watchers <u>will</u> be able to get away from the media easily; they <u>can never</u> become addicted.

7 **Discussing the Reading** In small groups, talk about your answers to the following questions. Then tell the class the most interesting information and ideas.

1. In your opinion, is it a good use of time to watch TV, download music and other entertainment, and/or make use of videos and DVDs? Why or why not?

2. In general, do you believe that television and other visual media improve or damage the brain? Do they increase or reduce learning, logical thinking skills, concentration, memory, and the like? Give reasons for your opinions.

3. In your view, why is there so much violence on TV? What effects does it have on individuals and society? Explain your reasoning.

4. Have you ever watched the talk shows of "trash TV"? Do you enjoy reality TV? If not, why not? If so, what do you think of the people on those shows? Why?

5. Look back at the list of questions about TV addiction on pages 163–164 of the reading. For how many of the questions do you have to answer *yes*? Do you believe you are addicted to TV? Give reasons for your answers.

Media Stories

1 Previewing Vocabulary Read the vocabulary items below from the next reading. Then listen to the words and phrases. Put a check mark (✓) next to the words you know. You can learn the other words now or come back to them after you read.

Nouns	Verbs	Adjectives	
❏ adulthood	❏ captured	❏ bloody	❏ shadowy
❏ adventure	❏ inherited	❏ computerized	❏ suspenseful
❏ bankruptcy	❏ investigate	❏ decent	❏ wealthy
❏ drama	❏ recover	❏ desperate	
❏ investigator	❏ sinks	❏ natural	
❏ murderer	❏ stabs	❏ powerful	
❏ passion	❏ transport	❏ pregnant	
❏ relationship		❏ run-down	
		❏ scary	

2 Classifying Stories and Putting Events in Order Most programs in the visual media include stories that tell what happened, most often in time order. Below are the kinds of stories that most often appear in movies and TV series.

1. _____ adventure or action
2. _____ crime or mystery
3. _____ authentic history
4. _____ serious drama
5. _____ suspense or horror
6. _____ science fiction or fantasy
7. _____ comedy
8. _____ animated cartoon
9. _____ musical
10. _____ biography or people's personal experiences

Skim the four story plots of well-known movies and TV shows. (Story plots are short descriptions of the actions or events of a real movie or TV show.) On the lines before some of the listed story types above, write the letters of the story plots A, B, C, and D. You can write the same letter more than once, but you will not find stories of all 10 types.

Read

3 Finding the Main Idea After you read each plot description, answer the question that follows each. Fill in A, B, or C for the movie title or name of the TV show that—in your opinion or experience—best fits the story plot.

Media Stories

Story Plot A

Marion, who works in a real estate office, is depressed about her life—especially her unhappy love **relationship**. Because she is feeling ill, her supervisor lets her leave early; he gives her $40,000 in cash from a house sale to put in the bank on her way home. However, temptation gets the best of the 5 moody young woman. With the cash in an envelope, she packs her bags and drives out of town. On a dark lonely road, a severe thunderstorm forces her to stop at the run-down Bates Motel. There is a **scary** old house high on a hill behind the motel, with the form 10 of an old woman in a rocking chair at the window. Norman Bates, the motel owner, is happy to sign in a guest, but his mother shouts at him angrily. After a conversation with Norman, Marion goes to her room.

▲ A scene from the movie *Psycho* by Alfred Hitchcock

When she is in the shower, the bathroom door opens. In a very famous, 15 very **bloody** murder scene, the **shadowy** figure of an old woman pulls aside the shower curtain and stabs the motel guest to death. Horrified, Norman cleans up the room, puts Marion's body in her car, and pushes the car into the swamp.

Worried about her and the stolen money, Marion's sister, lover, and boss 20 send out an investigator, who finally arrives at the Bates Motel. Suspicious of Norman's strange behavior, the investigator goes into the scary house, where the dark shape of an "old woman" at the top of the stairs kills him too—with a long knife. Others come to **investigate**. After many **suspenseful** scenes, they discover that Norman's "mother" is a skeleton. 25 The murderer in the old woman's clothes was Norman Bates himself, who has turned more and more into his mother.

In what movie does the sequence of events in Story Plot A above occur?
- Ⓐ *The Public Enemy* (a drama about the social forces that cause violent crime)
- Ⓑ *Psycho* (a psychological suspense film directed by Alfred Hitchcock in 1960)
- Ⓒ *Gone with the Wind* (a world-famous 1939 American Civil War drama)

Story Plot B

After a hurricane sinks their ship off the coast of Africa, a British couple finds their way to land with their baby son. However, the parents are killed by a wild animal. A gorilla (the largest of the humanlike monkeys) finds the baby, brings him home to her mate, and raises the helpless human in the jungle. As a result, he grows to **adulthood** in the **natural** ape community. Nevertheless, the young man's peaceful life in the jungle soon changes. To study African wildlife in its natural environment, Professor Porter arrives with his daughter Jane and a hunter named Clayton. When the explorers meet the jungle man, at first they think he is "the missing link" (a being halfway between an animal and a human being). Therefore, they are surprised to discover that he is as human as they are. When he begins to feel strange, unfamiliar emotions towards Jane, the man that grew up in the jungle becomes very confused. He wants to be with his own kind but doesn't want to leave the gorilla family that raised him—especially since Clayton sees the apes not as friends but as animals to hunt and kill. When Jane has to leave with her father, the ape man is very sad and upset. Even so, he saves the white people when they are captured, and Jane stays with him in the jungle.

▲ A scene from the movie *Tarzan*

In what movie (produced in many versions) do the events in Story Plot B happen?

- (A) *Tarzan, the Ape Man* (the first of a series based on the "Lord of the Jungle" characters)
- (B) *A Night to Remember* (the film about the sinking of the ship *Titanic*)
- (C) *Robinson Crusoe* (an adventure story about a man who lives alone on an island)

Story Plot C

The star ship *Enterprise* (a flying vehicle that travels to other galaxies at amazing speeds) stops at a space station for repairs. The four Bynars (beings with **computerized** brains) that are doing maintenance seem worried. Suddenly, they realize the ship is about to explode and order evacuation. Everyone leaves except Picard, the captain, and Riker, the second man in command, who don't hear the alert. After everyone else reaches the starbase (the space station), the problem mysteriously corrects itself, and the ship disappears. As the crew on the starbase try to figure out a way to recover the *Enterprise*, the captain and his helper discover what has happened. They instantly transport themselves to the bridge, where they find the Bynars unconscious, dying, and asking for help.

The ship reaches Bynarus, the Bynars' planet. Because of an exploded star that destroyed the planet's center computer, Bynarus is dead too. The Bynars needed the *Enterprise* to store the data from the planet 65 during the shutdown time. Picard and Riker manage to get into the Bynarus file and restart the computer. The Bynars come back to life. Undamaged, the ship returns to the starbase. 70

▲ The cast from the TV series *Star Trek: The Next Generation*

What popular American TV series are the events in Story Plot C from?

Ⓐ *The Twilight Zone* (amazing stories about the effects of the human imagination)

Ⓑ *Superman* (the adventures of a being from another planet with superhuman powers)

Ⓒ *Star Trek: The Next Generation* (futuristic adventures of travelers in space)

Story Plot D

It is the middle of the 19th century, a very romantic time of honor and passion. Matilde Peñalver y Beristan is an aristocrat, a member of the nobility (the most wealthy, powerful class in society). She falls in love with Adolfo Solis, an army solder with no fortune. Matilda trusts that her fair, kind father will let her marry her true love. However, Augusta (Matilda's 75 mother) objects; with her powerful connections, she sends Adolfo to prison. Lying, she tells her daughter that Adolfo is married with children.

Because their family is facing bankruptcy, Augusta wants Manuel Fuentes Guerra, an honorable and handsome young man who has just inherited a vast fortune, to be her son-in-law. Confused and desperate, 80 Matilde marries Manuel. Soon, Adolfo escapes from jail. After a frantic, intense search, he finds Matilde. Posing as the new ranch administrator, he recognizes her husband as an honest, fair, and decent man. At that point, 85 Manuel and Matilde discover Augusta's deceit in their marriage. But in the meantime, Matilde's feelings for Adolfo are beginning to disappear. She is starting to fall in love with Manuel. Heartbroken, Adolfo accepts reality 90 and leaves the ranch. Matilde announces she is pregnant. However, . . . To be continued. . .

▲ A scene from a soap opera

Which popular Mexican soap opera is the plot in Story Plot D from?

(A) *Rubí* (a modern melodrama about a beautiful, manipulative woman and her effects on the people around her. Rubí lies, cheats, and steals to get what she wants—especially from rich, sexy men.)

(B) *Amor Real* ("True Love," a historical drama about a young woman who breaks the social code when she falls in love with a poor commoner.)

(C) *Like Water for Chocolate* (a sad and funny love story set in Mexico with cooking as the central theme of passion. Many recipes are included.)

After You Read

Strategy

Summarizing a Story

A reading selection or paragraph that describes a plot (a sequence of events in a story) is most often organized in time order—that is, one event follows another.

- To prepare to summarize a plot, you might number the main events in the reading material.

- Then after an introduction to set the scene, you tell the most important things that happened.

Here is an example of possible event numbering from the first story in "Media Stories."

Marion, an employee in a real estate office, is depressed about her life—especially her unhappy love relationship. *(1)* Because she is feeling ill, her supervisor lets her leave work early; he gives her $40,000 in cash from a house sale to put in the bank on her way home. *(2)* However, temptation gets the best of the moody young woman. With the cash in an envelope, she packs her bags and drives out of town. *(3)* On a dark lonely road, a severe thunderstorm forces her to stop at the run-down Bates Motel. There is a scary old house high on a hill behind the motel, with the form of an old woman in a rocking chair at the window. *(4)* Norman Bates, the motel owner, is happy to sign in a guest, but his mother shouts at him angrily. *(5)* After a conversation with Norman, Marion goes to her room.

4 **Summarizing a Story** Work in groups of three. Choose a plot description (Story B, C, or D) from the selection "Media Stories" on pages 168–170. Read it carefully. Number the events like the example in the Strategy Box shows. Then write a summary of the story. After a short introduction, list the main events needed to understand the story in as few words as possible. Then tell or read your plot summary to your group.

5 Discussing the Reading In small groups, talk about your answers to these questions. Then tell the class the most interesting information or ideas.

1. Of the ten media story types in Activity 2 on page 167, which is your favorite, your second favorite, and so on? Give reasons for your preferences.

2. For several of the kinds of stories, tell the titles of some well-known movies or television series. How many of each media type can your group name within a time limit?

6 Talking It Over What are your preferences in media entertainment? Read the choices for each category below. Number your preferences from favorite (1) through least favorite (6). Then explain the reasons for the order you chose. Compare your choices with your classmates' preferences.

Media

_____ television (network, cable)

_____ prerecorded videotapes, DVDs

_____ feature films in theaters

_____ media on the Internet

_____ radio programs

_____ other kinds of media

Movies

_____ comedies or animated features

_____ romance

_____ action or thrillers

_____ horror or suspense

_____ serious drama

_____ other kinds of movies

TV Series

_____ situation comedies

_____ science fiction

_____ crime or detective shows; law or hospital dramas

_____ soap operas (highly emotional dramas with continuing story lines)

_____ reality shows

_____ other kinds of series

Other Programming

_____ news or current events

_____ talk shows

_____ quiz shows

_____ educational programs

_____ travel shows

_____ other kinds of programs

Music

_____ classical music

_____ jazz or blues

_____ popular singers and groups

_____ country music or dancing

_____ international folk music

_____ other kinds of music

Other Entertainment

_____ live theater (plays)

_____ cabarets or dinner theater

_____ stand-up comedy clubs

_____ dance clubs or discos

_____ casino gambling

_____ other _____

| **Part 3** | Vocabulary and Language-Learning Skills |

Strategy

Getting Meaning from Context
Getting the general meaning of new or difficult words or phrases can help you understand the meanings of the sentences. You may then be able to understand the details and their relationship to the main ideas of the material.

1 **Understanding New Vocabulary from Context** Read the outline below from the reading selection "How the Visual Media Affect People" on pages 161–164. Then read the details that follow. In the questions below, choose the answer that is closest in meaning to the underlined word or phrase. Identify where each detail belongs in the outline and write the number and letter from the outline (e.g., I.A.) in the parentheses after the sentence. The first answer is provided.

Effects of the Visual Media

I. *Advantages: Television and videos*
  A. *Provide learning in many subjects*
  B. *Benefit the old and the sick*
  C. *Help with language instruction*
  D. *Offer ways to relax*

II. *Disadvantages: The media*
  A. *Take time from family and other activities*
  B. *Can decrease people's concentration and reasoning abilities*
  C. *Produce strong or dangerous emotional reactions in people*
  D. *May create dissatisfaction or boredom in everyday life*
  E. *Can addict people*

---

1. At all hours, the media offer language learners "real-life" audiovisual instruction and practice in <u>aural comprehension</u>. (*I.C*)
   - (A) the answers to test questions
   - **(B)** understanding spoken language
   - (C) hospital and health information
   - (D) real-life experience

2. Moreover, television helps <u>elderly</u> people who can't go out often, as well as patients in hospitals and residents of <u>nursing facilities</u>. (   )

   <u>elderly</u>
   - (A) sick people
   - (B) old people
   - (C) people who need help
   - (D) busy people

   <u>nursing facilities</u>
   - (A) homes for doctors and nurses
   - (B) centers for public entertainment
   - (C) normal housing for average people
   - (D) places for older and very sick people

3. High-quality TV <u>programming</u>—a good plan of shows about various fields of study—can increase people's knowledge and improve their thinking abilities. (   )
   - (A) scientific and medical shows
   - (B) academic lecture courses
   - (C) choice and organization of shows
   - (D) movies with good music

4. Television and video provide almost everyone with good entertainment—a pleasant way to relax and spend free time at home. (   )

- Ⓐ relaxation through exercise
- Ⓑ amusement or pleasure
- Ⓒ fun through serious study
- Ⓓ freedom from worry and tension

5. Children who watch a lot of TV may lose their ability to concentrate or focus on a subject for very long; sometimes they develop "attention deficit disorder." (   )

concentrate

- Ⓐ direct their attention
- Ⓑ reduce or decrease
- Ⓒ communicate
- Ⓓ improve

deficit

- Ⓐ criticism or anger
- Ⓑ lack of money
- Ⓒ inability or shortage
- Ⓓ difficult confusion

6. Because of the time it consumes, television and video can easily replace family communication as well as physical activity and other interests. (   )

- Ⓐ take the place of
- Ⓑ go back to
- Ⓒ find the location of
- Ⓓ contribute to family time

7. Images of violence on the screen scare people, giving them terrible nightmares when they sleep. (   )

violence

- Ⓐ bad conditions
- Ⓑ behavior that hurts people
- Ⓒ dark, stormy weather
- Ⓓ physical disabilities

nightmares

- Ⓐ frightening dreams
- Ⓑ the emotion of depression
- Ⓒ traditional visual images
- Ⓓ personality types

8. The talk shows of "trash TV" make instant "stars" of real people with strange or immoral ideas, who tell their most personal secrets, shout angrily, and attack one another. (   )

"trash TV"

- Ⓐ valuable programs
- Ⓑ shows without quality
- Ⓒ negative effects
- Ⓓ normal life stories

"stars"

- Ⓐ movie roles
- Ⓑ news magazines
- Ⓒ media addicts
- Ⓓ famous personalities

immoral

- Ⓐ not having values
- Ⓑ refusing help
- Ⓒ excited
- Ⓓ unusual or common

For more practice, you can look for and figure out the general meanings of other vocabulary items in the reading, such as *visual, action programming, likely, normal, boring, truthful,* and so on.

For each item, explain the logical reasoning for your guesses at definitions. Then use each word or phrase in a sentence that tells an advantage or disadvantage of TV watching.

UNDERSTANDING SUFFIXES

A useful clue to the part of speech of a word is its ending, or *suffix*.

- The noun suffixes presented in Chapter 7 were *-ance* or *-ence, -ity, -ment, -ness,* and *-sion* or *-tion*.

- The adjective endings were *-ant* or *-ent, -able* or *-ible, -ive, -ous, -ic,* and *-al*.

- The adverbs ended in *-ly* or *-ward(s)*.

Below are a few additional word endings that may indicate if a word is a noun, a verb, or an adjective. In parentheses are the general meanings of the suffixes. Examples are included.

Noun Suffixes	Examples
-er, -or, -ist (a person or thing that does something)	daughter, calculator, actor, scientist
-ship (having a position or skill)	citizenship, friendship
-hood (a state or time of something)	childhood, widowhood
-ism (a belief or way of doing something)	liberalism, Buddhism
Verb Suffixes	**Examples**
-ate, -ify, -ize, -en (to make something be a way or change it to that quality)	create, decorate, beautify, clarify, certain realize, energize, strengthen, widen
Verb Suffixes	**Examples**
-al, -ar (relating to something)	dental, financial, muscular
-y (full of or covered with something)	rainy, angry, moody
-ful (full of)	careful, beautiful
-less (without something)	careless, endless
-ing (causing a feeling)	interesting, exhausting
-ed (having a feeling)	interested, exhausted

2 **Practicing More Word Endings** Here are some of the important nouns, verbs, and adjectives (or related words) from the reading selections before or in Chapter 8. In these words, the suffix (ending) clearly indicates the part of speech. On the line before each item, write *n* for "noun," *v* for "verb," or *adj* for "adjective." Underline the suffix. A few words are done as examples.

1. _*n*_ chapter
2. _____ behavior
3. _____ classify
4. _____ addicted
5. _____ psychologist

6. _____ concentrate
7. _____ computerized
8. _____ unlimited
9. _*v*_ visualize
10. _____ visual

11. _____ boring
12. _____ nuclear
13. _*adj*_ truthful
14. _____ childhood
15. _____ bloody

16. _____ simplify	**21.** _____ personalize	**26.** _____ shadowy
17. _____ organize	**22.** _____ relationship	**27.** _____ investigate
19. _____ viewer	**23.** _____ emotionalism	**28.** _____ sadden
19. _____ baby-sitter	**24.** _____ exciting	**29.** _____ natural
20. _____ dissatisfied	**25.** _____ specialist	**30.** _____ adulthood

Strategy

Understanding Word Families

Word families are groups of related words of various parts of speech. Read below about word families.

- Within a word family of related forms, some words can be used as more than one part of speech. For example, *increase* can be used both as a noun and a verb.

- There may be two or more nouns with different suffixes: often, one noun names an idea, while a related noun with a different ending is a word for a person—like *psychology* (a field of study) and *psychologist* (a specialist in psychology).

- There may be related words of the same part of speech with meanings that are a little different from each other. Some examples are *vision* (*noun*: a mental picture) and *visionary* (*noun*: a person with clear ideas of the future), *criticize* (*verb*: to judge negatively) and *critique* (*verb*: to evaluate the quality of), *classic* (*adjective*: long important and popular) and *classical* (*adjective*: based on traditional ideas).

3 **Choosing from Word Families** Read the sentences below about the topics in Chapter 8. Circle the correct word form in parentheses. Then write the missing words in the charts that follow—except for the boxes with Xs. There may be more than one possible word for some of the boxes—maybe one noun for a person and another for an idea.

1. Which kinds of shows do you (preference /(prefer)/ preferable)? Do they decrease your ability to (concentration /(concentrate)/ concentrated)?

2. Are you (addiction / addict / addicted) to television or other (visions / visualize / visual) media?

3. Many TV critics and viewers (criticism / criticize / critical) the amount of (violence / violate / violent) in the media.

4. Psychologists worry about the (behavior / behave / well-behaved) of young people who watch a lot of TV during their (children / childhood / childless).

5. (Frequency / Frequent / Frequently) TV watchers may become (dissatisfaction / dissatisfy / dissatisfied) with their normal or average lives.

6. They might (envy / enviable / envious / enviously) the lives of TV or screen actors because their lives seem (excitement / excite / excitable / exciting).

7. "Trash TV" brings (reality / realism / realize / real) people to talk shows—people with behavior that may be (immorality / immoral / immorally).

8. Are the guests on these shows telling the (truism / truth / true / truthful) about their lives? Are the people on reality TV showing their real (person / personalities /personalize / personal)?

9. Many of the films of the director Alfred Hitchcock are (psychology / psychologists / psycho / psychological) thrillers. They are very (suspense / suspend / suspenseful / suspensively).

10. Hitchcock usually (strength / strengthens / strong) the (scare / scary / scared) mood of his movies with frightening details.

Noun	Verb	Adjective
preference(s)	*prefer*	preferred preferable
	concentrate	concentrated
addiction(s) addict	addict	
vision(s)		
		critical
	x	violent
behavior		(well-) behaved
	x	childish childless
	frequent	
		dissatisfied

Noun	Verb	Adjective
envy		
	excite	
		real
	x	immoral
truth	x	
personality personalities		
	x	psychological
	suspend	
		strong
scare		

For more vocabulary practice with word endings that indicate parts of speech, try to think of more words (nouns, verbs, and adjectives) with the suffixes listed on page 176. You can check your guesses in a dictionary. Can you use your words in sentences that show their meanings?

4 Focusing on High-Frequency Words Read the paragraph on page 179 and fill in each blank with a word from the box. When you finish, check your answers on page 161.

average	improve	practice
elderly	medicine	programming
hospitals	nursing	

Introduction: Benefits of the Visual Media

A   How do television and the other visual media affect the lives of individuals and families around the globe? The media can be very helpful to people (and their children) who carefully choose what they watch. With high-quality _____ in various fields of study—science,
1
_____, nature, history, the arts, and so on—TV, videotapes,
2
and DVDs increase the knowledge of the _____
3
and the well-educated person; they can also _____
4
thinking ability. Moreover, television and other visual media benefit
_____ people who can't go out often, as well as patients
5
in _____ and residents of _____
6   7
facilities. Additionally, it offers language learners the advantage of "real-life" audiovisual instruction and aural comprehension
_____ at any time of day or night. And of course, visual
8
media can provide almost everyone with good entertainment—a pleasant way to relax and spend free time at home.

 5 Making Connections Do an Internet search on a TV show or movie that you especially enjoy or would like to see. It can be a comedy, a soap opera, a drama, a mystery, a talk show, or any other kind of popular entertainment.

You can use a search engine and type in the name of the show and—if appropriate—the name of the TV network or movie studio. Take notes on the plot or topic(s) of the show, the actors or celebrities in it, and other interesting aspects of the show. You can use the model on the next page.

Describe what you learned to a partner, a group of classmates, and/or the whole class. Try to persuade (convince) them that the show is good. Did you persuade them to watch the show? Why or why not?

Website: _____

Name of show: _____

Type of show: _____

Interesting information: _____

_____

_____

_____

What is good about the show? _____

_____

_____

_____

_____

Part 4 | Focus on Testing

TOEFL® iBT FOCUSING ON COMPARISON AND CONTRAST IN READINGS
Part 1 of this chapter focuses on comparison and contrast. Standardized tests, including the TOEFL® iBT, expect readers to recognize similarities and differences in meaning between ideas, opinions, points of view, and pairs of sentences.

Practicing with Comparison and Contrast Read the following short personal stories about the topic of this chapter's first reading, "How the Visual Media Affect People." Try to recognize the similarities (points in common) in and the differences between the two stories. Then answer the questions that follow.

Story 1

My television set is an important piece of equipment for me. I can't get out of the house very often, but my TV brings the whole world to me. From the evening news and the all-news channels, I learn about events in the outside world: politics, the environment, recent changes in technology and medicine, and so on. I like game shows and travel programs, too. Even the talk shows are exciting—all of these strange people telling their life stories and secrets to the whole world! And I love comedies; I think it's important to be able to laugh. I can even watch shows in other languages and "go shopping" by TV. With the major national networks, the educational and cable channels—and the extra sports, movie, science fiction, history, music, and other specialty channels, I have a choice of 50 different programs at the same time! The only programs I don't watch regularly by myself are the children's shows, but when my niece visits, those are fun, too! Maybe I'll get a satellite dish. Then I'll have even more TV choices; and if those aren't enough, I can buy or rent a video or DVD, listen to radio programming, and so on. How can I ever feel lonely or bored with so much media?

Story 2

We used to have a television set in every room of our house. Our eight-year-old son used to spend *hours* each day in front of the "boob tube." He was beginning to get strange ideas about reality from the violence and sex on many programs. He was having nightmares; he was losing interest in school, in creative play, in other children, and in his family! We (his parents) were watching too much TV, too. We stopped inviting our friends and relatives to our home and we stopped visiting them. We preferred to watch TV. We didn't even talk to each other that much. Because we weren't communicating enough, our marriage was suffering. Our health was suffering, too. We were getting lazy and becoming old and tired very quickly. So one day we decided to "pull the plug" on our dangerous family addiction. We quit TV "cold turkey"—from that time on, there was no television in our lives! It was a *very* difficult time for all of us. Like most recovering addicts, we had all the signs of withdrawal—feelings of boredom, of loneliness, of emptiness. Our son was always running to the refrigerator to satisfy his need for pleasure. My wife and I went back to smoking, to drinking alcohol, and to some other bad habits. But we finally recovered—and found the perfect solution to our discomfort and emptiness. Now we each have our own computer at home, and we spend all our free time in front of another screen. We are addicted to the Internet.

1. Which of the previous stories is about the topic "views of the visual media, especially TV?"
   (A) Story number 1
   (B) Story number 2
   (C) both of the stories
   (D) neither of the stories

2. Which of the following might be a good title for Story 1?
   (A) How TV Changes Politics
   (B) Why I Can't Live Well Without TV
   (C) How to Get on a TV Talk Show
   (D) Why Shopping on TV Is Convenient

3. Which of the following statements describes the main idea of Story 2?
   (A) There are many kinds of television programs—political, educational, commercial, and musical.
   (B) Television is an important element of a healthy and communicative family life.
   (C) Cold turkey is an excellent cure to feelings of boredom, loneliness, and emptiness in people's lives.
   (D) Addiction to television is difficult to overcome without a replacement or substitute.

4. According to both Stories 1 and 2, TV and visual media _____
   (A) have very little influence on most of their viewers
   (B) are not a good distraction from real life
   (C) can greatly affect viewers' lives
   (D) are becoming less popular

5. What is the main difference between the points of view of the writers of the first and second stories?
   (A) The first writer views television and video as beneficial, but the second focuses on their harmful effects on people.
   (B) In contrast to the first writer, the second values the Internet over TV programming.
   (C) The first writer's view is overwhelmingly negative; the second's feelings are exactly the opposite.
   (D) There is little difference between the two opinions; both writers see the visual media in similar ways.

Self-Assessment Log

Read the lists below. Check (✓) the strategies and vocabulary that you learned in this chapter. Look through the chapter or ask your instructor about the strategies and words that you do not understand.

Reading and Vocabulary-Building Strategies

❏ Recognizing reading structure: using an outline
❏ Understanding the point and recognizing supporting details
❏ Classifying stories and putting events in order
❏ Summarizing a story
❏ Understanding new vocabulary from context
❏ Understanding suffixes
❏ Understanding word families

Target Vocabulary

Nouns

❏ addiction
❏ adulthood
❏ adults
❏ behavior*
❏ hospitals*
❏ personalities*
❏ programming*
❏ reality*
❏ relationship*
❏ stars*

❏ viewers
❏ violence*
❏ visual media

Verbs

❏ concentrate
❏ envy*
❏ improve*
❏ investigate
❏ practice*
❏ replace*

❏ scares

Adjectives

❏ addicted
❏ aural
❏ bloody*
❏ boring
❏ computerized
❏ dissatisfied*
❏ elderly*
❏ emotional

❏ envious
❏ exciting*
❏ immoral
❏ natural*
❏ nursing*
❏ reality
❏ scary
❏ shadowy*
❏ suspenseful
❏ unlimited*

*These words are among the 2,000 most frequently used words in English.

Social Life

In This Chapter

The readings in this chapter are about social relationships. The two selections are from a fictional story called, "Meeting the Perfect Mate." You will read about a woman who talks to different people about their ideas on the best way to meet the perfect mate. Their ideas range from Internet dating, to speed dating, to arranged marriages.

❝ The only way to have a friend is to be one. **❞**

—Ralph Waldo Emerson,
American author, poet, and philosopher (1803–1882)

Connecting to the Topic

1 Look at the people in the photo below. What do you think their relationship is to one another?

2 How do young people typically socialize in your country?

3 What do you think are the three best ways for people to meet a potential boyfriend or girlfriend?

Meeting the Perfect Mate

Before You Read

1 **Previewing the Topic** Discuss the pictures and questions that follow in small groups.

I joined a computer dating service last week. It will be wonderful! Soon dozens of men will be asking me for dates!

A computer dating service? YECH! That's not very romantic. I prefer to go to clubs or do speed dating. I meet lots of men that way.

Clubs? Speed dating? How awful! How unnatural! I think it's terrible to plan a romance. Romance should come naturally.

A computer program can't lead to true love. Did Romeo and Juliet have a computer? Did they go to a dance club? Of course not!

Can real love develop over the internet? Can you fall in love with words and photos? No way! I will NEVER go out and try to find a boyfriend!

These things happen naturally.

So when was your last date?

Three years ago.

1. Who are the people and what are they talking about? How are the three people different from one another?

2. Do you agree with any one of them? Why or why not?

3. How do young people you know usually meet their boyfriends/girlfriends or their future mates?

2 Predicting Think and talk about possible answers to these questions. What will the reading say? Make predictions. When you read "Meeting the Perfect Mate," look for the answers.

1. What was a common kind of marriage in India in the past that still exists today?

2. How do some young people around the world meet the people who become their boyfriends or girlfriends, or fiancés (future spouses)?

3. What is an advantage to each method (way) of meeting people? What is a disadvantage?

3 **Previewing Vocabulary** Read the vocabulary items below from the first reading. Then listen to the words and phrases. Put a check mark (✓) next to the words you know. You can learn the other words now or come back to them after you read.

Nouns
- ❑ arrangement
- ❑ atmosphere
- ❑ cafés
- ❑ cell phone
- ❑ cyberspace
- ❑ dormitory
- ❑ guy
- ❑ match
- ❑ mates
- ❑ power notebook
- ❑ search
- ❑ socks
- ❑ speed dating
- ❑ spouses

Verbs
- ❑ arranged
- ❑ examine
- ❑ exercise
- ❑ hang out
- ❑ interviewing
- ❑ match
- ❑ replied (reply)
- ❑ volunteered

Adjectives
- ❑ aggressive
- ❑ arranged
- ❑ discouraged
- ❑ perfect
- ❑ popular
- ❑ potential
- ❑ speedy
- ❑ worried

Adverbs
- ❑ enthusiastically
- ❑ fortunately

Read

4 **Reading an Article** Read the following article. Then read the explanations and do the activities after the article.

Meeting the Perfect Mate, Part 1

For the past month, I've been taking a university graduate course called "Social Structure." It's a very popular class. We've been discussing friendship, social life, dating, marriage, and other relationships—through the generations and throughout the world. One of our assignments is to examine the ways that people meet potential spouses (husbands and wives). I've been interviewing students on campus all week as part of my study. I'm amazed at what I've been hearing. 5

First, I talked with my roommate in the dormitory, Usha, an international student from India.

"What's one way to meet a possible mate?" I asked her. 10

"Well," she said, "one method in my country is to have an arranged marriage."

"A what?" I asked. "I know you can match a tie to a shirt—or two socks after you do the laundry. Then they're a match. But people?"

"Sure," she **replied**. "There are still arranged marriages these days, and there were a lot more not too long ago. My parents, for example, met each other for the first time on their wedding day. My grandparents chose their children's spouses and **arranged** the weddings."

"Do you mean that the bride and groom weren't in love? That sounds awful! Weren't they **worried**?"

"Maybe a little bit," Usha said, "but they accepted each other. Then, **fortunately**, they learned to love each other. They've had a good, successful marriage for the past 30 years. This happens in a lot of arranged marriages. You know, even today some orthodox (very religious) young people—Jewish and Muslim and Christian—marry this way."

I shook my head. "Amazing!" I said.

* * * * * * * *

The next person that I interviewed was Bill, a **guy** in my business management class. "I meet a lot of women in dance clubs—at least I used to," he said. "The environment was exciting and I used to go every weekend, if possible, to dance or talk or just listen to music."

"That seems great," I said.

"I thought so, too, at first," he said a little sadly. "But on the other hand, the music at these places was *very* loud. Many people drank, so they didn't talk; they shouted—and didn't listen much. Both the men and the women got kind of **aggressive**. And it was *so* disorganized. So I've been trying speed dating instead of bars and clubs."

"What on earth is *that*?" I asked, amazed.

"Well, you go to a nice place with tables and chairs. You get to meet a new person every six minutes. Then you list the people you want to see again."

▲ An interview about dating

"Does it work?"

"No, it's much too fast for me. I don't move that quickly, and I'm not a **speedy** thinker or talker, either. You know, you ought to talk to my brother, Freddy. Here—you can get him by speed dialing my cell phone." Bill handed me the cellular telephone. I speed dialed Freddy.

"Oh, I do just about *everything* on the Internet—you know, the World Wide Web," volunteered Freddy, very quickly.

"You meet potential dates—and girlfriends—and *mates*—on the *Web*? On your computer?" I asked, not really so amazed any more.

"Yeah, there are plenty of people to communicate with in cyberspace," Freddy began, **enthusiastically**. "With the most up-to-date technology— laptops and power notebooks and even camera and video phones, you can do it anywhere—at home, at work and school, at cafés, in the library . . . You go into "chat rooms" and "talk" by typing."

Slowing down, Freddy paused to think. "On the other hand, . . . I'm not such a good writer. It's hard, you know, . . . to use those little computer devices. Anyway, well, um . . . who knows what is real there and what isn't? Who knows . . . like, who might be dangerous?" he continued, starting to sound a little **discouraged**. It seemed he was talking more to himself than to me. I thanked him, and we said good-bye so I could continue my search for the **perfect** way to find the perfect mate.

* * * * * * * *

"The Internet? Never!" said Julie, a student who works part-time in the campus bookstore. "I prefer to make new friends at places where people have the same interests. I met my boyfriend at the health club, for example, and it seems that the healthy atmosphere of the gym is continuing into the relationship that I have with him." We work out together, hang out at the pool and hot tubs, go to the health-food juice bar, and so on. There are so many active, attractive people there. Hmm . . . maybe you should try it."

"That sounds wonderful," I said.

"Yes," Julie said, "I guess so. But to be honest, there's one problem with this arrangement."

"What?" I asked.

"The truth is that I really hate to exercise, so I don't want to go to the gym anymore. What's my boyfriend going to think when he finds this out?"

To be continued . . .

RECOGNIZING THE STRUCTURE OF WRITTEN CONVERSATIONS

Even readings that are in conversational form—with the words of each speaker between quotation marks (" "), should be well organized. There should be a main topic and smaller topics, or subtopics. Each main topic should include details and ideas about the topic.

5 Recognizing the Structure of Written Conversations The chart below will help you organize the main topics and supporting ideas of the reading selection "Meeting the Perfect Mate." First, in the column after the speakers' names, write what the person talked about. Choose from the phrases below. (Tip: One person talks about two topics.)

- Meeting people in dance clubs
- Arranged marriages
- Going to "speed dating" sessions
- Finding friends in cyberspace
- Meeting in health clubs or the gym

Interviewer's Question: *What's the best way to meet a perfect mate?*

Interviewee	His or her method (= main idea)	Speaker's Pros	Speaker's Cons	Your Opinion
Usha	*Arranged marriages*			
Bill				
Freddy			*You don't know what is unreal or dangerous about people you meet on the Web.*	
Julie		*You can meet people with common interests.*		

Next, write the pros (advantages) and cons (disadvantages) each person talks about in the chart. Choose from the list on page 192. You can look back at the reading for help. Some answers are in the chart as examples.

- The club atmosphere is exciting, especially on weekends.
- You can dance, talk to people, or just listen to music.
- Husbands and wives may learn to love each other.
- You meet a different potential date every six minutes.
- You list the names of the people you met that you want to see again.
- Spouses may meet for the first time on their wedding day.
- You can go online at home, at work or school, in cafés, and in other places.
- If you're not a fast thinker or talker, there's not enough time to get to know people.
- You can use your power notebook and video cell phone.
- You can meet people with common interests.
- Some very religious (orthodox) young people may marry this way today.
- You don't know what is unreal or dangerous about people you meet on the Web.
- People may drink, and shout instead of talk, and become aggressive.
- There are many attractive, active people there to meet.
- If you're not really interested in exercise, there might be a problem.

To tell the main (the most general) idea of the reading, finish this sentence:

There are _____ and disadvantages to the various

ways _____ .

6 **Understanding the Main Idea** The main idea of the reading selection "Meeting the Perfect Mate" is in the first sentence of the following paragraph, but it is not quite true. Change the underlined words so that the paragraph correctly tells the point of the reading. A few items are done as examples.

advantages and disadvantages
There are (1) ~~only disadvantages~~ to the various possible ways of
mates
meeting potential (2) ~~classmates or roommates~~. (3) An advantage of
arranged marriages is that mates may not meet until their wedding day;
even so, through the years they may learn to (4) take graduate courses
anyway. (5) At stand-up comedy clubs, you can talk or just listen to (6) soft,
relaxing music; on the other hand, the people in such places tend to (7)
listen too much, so they often act (8) passive. "Speed dating" is an
organized way to meet potential friends, but it's probably most effective for
(9) slow-talking, thoughtful people. Getting to know people in cyberspace is
(10) inconvenient because computers and other electronic devices are (11)
nowhere; however, (12) it is easy to know what is unreal or unsafe about the
people online. If you meet potential dates at a place where you have (13)
nothing in common, like the gym, you can share your interest, but what
happens if one person (14) gets interested in the activity?

Understanding Left-Out Words and References

1. Left-Out Words

Often, a writer leaves out words because information in other sentences or sentence parts makes them unnecessary. The reader figures out the missing information from the context.

Example

"What's one way to meet a possible husband or wife?" I asked.

"Well," she said, "one method in my country is to have an arranged marriage."

> Full meaning:
>
> "One method _to meet a possible husband or wife_ in my country is to have an arranged marriage. "

2. References

Some words refer to ideas that came before them in the reading.

Example

"My parents have had a good marriage for the past 30 years. This happens in a lot of arranged marriages."

> Full meaning:
>
> The word *this* refers to having a good marriage.

7 **Providing Left-Out Words** In the following quotes there are missing words that readers can figure out from the context. Which words are missing? Write them in the blanks. See the Strategy Box above for more help.

1. "I know you can match a tie to a shirt—or _____ _match_ _____ two socks, too, after you do the laundry. But _____ people?"

2. "Sure," she replied. "There are still arranged marriages these days, and there were a lot _____ more not too long ago."

3. "Do you mean that the bride and groom weren't in love? That sounds awful! Weren't they worried?"

   "Maybe _____ a little bit," Usha said. "But they've had a successful marriage for 30 years."

4. "I meet a lot of women in dance clubs," Bill said. "At least I used to _____. The environment was exciting. I used to go _____ every weekend."

8 Identifying References In each of the following sentences, circle the words that the underlined word refers to. The first one is done as an example. See the Strategy Box for more help.

1. I've been taking a graduate (seminar) in social structure for the past month. It's a very popular course.

2. "One method is to have an arranged marriage," Usha said. "A what?" I asked.

3. "My grandparents chose their children's mates and arranged their weddings," she explained. "Do you mean they weren't in love?"

4. "Dance clubs seem great," I said. "I thought so too at first," he said a little sadly.

5. "Yeah, there are plenty of people to communicate with in cyberspace, . . . but who knows what is real there and what isn't?"

6. "It seems that the healthy atmosphere in the gym is continuing into our relationship," Julie said. "That sounds wonderful," I said. "Yes," she said. "I guess so."

7. "But the truth is that I hate to exercise. What's he going to do when he finds this out?"

9 Discussing the Reading In small groups, talk about your answers to the following questions. Then tell the class the most interesting information or ideas.

1. Do you know anyone who had or has an arranged marriage? Are there arranged marriages in your country or culture? What is your opinion of them?

2. Do you like to communicate with potential friends or dates in cyberspace? How do you do it?

3. Where might people with common interests usually meet in your community?

Part 2 Reading Skills and Strategies

Meeting the Perfect Mate (continued)

Before You Read

1 Previewing Vocabulary Read the vocabulary items below from the next reading. Then listen to the words and phrases. Put a check mark (✓) next to the words you know. You can learn the other words now or come back to them after you read.

Nouns		Verbs	Adjective
❏ background	❏ inches (″)	❏ filled out	❏ optimistic
❏ beach	❏ membership	❏ film	
❏ characteristics	❏ motorcycling	❏ made (make) a mistake	
❏ computer dating services	❏ personal ad	❏ miss	
❏ feet (′)	❏ statistics	❏ tell the truth	
❏ height	❏ supermarkets		

Understanding Literal Meaning and Inferences

The first time readers skim a piece of information, they usually read for *literal* meaning—that is to say, they find out quickly what the material *says*.

Beyond the basic meaning of the words, however, they may be able to *infer* (figure out) other ideas or opinions. On a second, more careful, reading they can recognize and understand thoughts that the writer did not state directly.

2 **Reading for Literal Meaning and Inferences Read** "Meeting the Perfect Mate," Part 2 for literal (basic) meaning. Then to better understand the writer's meaning, read the material a second time.

Meeting the Perfect Mate, Part 2

"What is the best way to meet the perfect husband or wife? Computer dating services are the answer!" said my friend Sara, who lives down the hall from me in the dormitory. "They provide a great way to meet people! The biggest advantage is that you have a lot in common with the people you meet through a computer. The computer can match you up with someone of your same intelligence, cultural background or religion, age, personality, values, and so on. If you want, you can meet someone who is famous, exciting, **optimistic**, healthy, polite—any characteristics that are important to you. You can match your preferences in lifestyle, food, nature, sports, movies, and everything else. And you can ask for a professor, a scientist, a computer specialist, an artist, or . . ." 5 10 15

▲ Woman at a laptop computer looking at an online dating website

"Have you had many successful dates so far?" I asked.

"To tell the truth," she said, "not really. I think I made a big mistake when I filled out the application form. I didn't want to miss a wonderful guy because of an answer that was too specific, so I was careful to write very general answers." 20

"What do you mean?"

"Well, there was a question about height. I said, 'anyone between 3'5" [3 feet, 5 inches] and 7'5".' Then there was a question about recreation. I answered 'yes' to 147 interests, from classic historical architecture to motorcycling. I wrote that I liked tennis, swimming, the beach, the mountains, the desert, health food, junk food, ethnic foods, eating out, cooking, staying home, traveling, the arts, TV comedies, quiz shows, crime dramas, family life, single life, and on and on and on . . . you know, I think that the computer got confused. It hasn't found a date for me since I sent in the application."

"And what about online video dating?" asked Sara's roommate, Sandra.

"Online video dating?" I asked. "How is that possible?"

"Well, I hear that you film yourself and talk about yourself . . . you know, your background and your interests and things like that. Then you post your video online and people can view it and you can view other people's videos and email the people you want to meet."

"Hmm . . . ," I answered. "More videos in my life."

"Well, you could place a personal ad," Sandra continued.

"In the newspaper?"

"Sure. A friend of mine did that. He wanted to get married, so he figured it out by statistics. He decided that out of every ten women, he liked one. And out of every ten women he liked, he might fall in love with one. Therefore, to get married, he just needed to meet one hundred women."

"Did it work?" I asked.

There was no answer.

Last, I interviewed a guy in the cafeteria. His name was Felix.

"Supermarkets," he told me.

"You're kidding," I said.

"No, I'm serious. I meet a lot of potential dates over the frozen pizzas in the convenience-food section. Also, it's easy to make small talk over the cabbage and broccoli in the produce section. We discuss chemicals and nutrition and food prices. Sometimes this leads to a very romantic date."

I slowly shook my head: it is strange . . . very strange. I didn't respond because I didn't want to be impolite.

That evening, I talked with my roommate, Usha.

"You know," I said. "I think maybe your parents and grandparents had a pretty good idea. An arranged marriage is beginning to seem more and more attractive to me."

After You Read

3 Identifying Literal Meaning and Inferences As you read in the Strategy Box on page 195, information in a reading can be literal (the author states it clearly) or inferred (the author implies or suggests it.) The reader can read for the literal meaning and infer (figure out) the implied meaning.

Read the sentences below. Put a check mark (✓) on the line in front of the ideas that the author stated (clearly said) or implied (suggested) in the reading. Put an X before the ideas that the writer did not state or imply. Look back at the reading selection if necessary.

1. __✓__ The writer's friend Sara is a student.

2. __X__ There is a computer dating service in the dormitory.

3. _____ Sara thinks that computer dating has many advantages.

4. _____ A computer application asks questions about height, interests, and other things, and the computer uses the information to match people for dates.

5. _____ Sara wants to have a date with a doctor who doesn't eat meat.

6. _____ Sara had a lot of success with computer dating so far.

7. _____ If you join an online video-dating club, you meet people on network TV or online.

8. _____ In online video dating, two people can arrange to get together if they like each other's videos.

9. _____ To place a personal ad, you write about yourself and pay the newspaper to print the information.

10. _____ Dating may be a matter of statistics.

11. _____ The student that the writer interviewed in the cafeteria likes computer dating services and online video dating clubs too.

12. _____ Felix makes small talk with potential dates in stores.

13. _____ On dates, Felix likes to eat pizza with broccoli and cabbage salad.

14. _____ The writer doesn't think that it is a good idea to date people you meet in the supermarket.

15. _____ The writer didn't tell her opinion to the guy in the cafeteria.

16. _____ She thinks that arranged marriages may have some advantages after all.

Strategy

Summarizing Stories by Identifying Pros and Cons
You learned to summarize stories in Chapter 8 by numbering the main events of a story. Another way to summarize a story is to tell the advantages (pros) and disadvantages (cons) of each side of the story. The story in Parts 1 and 2, "Meeting the Perfect Mate," is fiction, but it contains real information about possible ways to meet potential husbands and wives in many societies in today's world. For this story about ways to meet people, it's a good idea to write the pros and cons in your summary.

4 **Summarizing Stories by Identifying Pros and Cons** Work in groups. Each student should complete two or more of the following items taken from the reading on pages 195–196. Then read your sentences to your group. As a group, put your sentences together in a summary about the pros and cons of different ways to meet a mate.

1. The writer has been interviewing people about friendship, marriage, and other relationships. She found out that the mates in arranged marriages _____ _____.

2. The advantages of meeting people at dance clubs are that _____ _____.

   The disadvantages are that _____ _____.

3. Speed dating is _____.
   It may be effective if _____,
   but it probably won't work if _____.

4. It's easy to meet people online because _____.
   On the other hand, it can be a problem if _____ _____.

5. Some people make new friends at places where _____ _____
   such as a gym. But there might be a problem if _____ _____.

6. An advantage of computer dating is that _____ _____.
   But if you _____,
   the computer might not _____ _____.

7. For online video-dating, _____.
   If you place a personal ad in a newspaper, you can meet _____ _____.

8. Some people think the supermarket is a good place to meet potential dates because _____ _____.

9. After interviewing many people about a possible way to meet potential mates, the writer decided _____ _____.

5 **Discussing the Reading** In small groups, talk about your answers to these questions. Then tell the class the most interesting information or ideas.

1. Do you sometimes make conversation with people in places where you have similar interests? Do these people ever become your friends?

2. Do you have online video and/or computer dating services in your country? What do you think of this way of finding dates?

3. Where do you usually meet the people who become your friends? Where or how did or do you meet potential boyfriends or girlfriends?

6 **Talking It Over** Proverbs are old, short, well-known sayings about human nature and life. Here are some well-known English-language proverbs about social life, friendships, and love relationships. First, match the proverbs on the left with their meanings (the paraphrases) on the right. Write the letters on the lines. Then for each proverb, discuss your answers to the questions below.

Proverbs

1. _____ Love makes the world go 'round.

2. _____ Absence makes the heart grow fonder.

3. _____ All's fair in love and war.

4. _____ Better to love and lose than never to love at all.

5. _____ Love is blind.

6. _____ Any friend of yours is a friend of mine.

7. _____ A friend in need is a friend indeed.

8. _____ The best of friends must part.

9. _____ A woman without a man is like a fish without water.

10. _____ The course of true love never did run smooth.

Meanings

a. If you don't see someone for a while, you will miss that person.

b. In love relationships, anything is possible.

c. Love motivates people all over the globe.

d. Even after it ends, a failed relationship is better than no relationship at all.

e. When you are in love, you don't see the faults of the other person.

f. In times of need, you find out who your real friends are.

g. Even the closest friends cannot always be together.

h. Women need men in their lives.

i. If you like someone, I will like that person too.

j. There will always be hard times in a real love relationship.

1. Do you agree with the "wisdom" of the proverb? Why or why not? Give some examples from your own experience.

2. Is there a proverb with a similar meaning in your native language? If so, translate it into English for the class and explain it.

3. Do you know any proverbs with an approximately opposite meaning (in English or in any language)? If so, tell about them.

Strategy

Identifying Negative Prefixes

A *prefix* (a part added to the beginning of a word) does not show the part of speech; however, a prefix usually changes the *meaning* of the word it is attached to. (In contrast, as you learned in Chapter 8, a *suffix*, an ending added to a word, often indicates its *part of speech*—that is, if it is a noun, a verb, an adjective, or an adverb.)

These are some common prefixes that add negative meanings to words; that is to say, these word beginnings change a word to its opposite.

    dis-   *il-*   *im-*   *in-*   *non-*   *un-*

Example

    During our trip, we discussed our <u>dis</u>satisfaction with our relationship. He was <u>im</u>polite, and I was <u>in</u>direct. Even so, the talk was so important and interesting that the miles seemed to <u>dis</u>appear.

In the words *dissatisfaction, impolite*, and *indirect*, the prefixes *dis-, im-, and in-* add a negative meaning. However, the same letters are *not* negative prefixes in the words *discussed, important*, and *interesting*.

The prefix *im-* appears most often before the letters *b, m,* or *p*. Words beginning with the letter *l* may take the prefix *il-*. The most common negative prefix is *un-*.

1 **Identifying Negative Prefixes** Which of these words below from Chapters 1 to 9 contain a prefix with a negative meaning? Underline those prefixes and write *N* on the line before the word. Write *X* on the lines before the words without negative meanings. Use a dictionary if you need help.

1. _____ discourage
2. _X_ discussion
3. _N_ <u>dis</u>ease
4. _____ dishonesty
5. _____ disrespect
6. _____ distance
7. _____ illogical
8. _____ illustration

9. _____ images
10. _____ immediately
11. _____ immoral
12. _____ immortality
13. _____ impatience
14. _____ impolite
15. _____ inability
16. _____ independence

17. _____ indirectness

18. _____ individual

19. _____ industrialization

20. _____ informal

21. _____ international

22. _____ nonsense

23. _____ nontraditional

24. _____ non-Western

25. _____ understanding

26. _____ universal

27. _____ unlimited

28. _____ unrelated

29. _____ unusually

30. _____ unwelcome

2 Filling in the Negative Prefix
From your own knowledge of the vocabulary in this book, write the missing negative prefix (*dis-, il-, im-, in-, non-, un-*) in each blank, as in the example. Then you can check your answers in the dictionary.

1. _____ advantage

2. _*dis*_ appearance

3. _____ certain

4. _____ common

5. _____ consistent

6. _____ effective

7. _____ fortunately

8. _____ healthy

9. _____ legality

10. _____ mortality

11. _____ natural

12. _____ perfect

13. _____ politeness

14. _____ sense

15. _____ specific

3 Writing Opposites
To make the following paragraph accurate, write the contrasting word (a word with the opposite meaning) over all the underlined items. Be careful: not all words with opposite meanings include negative prefixes—or any prefixes at all.

    Some people looking for ~~impossible~~ [*possible*] husbands and wives try ~~unnatural~~ [*natural*] methods. For instance, they might find it <u>difficult</u> to make small talk with people that look <u>unfriendly</u> or <u>depressed</u> in the produce section of the supermarket, where they are choosing <u>rotten</u> fruits and vegetables. Or they might have a conversation at a <u>slow</u>-food restaurant, where they <u>dislike</u> eating hamburgers, French fries, or other items with <u>high</u> nutritional value. In a <u>similar</u> way, a computer service is <u>incapable</u> of matching singles with <u>married</u> people that are very much <u>unlike</u> them; men and women that get together in this <u>inconvenient</u> way often share many interests. A video-dating center may be <u>unhelpful</u> as well; meeting people on the Internet has benefits, but it can have <u>advantages</u> too. In any case, <u>many</u> ways of meeting people can be <u>unsuccessful</u> all the time.

For more vocabulary practice with the words that begin with prefixes, identify the parts of speech of the items in Activities 1–3 of Part 3. Can you use these words in sentences that show their meanings?

4 **Figuring Out Vocabulary from Prefixes and Suffixes: Reading Personal Ads** As you've read and discussed in this chapter, some people write personal ads to meet potential mates. Below are some ads of this kind. If many of the ads seem funny, it's because they were meant to be amusing to attract interest.

Read the ads and circle or highlight the words and phrases that are new or difficult for you. Work with a partner to figure out their general meanings from the word parts—their prefixes and suffixes. Can you think of words with opposite meanings for some of the items?

PERSONALS MEN SEEKING WOMEN	PERSONALS WOMEN SEEKING MEN
1. **MALE** Retired senior citizen wants female companion 70+ to discuss health conditions, illnesses, and diseases. Like complaining and sitting around watching a lot of television. Under 30 is also OK.	a. **FEMALE** 75-year-old grandmother, no money, no house, seeks handsome, strong male under the age of 35. Dislikes: loud music. Goal: marriage. I can dream, can't I?
2. **RELIGIOUS MALE** I am a serious student of religion. I plan to devote my life to God. I go to church every week and pray three times a day. I am looking for a fun-loving girl to share an exciting life in the fast lane.	b. **SINGLE FEMALE** Attractive and accomplished woman, college graduate, looking for handsome, successful European or Middle Eastern prince to save me from my parents' house. I don't cook, but I do love to shop.
3. **SINGLE MALE** 34, very successful, smart, independent, and self-made. Looking for a wife whose father will hire me.	c. **FEMINIST** Faithful feminist, devoted to women's liberation and female rights, seeking man who will accept my independence and strength—but you probably will not. Oh, just forget it.
4. **SINGLE MALE** I am an unmarried businessman with no shocking family secrets, no terrible past, no horrible life experiences, and no personality. So call me some time.	d. **FEMALE** Worried about the meddling interference of irritating in-laws and other relatives? I am an orphan with no brothers or sisters. Please write me.
5. **DIVORCED MALE** As a divorced Jewish man, I need someone who will do these things with me: keep kosher, attend synagogue, observe the Sabbath, celebrate all the Jewish holidays, and attend bar mitzvahs and other life events. Religion unimportant.	e. **FEMALE** I am a sensitive multicultural woman you can open your heart to and share your innermost thoughts and deepest secrets. Trust and confide in me. I'll understand your insecurities. No talkative guys, please.
6. **MALE** My favorite foods are sushi, soybean burgers, water bugs, and tiramisu. My main interests are unusual laws about jaywalking, twelfth-century Ethiopian literature, weather, and eternal life or immortality. Also, I like to go barefoot in elevators, warm my feet in a hot bath, and collect art objects of the Egyptian pharaohs. Seeking a like-minded soul mate to live with me in a fixer-upper castle in the Sahara Desert. No strange individuals, please.	f. **EDUCATED FEMALE** Kind Taiwanese professor, 41, with 18 years of teaching behind me. Looking for a Latin-American romantic who likes to sit around and speak Spanish. Unappealing characteristics: impatience, impoliteness, and disrespect.

5 **Recognizing Words with Similar Meanings** Read the words in each row below. Three of the words have the same or similar meanings. One of the words has a different meaning. Circle the word with a different meaning.

1.	aggressive	calm	assertive	strong
2.	fast	quick	slow	speedy
3.	guy	gal	male	man
4.	joyfully	enthusiastically	quickly	happily
5.	husband	daughter	spouse	wife
6.	inches	pounds	feet	arms
7.	question	reply	say	respond
8.	arrange	organize	plan	disrespect
9.	pessimistic	positive	optimistic	hopeful
10.	well-liked	popular	pleasing	unpopular

For fun, you can try to match the women and men in the ads that you think should meet. Which people should not meet? Use words with opposite meanings to explain the reasons behind your matchmaking decisions.

6 **Focusing on High-Frequency Words** Read the paragraphs below and fill in each blank with a word from the box. When you finish, check your answers on pages 188–189.

arranged	grandparents	lot	socks	worried
bit	international	match	tie	

First, I talked with my roommate in the dormitory, Usha, an

_____ student from India.
₁

"What's one way to meet a possible mate?" I asked her.

"Well," she said, "one method in my country is to have an

_____ marriage."   5
₂

"A what?" I asked. "I know you can _____ a
                                                              ₃

_____ to a shirt—or two _____ after
₄   ₅

you do the laundry. Then they're a match. But people?"

"Sure," she replied. "There are still arranged marriages these days, and there were a lot more not too long ago. My parents, for example, met each other for the first time on their wedding day. My ——————— chose their spouses and arranged the weddings."

"Do you mean that the bride and groom weren't in love? That sounds awful! Weren't they ———————?"

"Maybe a little ———————," Usha said, "but they accepted each other. Then, fortunately, they learned to love each other. They've had a good, successful marriage for the past 30 years. This happens in a ——————— of arranged marriages. You know, even today some orthodox (very religious) young people—Jewish and Muslim and Christian—marry this way."

I shook my head. "Amazing!" I said.

 7 **Making Connections** Do an Internet search to find love poems, quotes, or proverbs about love. You can type *love poems* or *love quotes* in a search engine. Find a few that you like. What do they mean? Is there a similar poem or proverb in your language? Choose a favorite one, write it down and explain it to your classmates.

Website: _____

Poems, Quotes, or Proverbs:

_____

_____

_____

_____

_____

_____

TOEFL® iBT

UNDERSTANDING INFERENCES AND POINTS OF VIEW IN READINGS

Parts 1 and 2 of this chapter are a fiction story with a point of view. Standardized tests, including the TOEFL® iBT expect readers to understand sentences, paragraphs, and passages beyond their literal (exact) meaning. Test-takers should be able to make inferences by figuring out answers from the events and ideas in a story. They also need to recognize the writer's point of view.

Practicing Inferences and Points of View Read this passage about the topic of Chapter 9, Social Life. Try to recognize the real meaning of the story. Then answer the testlike questions that follow.

The Beginning of a Friendship

A   Lucy was a shy and frightened little girl when she first stood in front of Mrs. Campbell's third-grade class. It was Monday. "Now, children, we are very lucky today. I would like you to meet Lucy. She and her family just moved here from Guam. She will be in our class for the rest of the year." Pointing to a two-student desk that was empty, the teacher addressed the new student. "You can have that desk over there."

B   Looking only at the floor and holding her books close to her, Lucy walked over to her desk. However, she stumbled slightly and her books fell on the floor. Some of the kids in the class laughed—because that's the way some kids were. Lucy picked up her books and sat down, alone. The class had an odd number of students, so she was the only one without a desk partner.

C   When it was time for the first recess, all the kids hurried out of the classroom—all the kids but Lucy, that is. She waited until they were gone, got the snack out of her lunchbox, and walked slowly out to the playground. All the children were laughing, running, and playing. Unnoticed, Lucy made her way to a big tree, where she sat down on a bench and ate, alone. She watched the others play, but nobody came over to ask her if she wanted to join them.

D   When lunchtime came, the situation was the same. The girls played hopscotch and the boys played ball, and Lucy sat alone on the bench under the big tree. The only thing any of the kids said to her all day was, "Guam? I've never heard of Guam. I'm from America." Lucy was too shy to say anything. The little boy ran off to tell his friends that people from Guam didn't talk. That's the way some kids were.

E   The next day Lucy told her mom she didn't want to go to school anymore because she didn't have anybody to play with. She wanted to go back to Guam, to her friends. Her mother told her she would make new friends—and to hurry up and get ready. She shoved her lunchbox into her hands and led her out the door. Lucy's second day went just like her first. During recess, she went out to the bench under the big tree to eat her snack. She didn't look up much, but she could hear the sounds of laughter coming from the playground. She was lonely and very homesick. Then, halfway through her apple, she started to cry. Some of the other kids saw her crying, but they didn't ask her what was wrong. They just whispered to one another and pointed at her. Some laughed, because that's the way some kids were.

F   The third day of the week went pretty much the same—and the fourth day too. Lucy talked to nobody. Nobody talked to her. She sat alone during all the recesses and lunch periods. Then she went home and cried.

G   Then on Friday something different happened. In the middle of math class, the teacher was called out of the room. When she returned, she had a little boy with her. She said, "Class, this week we are very, very lucky. We have another new student. His name is Henry. Henry, you can take the other seat at that desk, next to Lucy." The little boy came over and put his book bag on Lucy's desk. He looked at her before he sat down, and he smiled. He smiled at her. It was a shy kind of smile, but it was a nice smile. She smiled back.

H   When lunch time came, Lucy sat on the bench under the big tree eating her peanut butter sandwich. She didn't feel like crying. She was looking for Henry. There he was—playing ball with some boys. Henry made friends quickly, it seemed. Then he looked over at Lucy and saw her looking at him. Shyly, she looked down, but when she looked up again, there was Henry—standing right in front of her, his lunch bag in his hand. "Can I sit on this bench with you?" he asked. She nodded. For a few minutes they didn't talk at all. But right away Lucy new she had a friend. Henry was nice. Some kids were just that way . . .

By Andrew Kirn, 1995

1. What kind of reading passage is this?
   A science fiction or fantasy story
   B a personal story—either fiction or a narrative based on a real situation
   C a factual history of elementary school education in the United States
   D an opinion essay about conditions in our public schools today

2. According to the passage, what is most important about Lucy, the main character of the story?
   A She couldn't relate to the other children because of her poor English skills.
   B She missed her family and friends and home, so she paid no attention to the kids on the playground.
   C She needed time—and a friend—to get over her shyness and discomfort in a new situation.
   D She didn't like the lunches and snacks at her new elementary school.

3. According to the passage, what is most important about the other characters in the story?

    (A) They were all mean, vicious children that needed discipline and punishment from school officials and their parents.

    (B) They treated Lucy as she deserved to be treated—like an outsider that didn't belong to their group.

    (C) They were as nice and kind to Lucy as possible, but she didn't respond to their efforts.

    (D) They acted like typical kids their age when they meet someone new or different—except for a friendly boy that understood Lucy's feelings.

4. A good title for this story might be _____.

    (A) Changing Children's Attitudes Toward Newcomers

    (B) The Mistakes of Teachers and Parents of Third-Graders

    (C) The Differences of Girls and Boys in a Typical School

    (D) How Friendship Can Make a Difference

5. Who might most appreciate and learn from the point of this story?

    (A) shy people at any age that feel uncomfortable in a new environment

    (B) students that don't know how to relate to people from other cultures

    (C) both A and B

    (D) teachers of classes in which all students have the same native culture and language

Self-Assessment Log

Read the lists below. Check (✓) the strategies and vocabulary that you learned in this chapter. Look through the chapter or ask your instructor about the strategies and words that you do not understand.

Reading and Vocabulary-Building Strategies

❏ Recognizing the structure of written conversations
❏ Understanding left-out words and references
❏ Understanding literal meaning and inferences
❏ Summarizing stories by identifying pros and cons
❏ Identifying negative prefixes
❏ Figuring out vocabulary from prefixes and suffixes
❏ Recognizing words with similar meanings

Target Vocabulary

Nouns
❏ feet*
❏ guy
❏ inches*
❏ match*
❏ mates
❏ socks*

❏ spouses

Verbs
❏ arranged*
❏ interviewing
❏ match
❏ replied*

Adjectives
❏ aggressive
❏ discouraged
❏ optimistic
❏ perfect*
❏ popular*
❏ speedy*

❏ worried*

Adverbs
❏ enthusiastically
❏ fortunately*

* These words are among the 2,000 most frequently used words in English.

10

Sports

The readings in this chapter offer information and opinions about competitive sports. The first reading compares and contrasts the ancient Greek Olympic Games with the modern worldwide Olympics. In opinion-letter form, the second reading offers opposing views on controversial issues in sports competition, such as the use of banned drugs, and the effects of commercialism on professional sports.

> ❝ The goal of the Olympic movement is to contribute to building a peaceful and better world by educating youth through sport practiced without discrimination of any kind. ❞
>
> —The Olympic Charter, paraphrased by the Amateur Athletic Foundation of Los Angeles, California

Connecting to the Topic

1 Look at the photo below. Where do you think this game is taking place?

2 What is your favorite Olympic event to watch? Why?

3 What do you think are some of the issues and problems with competitive sports?

The Ancient vs. the Modern Olympics

Before You Read

1 **Previewing the Topic** Work in groups. Look at the photos and pictures and read the questions below to compare the ancient and modern Olympics.

1. What do you see in the ancient pictures? What's in the modern photos?

2. What do the ancient and modern pictures have in common? (What similarities are there in the pictures?)

3. What is clearly different about the ancient and modern pictures? (What contrasts do you see?)

▲ Athletes competing in the ancient Olympics

▲ Athlete competing in the modern Olympics

▲ The ancient Olympics

▲ The modern Olympics

 2 **Predicting** Think and talk about possible answers to these questions. What will the readings say? You can make predictions. When you read "The Ancient Olympics" and "The Modern Olympics" look for the answers.

1. What events used to take place in the ancient Greek Olympics—during the opening ceremonies, the sports competitions, and the closing ceremonies? Which events are customary before, during, and at the end of the modern Olympics?

2. In which ways could girls and women take part in the original Olympic Games? How have they participated in the modern Games so far?

3. How did world politics affect the Olympic Games of the ancient Greek world? Since 1896, what effects have political conflicts had on the Olympics?

3 **Previewing Vocabulary** Here are some vocabulary items from the first reading selection. Listen to the words. Put a check mark (✓) next to the words you know. You can learn the other words before you read or come back to them after you read.

Nouns		Verbs	Adjectives
❑ achievement	❑ organizations	❑ awarded	❑ celebrated
❑ altar	❑ participants	❑ boycotted	❑ competitive
❑ ceremony	❑ peacefulness	❑ canceled	❑ equestrian
❑ chariot	❑ promise	❑ competed	❑ extreme
❑ competition	❑ representatives	❑ contributed	❑ international
❑ conflict	❑ sacrifices	❑ participated	❑ original
❑ coordination	❑ sanctuary	❑ re-create	❑ troubled
❑ demonstrations	❑ spectators		
❑ myths	❑ statue		
	❑ trainer		

Read

4 **Reading an Article** Read the following material. Then read the explanations and do the exercises after the reading.

The Ancient vs. The Modern Olympics

A   In a world troubled by political **conflict**, the Olympic Games have symbolized peace and unity throughout their history. In the ancient Greek Olympics, youthful athletes honored the gods with **demonstrations** of their speed and **coordination**. Based on the highest ideals, the Olympic Games were offered in the spirit of peace, for the love of sport, and honest, fair **competition**. Although the Olympics have changed over time, you might be surprised to learn that according to historians there are many similarities between the **original** Olympic Games and the modern ones. 5

Here are two articles to compare the Olympic competitions of past millennia with the widely celebrated Olympic Games of the 21st century. 10

B   **The Olympic Events, Athens, Greece, the 4th century A.D.**

As the greatest of our national festivals comes to a close again, here are some of its highlights and history:

- Since 776 B.C., our summer Olympic Games have been held every four years at the sanctuary of our ruler Zeus on Mount Olympus.
- As usual, this year's Games began with the promise of fairness by athletes and judges to Zeus. There was a ceremony before the statue and altar of the great god. There were contests for young boys. Participants and spectators met with old friends. There were speeches, poetry, tours, feasts, parades, and singing. 15

- Next came the **competitive** sports events: the pentathlon (five track and field events, including the discus throw, javelin throw, the long jump, running, and wrestling); boxing; the four-horse chariot race; horse racing; and an **extreme** combination of wrestling and boxing. Under a full moon, there were sacrifices to the King of the Gods.   20
- On the fifth and final day, prizes were awarded—wreaths made of a special olive tree branch from the sanctuary. Some winners received prizes worth money. There were more feasts for and by the winners. Then the competitors and spectators went home—mostly on foot through the mountains.   25

Women in the Olympic Games

C   Most of the athletes at this year's events were young men, of course. Even so, unmarried girls **competed** in foot races at the Festival of Hera   30 (Zeus' wife). They were also spectators at the Festival of Zeus. The owner of the winning chariot team and the trainer of the winning horse in the races, were female, too! On the other hand, married women were not allowed in the Sanctuary of Zeus. They didn't want to be thrown off a cliff, so no one broke this rule.   35

The Politics of the Olympics

D   In my opinion, the most important **achievement** of the Olympic Games has been its peacefulness—not only at the Games, but in all of the Greek world. Of course, the actual events fill only five short days. Even so, during the three months before and after the competitions, there is an agreement to protect travelers, so there is usually no fighting between or among   40 competing cities. Although there have been exceptions, in its long history of over a millennium, the Ancient Games have never been **canceled** for political reasons. In general, even during the times of major wars, the Games have **contributed** to the cause of peace for well over a thousand years.

The Olympic Events, Athens, Greece, August 29, 2004

A   As another wonderful worldwide Olympic festival comes to a close, here are some of its highlights and history:

- With a few exceptions, our modern Olympic Games have been held every four years in a different city around the world. This year, they again took place where they started—in Greece.   5

- As usual, this year's games began with the opening ceremony. Representatives of all athletes and judges made promises of fairness. For the first time in history, the Olympic flame had traveled to all continents before the Games. The opening ceremony ended with fireworks and the lighting of the Olympic Cauldron.
- For spectators and TV watchers, the most popular competitions were aquatics (swimming and diving), athletics (track and field), basketball, boxing, cycling, fencing, gymnastics, the modern pentathlon, soccer, volleyball, weightlifting, and wrestling. There were also 20 other sports, including the triathlon (swimming, biking, and running) and equestrian (horse) events.
- Prizes were awarded after each event—the gold medal for the first place winner, silver for second place, and bronze for third. On the 17th and last day, the athletes got together for the closing ceremony. There were musical performances and speeches. The head of the International Olympic Committee closed the 2004 Olympic Games.

Women in the Olympic Games

B   To this day, only about one-third of all Olympic competitors are female. Even so, the 2004 Olympics included the most women athletes ever. Women participated in events such as gymnastics, fencing, tae kwon do, basketball, beach volleyball, tennis, track and field, cycling, aquatics, soccer, hockey, triathlon, and others. For the first time in history, women competed in the shot put—held at its original site in Olympia! However, there is still concern about the low number of female leaders in national and international competitive sports **organizations**.

The Politics of the Olympics

C   In my opinion, the most important achievement of these Olympic Games was its peacefulness. In their 108-year history, the modern Olympics have been canceled three times because of World Wars. Some countries have **boycotted** the Games for political reasons. Furthermore, the IOC has kept certain nations out of the Games because of their policies. There were terrorist attacks during the 1972 and 1996 Games. In contrast, in spite of the host organizers' and participants' worry, there was no violence during the 17 days of the 2004 Olympics. Despite worldwide problems, the representatives of 202 lands got along well. The Games contributed to the cause of peace.

D   As we have seen, the worldwide Olympic Games **re-created** at the end of the 19th century have been different in many ways from the original Olympics of thousands of years ago. Even so, our modern competitions are more similar to the ancient ones than many people want to believe.

After You Read

5 **Recognizing Reading Structure: Similarities and Differences** The readings "The Ancient Olympics" and "The Modern Olympics" are two parallel articles, one after the other. The first article tells about the Olympic Games of the ancient Greek world. The second article gives information about the modern Olympic Games. Both articles, of approximately the same length, discuss the same subtopics.

Read the important ideas below from the reading. If the point is from the article on the *Ancient Olympics,* write *A* in the blank. If the point is from the article about the *Modern* Olympics, write *M* in the blank. Some ideas appear in both articles. Write *both* in the blank before those ideas.

1. ___*A*___ The Olympics were always held on Mount Olympus in honor of Zeus—not at different cities in the world.

2. ___*both*___ Some of the events of this year's Games were the opening ceremonies, the pentathlon, boxing, equestrian competitions, and the closing ceremonies.

3. _____ Many of the prizes awarded at the Games were symbolic. Wreaths honored some of the winners' achievements but didn't have monetary value.

4. _____ Most of the participants were young men. Married women couldn't participate in any of the sports or even watch them, but they could own and train horses.

5. _____ Although fewer women than men participated in the Olympic Games, there were both male and female teams in many of the sports. Olympic organizations included both sexes. Anyone could be a spectator—male and female, single and married.

6. _____ The Olympic Games were held every four years for over 1,000 years. There were no cancellations, boycotts, or acts of political terrorism.

6 **Understanding the Main Idea** Which of the following sentences best expresses the main idea, or point, of the reading "The Ancient vs. the Modern Olympics"? Circle letter *a, b,* or *c.* Can you tell a few facts from the reading to support that statement?

a. In contrast to the modern worldwide Olympic Games, the ancient Greek Olympics were purely noncompetitive demonstrations of speed and coordination; even so, they were often canceled because of political conflict and terrorism.

b. Both the ancient and the modern Olympic Games are known primarily for their problems: death for unmarried women, the violence of the sports events, cheating, doping, and so on; however, these beliefs about the competitions are largely myths.

c. The original ancient Greek Olympic Games were similar in many ways to the modern Olympic competitions in today's world.

Using a Venn Diagram to Organize Supporting Details
A Venn diagram can help you organize the details of two different topics you are comparing and contrasting. By separating the details that describe each topic and identifying the details that describe both topics, you can see their similarities and differences more easily.

7 Using a Venn Diagram to Organize Supporting Details

In each box are some details about the information in the two articles "The Ancient Olympics" and "The Modern Olympics." Some details are about the ancient Olympics; some are about the modern Olympics, and some are about both. Write the letters and/or the phrases of the details in the correct place in the Venn diagram.

The Olympic Events
A. take place every four summers
B. held at the sanctuary of Zeus on Mt. Olympus near Athens, Greece
C. held in various world cities
D. begin with promises of fairness by athletes and judges
E. include sacrifices in honor of Zeus as well as feasts
F. start with the lighting of the Olympic Cauldron as part of the opening ceremony
G. include some sports competitions = footraces, the pentathlon, equestrian events
H. include other events = four-horse chariot race, extreme wrestling, and boxing
I. include other events = aquatics, cycling, soccer, basketball, volleyball, gymnastics
J. offer prizes = olive tree wreaths
K. offer prizes = gold, silver, and bronze medals for 1st, 2nd, 3rd places

Ancient Olympic Games   **Modern Olympic Games**

- _____   - _____ A
- _____   - _____ D   - _____
- _____   - _____ G   - _____
- _____   - _____
                                    - _____

Women in the Olympic Games
L. more men than women participants
M. unmarried women only = in footraces and audience
N. women athletes in many sports
O. married women in sanctuary of Zeus were killed (thrown off a cliff)
P. small number of women in Olympic organizations is an issue

Ancient Olympic Games   **Modern Olympic Games**

- _O. Married women_
  in sanctuary of Zeus
  were killed
- _____

- _____
- _____

- _____
- _____

The Politics of the Olympics
Q. spirit of the Games = contribution to peace
R. three-month peace agreement among rival city-states to protect travelers to and from the Games
S. Olympics canceled because of hostilities during two World Wars
T. sometimes political boycotts of the Olympics and terrorist attacks during them

Ancient Olympic Games   **Modern Olympic Games**

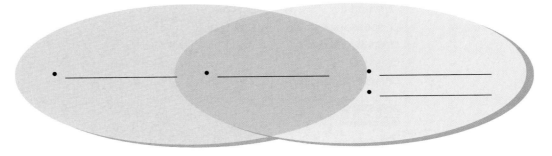

- _____

- _____

- _____
- _____

7 Discussing the Reading In groups of three, talk about your answers to these questions. Then tell the class the most interesting information or ideas.

1. Before you read the article, "The Ancient Olympics," did you have any images of or beliefs about ancient sports festivals like the Olympic Games in ancient Greece? If so, what were they? Have they changed? If so, how?

2. Have you ever been an Olympic competitor? Have you ever been a spectator at the modern Olympic Games? If so, when and where? If not, do you usually follow the summer or winter Olympics in the media? Why or why not?

3. What are some of your thoughts, ideas, and opinions about Olympic and other international sports competitions? How are they — or should they be — similar to and different from other (professional, school, and/or recreational) sports?

Part 2   Reading Skills and Strategies

Issues in Competitive Sports

Before You Read

1 Previewing Vocabulary Below are some vocabulary items from the next reading. Listen to the words and phrases. Put a check mark (✓) next to the words you know. You can learn the other words before you read or come back to them after you read.

Nouns	**Verbs**	**Adjectives**
❑ bribery	❑ cleaning up (their) act	❑ banned
❑ commercialism	❑ corrupted	❑ dedicated
❑ doping	❑ decrease	❑ dishonest
❑ fans	❑ disqualified	❑ intolerable
❑ influence	❑ expand	❑ nondiscriminatory
❑ nationalism	❑ influence	❑ performance-enhancing
❑ opposition	❑ preserve	❑ profitable
❑ patriotism	❑ promote	
❑ pride	❑ representing	
❑ purpose	❑ set (new) records	
❑ scandal	❑ solve	
❑ sponsors	❑ televise	
❑ sponsorship		
❑ sports		
❑ sportsmanship		

Read

2 Recognizing Point of View For every point of view about a topic, there is usually an opposing or contrasting opinion. These opposite views may be based on the same—and/or on different—facts and ideas.

Read the two letters on the next page. They present two opposing points of view on controversial issues in competitive sports. Which letter supports competitive sports? Which letter doesn't? At the top of each letter, fill in the blank of the title, "The World Should _____ Sports Competition," with either *Promote* or *Stop*.

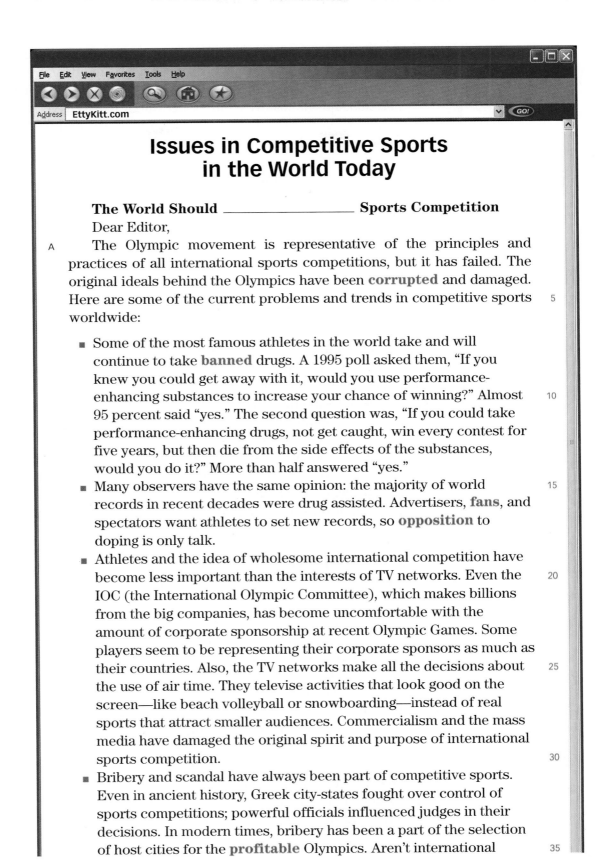

Issues in Competitive Sports in the World Today

The World Should _____ **Sports Competition**

Dear Editor,

A   The Olympic movement is representative of the principles and practices of all international sports competitions, but it has failed. The original ideals behind the Olympics have been **corrupted** and damaged. Here are some of the current problems and trends in competitive sports worldwide:

- Some of the most famous athletes in the world take and will continue to take **banned** drugs. A 1995 poll asked them, "If you knew you could get away with it, would you use performance-enhancing substances to increase your chance of winning?" Almost 95 percent said "yes." The second question was, "If you could take performance-enhancing drugs, not get caught, win every contest for five years, but then die from the side effects of the substances, would you do it?" More than half answered "yes."

- Many observers have the same opinion: the majority of world records in recent decades were drug assisted. Advertisers, **fans**, and spectators want athletes to set new records, so **opposition** to doping is only talk.

- Athletes and the idea of wholesome international competition have become less important than the interests of TV networks. Even the IOC (the International Olympic Committee), which makes billions from the big companies, has become uncomfortable with the amount of corporate sponsorship at recent Olympic Games. Some players seem to be representing their corporate sponsors as much as their countries. Also, the TV networks make all the decisions about the use of air time. They televise activities that look good on the screen—like beach volleyball or snowboarding—instead of real sports that attract smaller audiences. Commercialism and the mass media have damaged the original spirit and purpose of international sports competition.

- Bribery and scandal have always been part of competitive sports. Even in ancient history, Greek city-states fought over control of sports competitions; powerful officials influenced judges in their decisions. In modern times, bribery has been a part of the selection of host cities for the **profitable** Olympics. Aren't international

5

10

15

20

25

30

35

sports supposed to promote moral development, individual achievement, cooperative sportsmanship, and multicultural understanding? Instead, the patriotism of sports has often become nationalism—unhealthy group pride. Unfair judges have awarded medals because of national pride rather than true athletic performance. This is not a healthy practice in the search for world peace.

- In conclusion, the situation of the modern Olympic Games and other sports competitions has become **intolerable**. Competitive sports are sending the wrong message to athletes and young people around the world. They should therefore be stopped.

Regards,
Sophia Martin

The World Should _____ Sports Competition
Dear Editor,

The Olympic movement, representative of the principles and practices of all international sports competitions, has had a positive influence on individual people and societies around the world. Here are some of the current benefits of and trends in competitive **sports** worldwide:

- Doctors, laboratories, and sports officials are trying to **solve** the problem of illegal drug use by competitive athletes. In 1999, the IOC (the International Olympic Committee) formed the World Anti-Doping Agency to prevent drug use in international competition. Each country has an agency to test its own athletes. Scientists are developing tests to discover new forms of doping. At the 2004 Summer Olympic Games, more than 20 athletes were **disqualified** for drug use.
- Drug testing is becoming common in competitive sports. This will continue to protect young people from the dangerous side effects of doping. The testing also contributes to the ideals of fair play and good sportsmanship.
- In order to survive, international sports organizations have become more business-like. In the early and mid 20th century, the IOC—as well as national and local organizing committees —used to depend on dedicated staff members, volunteer workers, and local fundraising. Their budgets were small. Commercial interests and money from TV networks have changed all that. Beginning in the mid 1980s, for example, huge payments from corporate sponsors and the media have allowed the Olympic movement to **expand**. Scholarships, sports education programs, and direct financial aid to developing countries have helped spread the ideals of competitive sports. These ideals include improved health, development of personal character, and good sportsmanship throughout the world.

- Bribery and other kinds of scandal **decrease** spectators' interest in (and money from) sports competitions. The attention has forced dishonest officials to quit, and international organizations have been "cleaning up their act." Are stronger rules making athletes, coaches, judges, and fans change their attitude about international competitive sports? I hope so! I want to see fair play and cooperation. And I want to see governments create more helpful, **nondiscriminatory** policies. Patriotism may become a healthy emotion based on the pride of achievement and international understanding—a necessary development in the search for world peace.

- In conclusion, international sports competition—based on the ideals of the ancient and modern Olympic Games—are a positive force. They are sending a healthy message to athletes and young people around the world. We should preserve and promote competitive sports.

Sincerely,
Ali Badawi

After You Read

Strategy

Distinguishing Opinion from Fact
Most views about a topic include both facts and opinions as supporting detail. How can you distinguish between the two?

- A fact is supported by evidence. It does not include personal feelings; it is objective. It can be proven—perhaps through historical data, scientific research, or statistics.

- An opinion is based on individual beliefs, emotions, or ideas. It may be based on fact but cannot be proven. It is a personal conclusion or judgment; it is subjective.

3 Identifying Opinions and Facts Identify each of the following items about competitive sports as an objective fact (*F*) or a subjective opinion (*O*). You may look back at the reading selection if necessary. Can you tell the reasons for your answers?

1. _____ In 1995, 95% (percent) of polled athletes said that if they wouldn't get caught, they would take performance-enhancing drugs to increase their chances of winning in competition.

2. _____ Advertisers, fans, and spectators don't oppose doping (the use of performance-enhancing drugs) because they like to see athletes set exciting new records.

3. _____ The purpose of drug testing and the formation of world and national anti-doping agencies is to prevent and/or to punish the use of banned substances in international competitions.

4. _____ More and more, the IOC and other competitive sports organizations are bringing in huge sums of money from commercial sources such as corporate sponsorships and the sale of broadcast rights to TV networks.

5. _____ Sports competitions should be financed by local fundraising only; they should not be broadcast worldwide.

6. _____ Bribery and scandal—such as in the choice of host cities and the judging of events—have always been a part of competitive sports. So have nationalistic bias and patriotic pride.

7. _____ International sports competition is supposed to support and promote moral development, athletic achievement, team cooperation, and cultural understanding at local, national, and international levels.

8. _____ Olympics and other international sport competitions can and should be made more positive forces in the troubled modern world. It doesn't matter if they've succeeded or failed in the past.

Strategy

Summarizing Opinions

The letters in "Issues in Competitive Sports in the World Today" give reasons for and against the preservation and promotion of worldwide competitive sports as they are now. Here are some possible steps to follow to summarize letters of opinion like these:

- From the title, introduction, or conclusion of each letter, compose a main-idea statement of the writer's point of view—the main point of his or her opinion.
- State the important supporting points for that viewpoint. If necessary, include connecting words or other transitions from Chapter 7 that explain the logic of the writer's conclusion.
- Do you think the writer "made the case" for his or her opinion? Tell why or why not.

 4 Summarizing Opinions Work in small groups of an even number of participants—four or six. Half of each group cooperates in writing a summary of the letter "The World Should Stop Sports Competition." The other half writes a summary of the opposite viewpoint—"The World Should Promote Sports Competition." Each group reads or tells its summary to the other.

Choose the two most convincing points of view. All group participants work together to rearrange, change, and/or add supporting detail (arguments) to the summary of the most convincing points of view. Then they can present their arguments and conclusion to the whole class.

5 Discussing the Reading Talk about your answers to these questions.

1. How important are competitive sports in the world today—especially in worldwide festivals? Why do you think so?

2. Suppose you are on an international, national, or local sports committee. How would you change the rules, practices, customs, and/or attitudes connected with competitive sports? For what purposes would you make these changes?

6 Talking It Over People often debate ideas, expressing opposing points of view. Below are some statements about current issues in worldwide competitive sports. First, match each statement in Column A with its opposite (contrasting) opinion in Column B. Write the letters on the lines.

Then work in groups of four. For each pair of statements, two people choose one side. The other two people choose the other side. With your partner prepare all the possible reasons you can think of for your point of view. Your "opponent" or "opposing team" will compile the opposite or contrasting reasoning. Then tell your classmates your opinions.

After you debate your issue, class members can vote on the "winning team."

**Column A:
Statements, Opinions, Viewpoints**

1. _____ Performance-enhancing drugs should be banned from sports. Athletes found using them should be punished.

2. _____ Whether it is pride for a city or a country, patriotism has a negative influence in the world. People should support everyone rather than just one nation.

3. _____ Bribery, corruption, and scandal are elements of sports competitions and other areas of life. They have existed since ancient times and will continue to exist in the future.

4. _____ Women and men should be equally represented in all areas of competitive sports. There should be equality in money, corporate sponsorship, and media air time.

5. _____ Politics should be like sports contests. Politics should have judges and be based on rules, penalties, competition, and winning.

**Column B:
Opposing Statements, Opinions, Viewpoints**

a. With stronger rules and media involvement, we can stop bribery and corruption. This is important for competitive sports as well as politics.

b. Equality between the sexes is impossible in sports. Male and female competitors have always had different abilities. Fans, corporate sponsorship, and media will always support male athletes more than females.

c. Athletes should be allowed take supplements and other substances to improve their athletic ability. They shouldn't be punished.

d. Politics ought to be based on cooperation rather than competition. Politics shouldn't be anything like competitive sports.

e. The idea of pride toward all humans instead of any one nation just doesn't work. Societies are based on different principles and ideals, so patriotism toward one nation is important.

Strategy

Understanding Prefixes

In addition to the negative prefixes *dis-, il-, im-, in-, non-,* and *un-*, there are other common syllables that change or add to the meaning of base words when they are added to the beginning. Here are some of them—with their general meanings and examples.

Prefix	General Meaning	Examples
com-, con-, co-, cor-	with; together	compassion, convenient, co-worker, corporation
de-	down or away from	decrease, decline, detach
ex-, e-	out of, away from	exit, expand, emit
inter-	between; among	interview, intermission, Internet
pre-	before, in advance of, earlier	prepare, prefix, prepaid, precede
pro-	for, favoring, supporting	promotion, progress, propel
re-	again, back	repairs, repeat, re-created

1 **Understanding Prefixes: Matching** Paying attention to the underlined prefix and other word parts, match the vocabulary items and their parts of speech in Column A with their possible explanations in Column B.

Column A

1. __c__ contribute (verb)
2. _____ predictions (noun)
3. _____ conflict (noun)
4. _____ compete (verb)
5. _____ coordination (noun)
6. _____ professional (noun)
7. _____ international (adj.)
8. _____ corrupt (adj.)
9. _____ extreme (adj.)
10. _____ rewards (noun)

Column B

a. the farthest possible; very great or intense

b. prizes given for winning or other behaviors

c. to give to something other people are also giving to

d. a person who has special education or training

e. a disagreement

f. involving two or more countries

g. dishonest; willing to lie, cheat, or steal

h. organized activity of muscle groups in athletics

i. to go against in order to win

j. acts of telling the future in advance of it

REVIEWING PREFIXES

Below is a review list of common word beginnings with their general meanings. In the paragraphs that follow, you can use the prefixes as clues to unfamiliar words—and you can look up words in the dictionary.

Prefixes	Approximate Meanings	Prefixes	Approximate Meanings
a-, ab-	away from	intro-	inward
a-, ad-, ap-	to	mis-	wrong
con-, com-, co-, col-, cor-	with; together	non-	not
de-	from, away	ob-	against
dif-, dis-	apart; not	pre-	before
e-, ex-	out (of); former	pro-	for, on behalf of
in-	into; very; not	re-	again
inter-	between	uni-	one; single

2 **Understanding Prefixes: Fill in the Blank** Within each pair of parentheses ( ), circle the vocabulary item that best fits the meaning of the context.

1. A sport (consists / contributes) of a physical activity for the purpose of (procreation / recreation) and/or (competition / petition). Many people participate or (compete / repeat) in sports to (achieve / deceive) excellence or to develop a skill.

2. Archaeologists have uncovered examples of prehistoric cave art that show activity (resembling / assembling) sports from over 30,000 years ago. Some (objects / interjects) and structures suggest that Chinese people took part in gymnastics (events / prevents) as early as 4000 B.C. Activities like swimming and fishing (evolved / involved) into regulated sports with rules in ancient Egypt. Other sports (excluded / included) javelin throwing, high jump, and wrestling. Ancient Persian sports were (connected / corrected) to combat skills. In fact, military culture (inversely / universally) prevailed in sports in those days. The situation wasn't much (different / indifferent) in ancient Greece. In (addition / edition) to traditional sports, the Greeks (deduced / introduced) chariot and other races—including marathon (delays / relays).

3. The Industrial Revolution and mass (deduction / production) of the 18th and 19th centuries greatly changed the lives of ordinary people. People were provided with (decreased / increased) leisure time, which (disabled / enabled) them to play or (observe / preserve) team sports as spectators. Sports became (confessional / professional), which made them even more popular. So did the (advent / invent) of mass media.

Strategy

Understanding Prefixes, Stems, and Suffixes
To review, a suffix (word ending) often indicates the part of speech of a word. A prefix (word beginning) may change the meaning of the base word or stem (the main part of a longer word). With knowledge of these three elements, readers may be able to figure out new or difficult vocabulary, especially long words with several parts.

3 Practicing Prefixes, Stems, and Suffixes In the following paragraphs, use your knowledge of word parts to choose the best and most appropriate missing vocabulary items. Choose from the words in the box before each paragraph.

commonly (adverb)	environmentally (adverb)	professional (adjective)
describes (verb)	individual (adjective)	recreation (noun)
development (noun)	invention (noun)	transportation (noun)

1. *Cycling* is a word that ___*describes*___ the riding of bicycles not only for

_____ and fun, but also as a _____ sport. It

has a number of benefits both to the _____ person and society

in general. It is healthy _____ (to and from work) as well as an

_____-friendly means of exercise. The activity probably began

in the early 1800s, with the _____ and _____

of the earliest bikes. These were _____ made of wood and had

three wheels. The modern bicycle was first produced in 1892.

concept (noun)	event (noun)	prevent (verb)
constructed (verb)	involves (verb)	promote (verb)
different (adjective)	prevails (verb)	renowned (adjective)

2. Since the beginning of the 20th century, the bicycle has evolved enormously with the _____ of cycling as a sport and the demands of _____ kinds of terrain (ground). Probably, the most _____ (famous) cycling _____ in history is the Tour de France, which _____ cyclists from around the world riding over many types of land to the center of Paris. Also, governments have tried to _____ cycling as a healthy alternative to cars. Bike lanes have been _____ and lockers have been provided to _____ the theft of bicyclists' belongings. In fact, in some countries a "cycling culture" _____.

4 **Identifying Antonyms** Read the vocabulary words in Column A. Choose the word in Column B that has the opposite meaning from the vocabulary word.

Column A

1. __*f*__ corrupt

2. _____ disqualify

3. _____ expand

4. _____ banned

5. _____ opposition

6. _____ fans

7. _____ intolerable

8. _____ profitable

9. _____ solve

10. _____ boycott

11. _____ cancel

12. _____ competitive

Column B

a. support

b. losing money

c. contract, make smaller

d. schedule

e. athletes

f. honest

g. cooperative

h. question

i. allowed

j. acceptable

k. buy, purchase

l. qualify

5 **Focusing on High-Frequency Words** Read the paragraph on page 228 and fill in each blank with a word from the box. When you finish, check your answers on page 214.

competed	fencing	organizations	sports
female	international	original	track

B   To this day, only about one-third of all Olympic competitors are

_____. Even so, the 2004 Olympics included the most
          1

women athletes ever. Women participated in events such as gymnastics,

_____, tae kwon do, basketball, beach volleyball,
          2

tennis, _____ and field, cycling, aquatics, soccer,   5
          3

hockey, triathlon, and others. For the first time in history, women

_____ in the shot put—held at its _____
          4   5

site in Olympia! However, there is still concern about the low number

of female leaders in national and _____ competitive
                                            6

_____ _____.   10
          7   8

6 Making Connections Do an Internet search about a sport, a team, or an athlete that you are interested in. Type in the name of the sport, person, or team, and then another word like *biography* or *facts*. For example, *David Beckham biography*, or *tennis facts.* Find out what you can about that sport, person, or team.

Write down what you learn. It can be in list form—it doesn't have to be a paragraph. Now that you are an "expert" on the topic, tell the class what you have learned. Do you think your sport, person, or team is worth following or participating in? Try to convince your listeners of your point of view.

Topic: _____

What you learned: _____

_____

_____

_____

Your point of view about the topic and why: _____

_____

TAKING NOTES AND RECOGNIZING CONTRASTS
IN READING PASSAGES

The two readings in Part 2 of this chapter ("Issues in Competitive Sports in the World Today") showed opposing points of view in two separate letters. Sometimes opposing viewpoints appear within a *single* reading on the Internet-based TOEFL® iBT. If you recognize this point-by-point approach, you can take helpful notes.

You are allowed to take notes during the TOEFL® iBT. Each reading in the reading section stays on screen until you decide to move to the next reading or until the time limit (20 minutes) has expired. Because you can look back at the reading as you answer questions, you do not have to take notes about most things, but any contrasts should be put into a list. This will help you see the structure of a reading, understand the flow of ideas, and answer some questions about contrasts.

If a TOEFL® iBT reading shows point-by-point contrasts, divide part of your notepaper (provided by the test supervisors) into two columns. Use the left column for points made on one side of the argument, and use the right-hand column for points on the other. Try to arrange them so points that are in direct contrast appear next to each other, as they do in "Issues in Competitive Sports in the World Today."

Practicing Taking Notes About Contrasts Read the following passage about street sports. Take notes about contrasts, using the two-column style described above. Then using only your notes, answer the questions that follow.

Street Sports and the Olympics

A   Most cultures have at least one popular street sport. This is a game that children or adults may play informally whenever they can get enough players together. Typically, even the poorest members of society can play a street sport because it involves very little equipment. It also involves very little planning or organization.

B   In the United States, for example, basketball is probably the most commonly-played street sport. Since it requires only a basket, a paved surface, and a basketball, it can be played in nearly any city park or home driveway. In Canada and parts of the U.S., the everyday sport is ice hockey, played in winter with ice skates on a frozen pond and in summer with in-line skates in a parking lot. In most of the world, soccer is the informal sport of choice. Even easier to organize than street basketball, it requires only a ball and a wide-open space. In Thailand, Malaysia, and Vietnam, a game called *sepak takraw* is played by children and adults in nearly every town or village. It involves kicking a simple wicker ball over a head-high net, like volleyball played with the feet.

C Street sports are great for neighborhood games, but are they suitable for international competition? Fans of any given street sport would like to see it in the Olympic Games. Other people may say the Olympics should keep it out. Typical objections are that the street sport is not really a sport, or it is too local, or the Olympics simply have enough events already.

D The controversy is less about basketball, ice hockey, or soccer than it is about other street sports. Basketball, no longer a mostly North American game, has been an Olympic sport since 1936. Soccer (officially called football) was the first team sport to become a regular Olympic event (1908). Ice hockey has been part of the Winter Games ever since the league's establishment in 1924.

E Sports like sepak takraw are another story. Those who love this game hope to see it added to the Olympic line-up in 2008. Its athleticism is obvious, sepak takraw's supporters say. As an Asian sport, it can provide some balance to the Olympics' European and North American events. It is as well-organized and popular as any other sport, according to its fans. Those who would keep the game out of the Olympics argue mostly that it is simply too local. Few people outside one region play it. Although there are sepak takraw associations in Canada, Australia, and elsewhere, most of them are very small. Olympic medals in sepak takraw, its opponents say, would simply be gifts to a few Southeast Asian nations.

F A different kind of controversy surrounds such "extreme" street sports as skateboarding. Its proponents say that it is one of the few real sports played by actual amateurs. (The modern Olympics began as an event for nonprofessional athletes.) According to skateboarders, it is a true sport of the people, unlike synchronized swimming or ballroom dancing (both Olympic events). It is also far more athletic. And its supporters claim that it is kept out of the Olympics simply because skateboarders do not look very "Olympic." They favor odd hairstyles, often behave recklessly, and try not to look like other Olympic athletes. This is a complaint voiced by players of many sports—if you look too poor, you cannot enter the rich man's Olympics.

G On the other side, Olympic purists argue that it is very fair to keep scruffy looks and wild behavior out of the Games. The Olympic Games are the visible part of a movement, they say, to encourage peace and civility around the world. Athletes who do not live by Olympic ideals do not belong. Furthermore, skateboarding's opponents claim, it is not a sport. It doesn't have a well-established network of associations around the world. It has few rules, and skateboarders have few lower-level international tournaments. Skateboarders argue this. They are very well-organized, they say. They point out that the somewhat-related sport of snowboarding has

H made a fine addition to the Winter Games. Its addition to the winter line-up has not damaged the Olympic spirit, they say, but has updated it.

As badly as sepak takraw players or skateboarders think they are treated, players of several other street sports feel they have a stronger complaint. Rugby, American football, and cricket, for example, are immensely popular in the nations that play them. They are also quite accessible as street sports. They represent long traditions among the common people, their supporters say. Rugby and cricket fans feel especially hurt because these sports were once Olympic events but were dropped to make room for other sports.

1. Which of the following best expresses the main idea of the passage?
   - (A) Street sports make good Olympic sports because they are played by nonprofessionals.
   - (B) Once a street sport enters the Olympics, it loses popularity among common people.
   - (C) Olympic officials are biased against sports that are played by ordinary people.
   - (D) Controversy surrounds the hopes for some street sports to become Olympic sports.

2. Which of the following is NOT mentioned in the passage as a street sport?
   - (A) soccer
   - (B) volleyball
   - (C) skateboarding
   - (D) cricket

3. According to Paragraphs B and D, what do basketball, ice hockey, and soccer have in common?
   - (A) They are all North American street sports.
   - (B) They have strong positions as Olympic sports.
   - (C) Their supporters are trying to get them accepted as new Olympic sports.
   - (D) There is disagreement about whether they should be Olympic sports.

4. Which of the following is an argument against sepak takraw as an Olympic sport, according to Paragraph E?
   - (A) It is not international enough.
   - (B) It goes against Olympic ideals.
   - (C) It is not very athletic.
   - (D) It is not a sport.

5. According to Paragraphs F and G, skateboarders believe that Olympic officials keep them out because of their unusual looks and wild behavior. Which argument do skateboarding's opponents make in response, according to the passage?

- (A) that there is no prejudice against skateboarders because of their looks and behavior
- (B) that several Olympic sports already allow people with unusual looks and behavior
- (C) that skateboarders' looks and behavior would lead to fighting at the Games
- (D) that it is OK to keep certain unusual looks and behaviors out of the Games

6. Which of the following sports was once part of the Olympic Games, but was then dropped?

- (A) baseball
- (B) soccer
- (C) rugby
- (D) American football

Self-Assessment Log

Read the lists below. Check (✓) the strategies and vocabulary that you learned in this chapter. Look through the chapter or ask your instructor about the strategies and words that you do not understand.

Reading and Vocabulary-Building Strategies

❏ Recognizing reading structure: similarities and differences
❏ Understanding the main idea
❏ Using a Venn diagram to organize supporting details
❏ Recognizing point of view
❏ Distinguishing opinion from fact
❏ Summarizing opinions
❏ Understanding prefixes, stems, and suffixes
❏ Identifying antonyms

Target Vocabulary

Nouns	Verbs		Adjectives
❏ achievement	❏ boycotted	❏ decrease*	❏ banned
❏ competition*	❏ canceled	❏ disqualified	❏ competitive
❏ conflict	❏ competed*	❏ expand	❏ extreme*
❏ coordination	❏ contributed	❏ re-created	❏ international*
❏ demonstrations	❏ corrupted	❏ solve*	❏ intolerable
❏ fans*			❏ nondiscriminatory
❏ opposition			❏ original*
❏ organizations*			❏ profitable*
❏ sports*			

---

* These words are among the 2,000 most frequently used words in English.

Vocabulary Index

---

*These words are among the 2,000 most frequently used words in English

residents
restaurants*
robbery
seldom*
serious*
smoking*
strange*
teenagers
travelers
turn*
vehicles
wine*

Chapter 5

ancestor
arranged*
asleep*
birthrate
blended families
communal
community
cooking*
cottage*
crowded*
decades
decline
developing*
divorce rate
divorces
during*
economic
females*
fields*
future*
goats*
has (have) custody of
history*
housework*
improve*
independence*
industrialized
loosely-related
master*
meals*
modestly*
occur
previous
protection*

pushed aside
relatives*
single-parent families
slaves*
social* institution
stay-at-home mother
straw mat
structure
traditional
widowed*
widows*
years*
younger*

Chapter 6

agree*
amazing
annoyed*
architecture
attention*
civilization
clear*
contradict
contradiction
convincingly
customer*
describe*
develop*
enthusiastic
excellent*
experience*
greet*
invented*
knowing*
legacy
loudly*
media
medicine*
opposing*
pain*
patiently*
pleasant*
politely*
proud*
rude*
rudely*
scientific*
social*

societies*
soft*
successful*
terrible*
tourist*

Chapter 7

accurate
claims*
combination*
correct*
cure*
damage*
decisions*
disease*
dishonest*
elderly*
engineering*
environment
famous*
genes
genetic
inhabitants
length*
longevity
long-lived
moderate*
oppose*
patients
population*
prevent*
proven*
solve*
sour*
streams*
unpolluted
valid

Chapter 8

addicted
addiction
adulthood
adults
aural
behavior*
bloody*
boring
computerized

---

*These words are among the 2,000 most frequently used words in English

concentrate
concentration
dissatisfied*
elderly*
emotional
envious*
envy*
exciting*
hospitals*
immoral
improve*
investigate
natural*
nursing*
personalities*
practice*
programming*
reality*
relationship*
replace*
scares
scary
shadowy*
stars*
suspenseful
unlimited*
viewers
violence*
visual media

Chapter 9

aggressive
arrange*
discouraged
enthusiastically
feet*
fortunately*
guy
inches*
interview
match*
mates
optimistic
perfect*
popular*
replied*
socks*
speedy*
spouses
worried*

Chapter 10

achievement
banned
boycotted
canceled
competed*
competition*

competitive
conflict
contributed
coordination
corrupted
decrease*
demonstrations
disqualified
expand
extreme*
fans*
intolerable
nondiscriminatory
opposition
organizations*
original*
profitable*
re-created
solve*
sports*

---

*These words are among the 2,000 most frequently used words in English

Skills Index